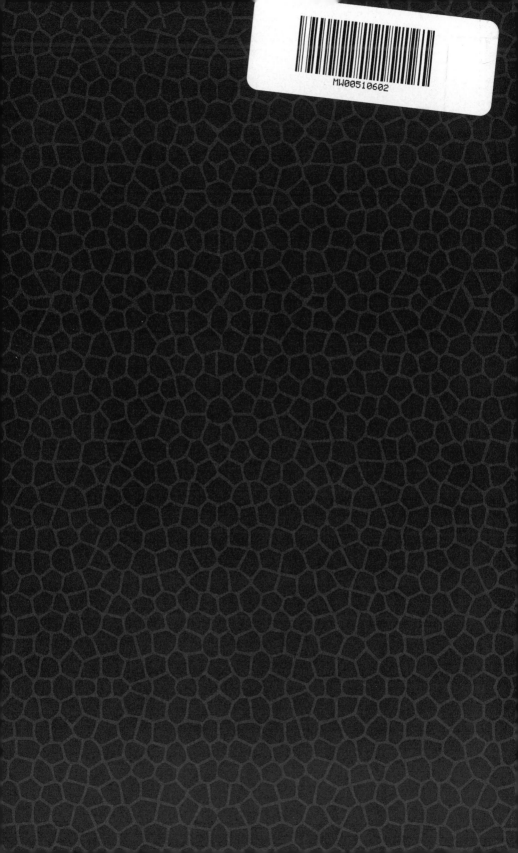

SPARKS OF CLARITY

חזון
עובדיה

MOSAICA PRESS

RABBI ZEV "BUDDY" BERKOWITZ

SPARKS OF CLARITY

חזון
עובדיה

NOVEL, UPLIFTING,
AND ENCOURAGING
TORAH THOUGHTS BASED
ON DIVREI CHAZAL

Published by Mosaica Press, Inc.
www.mosaicapress.com
info@mosaicapress.com

I would like to dedicate this *sefer*
in memory of my parents

משה דוד בן שרגא פייבל

כ״ד ניסן תשע״ט

אסתר ליבא בת אפרים מיכל הלוי

כ״ד אדר תשע״ה

It was a privilege to have been raised by you. The simplicity with which you led your lives is amazing. You never owned a home and you didn't own a car. The message you sent to our family was loud and clear: "The most important things in life are Torah and mitzvos." *Tzedakah, hachnasas orchim, tzniyus,* and *chessed* were the vehicles with which you served Hashem in this world. You were great role models for your children, grandchildren, and great-grandchildren. Much of this *sefer* reflects the values by which you lived. In reference to Rabbi Yehoshua ben Chananyah, the Mishnah in *Pirkei Avos* says: "*Ashrei yoladeto*—Fortunate are the parents who gave birth to him." However, I feel that to you the title may be applied: "Fortunate is the child that had you for parents." You both invested so much into me. I hope to continue to make you proud.

באהבה רבה והכרת הטוב,
BUDDY

Haskamah from R' Berel Wein, shlit"a

Rabbi Buddy Berkowitz is one of the most creative and beloved teachers of Torah that the Jewish people possess in the United States at this time. His devotion, wisdom, sense of humor and sparkling personality have captivated hundreds of students and brought them closer to the God of Israel and the people of Israel. I have always felt he is a soon-to-be heroic personality whose influence exists upon his students far beyond the time that they spend with him in the classroom.

Rabbi Berkowitz has composed a number of essays and insights into Jewish scholarship, values and lifestyle. They are sure gems that deserve wide attention and appreciation. I hope that they will reach a wide public so that the Jewish world will be able to benefit even more greatly from Rabbi Berkowitz.

All blessings,
Berel Wein

Haskamah from R' Chaim Mintz, shlit"a

Dear Reb Zev Yehuda (Buddy) יחי׳,

I read over the *shticklach* of Torah that you sent to me. It was a *mechayeh* to go through them—"*mechayeh*" literally, because you give life and meaning to some of the difficult *inyonim* in the Torah. You also bring out much *mussar haskeil*, practical lessons which we should incorporate into our day to day living in order to live a life of Torah values. All of this you accomplish while sticking to *pshat*, making it an enjoyable learning experience.

May Hashem continue to give you *ko'ach* and good health to be *mezakeh* the *rabbim* with more gems of Torah.

בכבוד רב ובהוקרה,
Chaim Mintz

מכתב ברכה

K'hal Zichron Mordechai
9 Fosse Court, Monsey, New York 10952

על שם ר' מרדכי ליבמן ז"ל

Rabbi Ben Tzion Kokis
Mora D'Asra

Nisan, 5779

To my dear friend, Rabbi Zev Yehuda (Buddy) Berkowitz, shlit"a-

What a pleasure it was to see the divrei Torah that you sent me, and thank you for the opportunity to record my impressions.

The famous words of the Kotzker Rebbe zt"l came to mind as I read the pieces that you have written.

The Rebbe asked, we are commanded in Krias Sh'ma to place the words of Torah "*on* our hearts". Wouldn't it be more appropriate to place Torah *in* our hearts?

The Rebbe answered, of course the goal is that divrei Torah should be absorbed within our hearts; but sometimes the heart isn't ready to open, because various barriers hold it closed. The Torah is telling us that even then, though the enthusiasm may not be there, we should still study Torah. Let the words remain *on* our heart, because the time will come when the gates will open again, and the words of Torah will fall right in.

R' Buddy, when I read your short but impactful divrei Torah, I felt that they have a unique power: besides their actual message, there is a *chein*, a charming quality, that emerges from between the lines. This invests your words with a special influence: they help us to *open* our hearts, so that the divrei Torah "fall" right in!

I can only offer my birkas hedyot that you will be able to continue to nurture many more students, both in the classroom and through the printed word, so that many more hearts will be opened and encouraged to grow in Torah, emuna, and yiras shomayim.

B'yedidus,

Ben Tzion Kokis

Ben Tzion Kokis

Rabbi Reuven Halpern
Rov, Bais Medrash of Westgate, Nusach Sfard
Mashgiach Ruchani at Beth Medrash Govoha
Lakewood, NJ

הר׳ ראובן הלפרין
רב, בית מדרש דוועסט-גייט, נוסח ספרד
משגיח רוחני בבית מדרש גבוה
לייקוואוד, נ.דז.

My dear friend, Rabbi Buddy Berkowitz, has authored a wonderful and original *sefer* about many topics in *avodas Hashem*. Each entry therein teaches an important and fundamental lesson in an engaging and enjoyable manner.

The author is someone who truly personifies these teachings, a quality which undoubtedly makes his words all the more impactful. They are truly instilled with the ability to influence and inspire others towards growth and change for the better. This *sefer* will be of value to all those who strive to come closer to Hashem and to walk in His ways.

With highest regard for Rabbi Berkowitz, and a *brachah* for his continued success in teaching and inspiring *acheinu B'nei Yisroel*.

Reuven Halpern

TABLE OF CONTENTS

Editor's Preface XV

Preface XVII

PART I

בין אדם לחברו

BEIN ADAM L'CHAVEIRO

1: The Angels' Missions 3

2: Rivkah's Test 5

3: Moshe Addresses the Fighters 10

4: Birth of Yosef 13

5: Noach, Avraham, and the Difference Between Them 16

6: Leah and Rachel: Sisterly Concern 20

7: Giving—and Receiving—Tochachah 23

8: Chosheid B'Kesheirim 27

9: Kavod Rabo, the Power of a Yid, and Moshe Smiting the Mitzri . . 33

10: Connecting to Hashem by Connecting to the Tzibbur 37

PART II

אמונה ובטחון
EMUNAH U'BITACHON

1: Pachim Ketanim. 45

2: Pachim Ketanim II: Visual Reminders 47

3: Righteousness of Noach: Full Compliance 50

4: Yosef's Response to Pharaoh 53

5: Akeidas Yitzchak and Emunah 56

6: Makkas Dam: Hitting the Water. 59

7: Cheit Ha'eigel: Danger of Distance 63

8: Sensitivity. 66

9: Eishes Ovadiah and the Miracle of the Oil. 70

10: Cheit Ha'meraglim 74

11: Lessons of Light 79

12: Moshe's Hands Were Heavy 82

PART III

תשובה, תפילה, צדקה
TESHUVAH, TEFILLAH, TZEDAKAH

1: Blessing for Wealth 89

2: Olam Haba through Ashrei 91

3: Perspectives on Giving 93

4: "A Gut Yor!" 95

5: Harchev Picha: Yesodos of Tefillah. 98

6: Nature of the Shofar 102

7: Avodah of Aseres Yemei Teshuvah 104

8: Tzaddik and Chacham: The Difference 107

9: Incarceration of Yosef. 111

10: Before Our Eyes 116

PART IV

שלום בית, חינוך
SHALOM BAYIS, CHINUCH

1: The Talmidim of Rabbi Akiva 123

2: Avraham and Sarah: Models of Shalom Bayis 126

3: Guiding B'nei Yisrael 129

4: Blessing the Sons of Yosef 132

5: Righteousness of Noach II 135

6: Pure Oil 138

7: Shalom Bayis and the Menorah 141

8: Lessons in Chinuch 146

9: Moshe Strikes the Rock 151

10: Nadav and Avihu 155

PART V

מידות, הכרת הטוב
MIDDOS, HAKARAS HA'TOV

1: Hakaras Ha'tov and the Makkos 161

2: Splitting the Sea 164

3: Rivalry of Yosef and His Brothers 168

4: Cheit Ha'eigel II: Shocking Betrayal 171

5: Cheit Ha'eigel III: Extent of Ingratitude 174

6: Impact of Leitzanus 180

7: Yeravam's Opportunity 185

8: The Sons of Aharon: Lessons in Silence .188

9: Cultivating and Spreading Simchah 190

10: Donation of the Nesi'im 194

PART VI

עשו, עמלק, המן

EISAV, AMALEK, HAMAN

1: Amalek and the Middah of Perfection 199

2: Learning from Amalek 203

3: Eisav's Cry. 206

4: Amalek, Chazaras Ha'shatz, and the Internet. 209

5: Learning Patience and Providence 213

6: Kiddush Hashem of Achdus. 217

7: Eisav's Kibbud Av. 222

8: Esther's Megillah 225

EDITOR'S PREFACE

THE moniker "Buddy" may not be completely unique to Rabbi Buddy Berkowitz; nonetheless, I highly doubt there is anyone to whom this description so aptly applies as to him. As all who know him can attest, he exudes warmth, vitality, and real *ahavah*—for Hashem, for Torah, and for his fellow Yidden. He is a true *"oheiv es ha'briyos u'mekarvan laTorah."* All of this, of course, has earned him his well-deserved reputation as "everyone's buddy." And of course, it has made it such a pleasure to know him, work with him, and enjoy his friendship.

At the same time, these qualities pose a certain challenge, from the standpoint of an editor. An editor's job, of course, entails fixing a bit here, rearranging something there, and polishing up where necessary to conform to publish-ready standards. In short, it is somewhat of an intrusion on the author's own words. But R' Buddy has an infectious personality, in only the most positive sense of the term—his exuberance, clear-eyed vision, and wit spill over on to his spoken and written words. Tampering with his output in any way thus ran the risk of diminishing the influence and flavor that was "pure Buddy." My only hope is that my own intrusions—which I have tried to keep to a minimum—did not overly dilute R' Buddy's inimitable imprint.

Kiddush Hashem is a prominent and recurring theme in R' Buddy's *divrei Torah*. In this sense, R' Buddy is truly a *"na'eh doresh v'na'eh mekayeim"* (*Chagigah* 14b), as he embodies the quintessential *mekadeish*

XVI   *Sparks of Clarity*

Sheim Shamayim as portrayed by Chazal: "מָה הַבְּרִיוֹת אוֹמְרוֹת עָלָיו, אַשְׁרֵי אָבִיו שֶׁלְּמְדוֹ תּוֹרָה, אַשְׁרֵי רַבּוֹ שֶׁלְּמְדוֹ תּוֹרָה...רְאוּ כַּמָּה נָאִים דְּרָכָיו, כַּמָּה מְתוּקָנִים מַעֲשָׂיו—What do people say about him? 'Fortunate is his father who has taught him Torah; fortunate is his *rebbi* who has taught him Torah...See how pleasant are his ways, how upright are his deeds!'" (*Yoma* 86a). And so it is that his words carry an extra potency as he aims to inspire others and awaken in them a love for Hashem and a desire to come closer to Him.

It has been a tremendous *zechus* being able to work with such a dear friend and have some *chelek* in this worthy project. This *sefer* in no way represents the culmination of R' Buddy's amazing journey, but one very significant milestone on a path of *aliyah* and *gadlus*—*b'ezras Hashem*, one of many, many, more.

Tzvi Hebel
Lakewood, 5780

PREFACE

THERE are three points I would like to clarify right at the outset. Firstly, I'm not a scholar. Secondly, I'm not a writer. Thirdly, my parents didn't name me Buddy.

Given my background and life story, the existence of this *sefer* is something of a miracle (something my high school *rebbeim* and English teachers would most likely attest to). Born and raised in the Bronx and living in Lakewood for the past fifteen years, it crossed my mind that the most fitting title would be *From the Hood to the Wood*. Always the sensible one, it was my wife who suggested instead the title *Sparks of Clarity*, which indeed most eloquently captures the essence of this work. As a *sefer*, I have likewise offered a *lashon kodesh* title which—in keeping with the custom of *mechabrim*—is reflective of the author. It is not only that "*Chazon Ovadiah*" is the haftarah for *Parashas Vayishlach*, my bar-mitzvah *parashah*. The title "חזון עובדיה" also contains all the letters of my real name, זאב יהודה (allowing for the interchangeability of the "ע" and the "א"). And, of course, right in the middle of "עובדיה" we find—"בְּדִי"!

Although this *sefer* took almost two years to write, it is based on notes from over thirty years of immersion in *chinuch*. One of my inspirations for this work was my *zaidy*, Aharon Asher Wolinetz, *zt"l*, a *mechaber* of many *sefarim*. Throughout the years, I would learn his *sefer* on *Chumash* and share its wisdom with my family at the Shabbos table.

I was only three years old when my *zaidy* passed away; nonetheless, because I learned his Torah, I have always felt a powerful closeness toward him. After all, there is no stronger bond among Jews than that formed by Torah—and that bond is even stronger when it involves family. I realized just how valuable it would be for my own family and myself to likewise enjoy such an unbreakable bond; and thus the idea for this project was conceived.

There are so many people to whom I extend sincere thanks for their assistance in the production of this *sefer*, and for helping me to develop and reach this seminal point. First and foremost, I would like to express my gratitude to my esteemed *rebbi*, Rabbi Berel Wein, *shlita*, whom I first met as a nineteen-year-old *bachur* when I entered Yeshiva Shaarei Torah in Monsey. I remember fondly how Rabbi Wein felt it important for every *talmid* to cultivate the skill of public speaking, regardless of where their future path may lie. The first assignment he issued was to choose a midrash with which to create four speeches for four different occasions—a wedding, funeral, bar mitzvah, and yeshiva dinner. My first reaction was total confusion; how could the same *maamar Chazal* be applied to both a wedding and a funeral? Looking back, I see that this public-speaking class may have been one of the greatest lessons I learned from my *rebbi*, as it taught us the skill of analyzing a *pasuk*, a Gemara, or any other *maamar Chazal* from a number of different angles. Being creative opens the mind to endless possibilities and helps one appreciate the Torah's limitless depth. May Hashem bless my *rebbi* with much *nachas*, and long years and good health to enjoy it.

As the years went by, I would apply this skill more and more, and was thereby able to develop various Torah insights. In hindsight, I see that it was most providential that I always wrote down my thoughts. Whether it was a *kashya*, a *teirutz*, or simply an inspirational point, I would jot it down on an index card or Post-it. This *sefer* is the product of this collection. I would start by trying to decipher my (sometimes cryptic) notes. Then I would build up each piece with an original Torah thought, including a message of *chizuk* or a practical lesson to be gleaned.

After I did the best I could, I would transfer the material to my dear friend, Rabbi Tzvi Hebel. R' Tzvi is a *talmid chacham* of the highest caliber. The wisdom and sterling character with which he graced this project cannot be overestimated. He polished each thought to a level far beyond my dreams. R' Tzvi is an amazing person and I am truly privileged to have a *chaver* like him. Hashem should bless him and his family with much *hatzlachah* and *berachah*.

The material in this *sefer* was filtered through many *talmidei chachamim*. This *sefer* was researched 99.9 percent internet-free. I mention this as a tribute to my *chaveirim*, for who needs Google when you have access to such stellar Torah scholars? My true pride is the fact that I am privileged to be connected to so many upstanding *b'nei Torah*. Much of this *sefer* was actually written in the Beis Medrash of Westgate, in the company of its many *chashuve* members. Of course, I thank all the *b'nei Torah* who helped me clarify the *divrei Torah* in this *sefer*. There are several individuals who truly went above and beyond, patiently listening to my ideas and offering their thoughts and suggestions: Rabbi Avrumi Berliner, Rabbi Avram Bogopulsky, Rabbi Shmuel Gelfand, Rabbi Yechiel Hess, Rabbi Shimon Koyfman, Rabbi Yosef Zalman Halevi Morgan, Rabbi Asher Neumann, Rabbi Moshe Aharon Sonnensohn, and Rabbi Moshe Spira.

U'mi'talmidai yoser mi'kulam. So many beautiful ideas in this *sefer* were generated by my students. The preparations and discussions were a major factor in developing my Torah thoughts. *Bli ayin hara*, there are too many students to name. Whether in the Jewish Foundation School in Staten Island, Yeshiva Bais Yitzchak in Hamilton, Moshe Aaron Yeshiva High School in Highland Park, Politz Day School in Cherry Hill, or the many youth/adult educational programs in which I was privileged to be a part, each student has a portion in this *sefer*.

I extend my deepest *hakaras ha'tov* to my in-laws, Rabbi Gavriel and Gelah Schechter. May Hashem bless them with good health and much *nachas* from the entire family. My father-in-law is an accomplished *talmid chacham* in his own right, and I greatly appreciate his review and comments of many of the *divrei Torah* in this *sefer*. And of course, I must thank my beautiful children. Many Shabbosos, I would share my Torah thoughts with them at the Shabbos table. Typically, I would deliver my remarks right before dessert was served—in the hopes that this would ensure a favorable reception. Upon concluding the *d'var Torah*, I would look to them and await their response of *"sefer*-worthy." My wife and I have tremendous *nachas* from each and every one of them. May Hashem continue to overflow their lives with *berachah* and *hatzlachah* in *ruchniyus* and *gashmiyus*.

As always, I turn to my dear wife, Rivka, the humblest person I know. Please forgive me for publicly thanking you. I know you truly don't want me to even mention you—but if I don't, people will think I'm single. I could cry tears of joy when I think of everything you do for me and our children. You constantly upgrade and uplift our family in ways that bring much *nachas* to Hashem. May He continue to bless us with all good things in *ruchniyus* and *gashmiyus*, and may we continue to make Him proud of us.

Acharon acharon chaviv. I thank Hashem for the life He has given me, and for the *siyata d'Shmaya* in bringing this dream to reality. My strongest desire is to bring honor to Hashem and Klal Yisrael.

Buddy Berkowitz
Lakewood, New Jersey, 5780

PART I

בין אדם לחברו

BEIN ADAM L'CHAVEIRO

1

THE ANGELS' MISSIONS

וַיִּשָּׂא עֵינָיו וַיַּרְא וְהִנֵּה שְׁלֹשָׁה אֲנָשִׁים נִצָּבִים עָלָיו.

And he lifted his eyes and he saw, and behold—three men were standing above him.

Bereishis 18:2

THE three "men" that Avraham hosted were really, as *Rashi* tells us, three *malachim*—each charged with a specific mission:

- Michael was to inform Sarah that she would give birth to a son.
- Gavriel was to overturn Sodom.
- Raphael would heal Avraham.

After relating this information, *Rashi* adds the following point: "שֶׁאֵין מַלְאָךְ אֶחָד עוֹשֶׂה שְׁתֵּי שְׁלִיחוּת—For a single angel does not perform two missions."

As we know, *Rashi* chooses his words very carefully, and only makes statements for a specific purpose. The question, then, is why *Rashi* felt the need to make this addition; what question was he coming to answer?

The conventional approach is that *Rashi* was addressing the need for multiple *malachim*; couldn't a single one carry out these tasks on his own? Thus, he explains that there is a "one-mission-limit" for a given *malach*.

3

4 Sparks of Clarity

However, if we take a closer look, we may discover that it was really a different matter that was bothering *Rashi*. His comments on this *pasuk* are based on a passage from the midrash.[1] The order in which the midrash listed these missions is somewhat perplexing—why was Raphael's placed last? It is very unlikely that the healing of Avraham actually took place *after* the other missions. After all, he was in such agony that he was even visited by Hashem Himself! The *malachim* were sitting right in front of Avraham who so desperately needed a *refuah*. It must be of course that the mission of healing Avraham was given top priority. Why, then, was Raphael's mission listed last?

It appears that this was the point *Rashi* was aiming to clarify. As he notes later on, Raphael actually had another task to perform—after healing Avraham, he was to save Lot from Sodom. But these were similar enough to be considered part of the same mission, as *Rashi* emphasizes: "אֵין מַלְאָךְ אֶחָד עוֹשֶׂה שְׁתֵּי שְׁלִיחוֹת." And based on this, we can see that the order listed above is indeed correct. True, Raphael healed Avraham right at the beginning. But his (one) mission was not yet over, being that it also included the rescue of Lot—something that didn't happen until much later. Thus, the missions were listed in order of their *completion*, and this is why Raphael's is placed last; for it was not fully completed until the end, when Sodom was overturned and Lot was saved.

---

1   *Bereishis Rabbah* 50:2.

2

RIVKAH'S TEST

וַיֹּאמַר...הִנֵּה אָנֹכִי נִצָּב עַל עֵין הַמָּיִם וּבְנוֹת אַנְשֵׁי הָעִיר יֹצְאֹת
לִשְׁאֹב מָיִם, וְהָיָה הַנַּעֲרָ אֲשֶׁר אֹמַר אֵלֶיהָ הַטִּי נָא כַדֵּךְ וְאֶשְׁתֶּה
וְאָמְרָה שְׁתֵה וְגַם גְּמַלֶּיךָ אַשְׁקֶה אֹתָהּ הֹכַחְתָּ לְעַבְדְּךָ לְיִצְחָק וּבָהּ
אֵדַע כִּי עָשִׂיתָ חֶסֶד עִם אֲדֹנִי.

*And he said, "...Behold, I am standing by the water fountain,
and the daughters of the city's people are coming out to draw
water. And it shall be [that] the maiden to whom I shall say,
'Please tilt your jug [toward me] so that I may drink,' and
she will answer, 'Drink; and also to your camels I will give
drink'—it is she whom You have designated for Your servant,
Yitzchak; and with her I shall know that You have performed
kindness with my master."*

Bereishis 24:12–14

THE Torah features a fairly extensive account of the search for a
wife for Yitzchak. Avraham sets his servant Eliezer on the task, with
some very explicit instructions: in no way may he select a wife from the
daughters of Canaan, nor may he bring Yitzchak himself to a foreign
land. Rather, Eliezer must go to Avraham's native land and bring back
from there a suitable *kallah* for his master's son.

5

Beyond Expectations

And so Eliezer travels to Aram Naharayim, and there by the well he devises his famous test: "וְהָיָה הַנַּעֲרָ אֲשֶׁר אֹמַר אֵלֶיהָ הַטִּי נָא כַדֵּךְ וְאֶשְׁתֶּה וְאָמְרָה שְׁתֵה וְגַם גְּמַלֶּיךָ אַשְׁקֶה אֹתָהּ הֹכַחְתָּ לְעַבְדְּךָ לְיִצְחָק—And it shall be [that] the maiden to whom I shall say, 'Please tilt your jug [toward me] so that I may drink,' and she will answer, 'Drink; and also to your camels I will give drink'—it is she whom You have designated for Your servant, Yitzchak."

Almost immediately, Rivkah appears, and proceeds to perform exactly as Eliezer had outlined: "וַיָּרָץ הָעֶבֶד לִקְרָאתָהּ וַיֹּאמֶר הַגְמִיאִינִי נָא מְעַט מַיִם מִכַּדֵּךְ, וַתֹּאמֶר שְׁתֵה אֲדֹנִי וַתְּמַהֵר וַתֹּרֶד כַּדָּהּ עַל יָדָהּ וַתַּשְׁקֵהוּ, וַתְּכַל לְהַשְׁקֹתוֹ וַתֹּאמֶר גַּם לִגְמַלֶּיךָ אֶשְׁאָב...וַתִּשְׁאַב לְכָל גְּמַלָּיו—And the servant ran toward her, and he said, 'Please allow me to drink a bit of water from your jug.' And she said, 'Drink, my lord'; and she hurried and lowered her jug upon her hand, giving him to drink. And she finished giving him to drink; and she said, 'I shall also draw [water] for your camels.'…And she drew for all of his camels."[1]

Actually, there is a slight (but significant) difference between Eliezer's outline and Rivkah's execution of the deed, as pointed out by my *zaidy*, Aharon Asher Wolinetz, *zt"l*. When Eliezer formulated the test, he grouped both elements—his own drinking and that of the camels—together in a single unit: "וְאָמְרָה שְׁתֵה וְגַם גְּמַלֶּיךָ אַשְׁקֶה." But we find with Rivkah that there was a separation, as evidenced by the fact that these items are placed in two different *pesukim*. The first *pasuk* contains the servant's own drinking: "וַתֹּאמֶר שְׁתֵה אֲדֹנִי וַתְּמַהֵר וַתֹּרֶד כַּדָּהּ עַל יָדָהּ וַתַּשְׁקֵהוּ,"[2] and only afterward does she tend to the camels: "וַתְּכַל לְהַשְׁקֹתוֹ וַתֹּאמֶר גַּם לִגְמַלֶּיךָ אֶשְׁאָב...וַתִּשְׁאַב לְכָל גְּמַלָּיו."[3]

What this indicates, my *zaidy* explained, is that not only did Rivkah pass the test, but she did so with flying colors. Eliezer was looking for someone whose *middah* of *chessed* would go above and beyond—offering water not only to himself in response to his request, but also to his thirsty animals. This Rivkah did, of course. But she went even a

---

1 *Bereishis* 24:17–20.
2 Ibid., v. 18.
3 Ibid., v. 19–20.

step further, displaying a sensitivity that Eliezer himself had not anticipated. Whereas Eliezer had grouped man and animal together, Rivkah
was particular to separate between the two. She felt it wasn't entirely
proper to offer sustenance to both a man and his animal in the same
breath; doing so revealed a certain disregard for the person's dignity,
as if both of their needs were on equal footing. Thus, it was her high
standard of *chessed*, coupled with her extra sensitivity to human beings,
that revealed her to be the perfect wife for Yitzchak.

Curious Omission

It certainly was a remarkable display of *middos* on Rivkah's part. But
here we find something interesting; for it appears that when relaying
the story, Eliezer completely skips over this aspect. When invited to
dine with Rivkah's family, he initially refuses to partake: "וַיֹּאמֶר לֹא אֹכַל
עַד אִם־דִּבַּרְתִּי דְּבָרָי—And he said: 'I shall not eat, until I speak my words.'"[4]
And so he proceeds to recount the events. But in retelling how Rivkah
passed his test, Eliezer sticks to his own version—not what Rivkah
actually did! Thus, he groups man and animal together, as if it really
happened that way. As he relates to his audience: "וַתְּמַהֵר וַתּוֹרֶד כַּדָּהּ מֵעָלֶיהָ וַתֹּאמֶר
שְׁתֵה וְגַם־גְּמַלֶּיךָ אַשְׁקֶה וָאֵשְׁתְּ וְגַם הַגְּמַלִּים הִשְׁקָתָה—And she lowered her jug from
her [shoulders], **and she said, 'Drink; and also to your camels I will
give drink'**; and I drank, and she also gave drink to the camels."[5] What,
indeed, is going on here? Eliezer's narration is noteworthy for its length,
as he includes a number of details. Why, then, does he choose to omit
one of the most impressive developments of the episode?

One could suggest that the whole matter was simply beyond Eliezer.
In other words, Rivkah's conduct indeed revealed a lofty level of character—so refined that Eliezer missed the significance. Such a level was
beyond his comprehension; in his mind, it was more than enough that
she offered more than he asked, giving his animals to drink in addition to himself. It would never occur to him to display such care and

---

4   Ibid., v. 33.
5   Ibid., v. 46.

sensitivity to avoid grouping man and animal together. When Rivkah did make such a separation, the gesture was lost on him. He simply didn't notice.

It is somewhat difficult, however, to make such a suggestion. After all, Eliezer was himself a great man, having served, watched, and learned from Avraham. Certainly, he was witness to the highest levels of *chessed* practiced in his master's house. There really can be no question that he picked up on Rivka's high level of *chessed* and concern for others. It would appear, then, that he deliberately sought to conceal Rivkah's heightened level of sensitivity.

Actually, for personal reasons, Eliezer had a strong motivation to do exactly that. As *Rashi* mentions, Eliezer himself had his eye on Yitzchak, whom he wanted for his own daughter. For his part, Avraham was distinctly uninterested. Great as Eliezer was, he was still a Canaani, and as such, the *shidduch* was not appropriate. But Eliezer wanted it badly and he seemed prepared to do what he could to scuttle the other prospects.

And so, when speaking to Rivkah's family, he insisted on using his own version. Such is alluded to in his statement—"עַד אִם דִּבַּרְתִּי דְּבָרָי—until I speak **my words**." Eliezer wanted to portray Rivkah's deed on a lower level, in accordance with his own conception of propriety. Thus he purposely omitted Rivkah's exemplary sensitivity for he was afraid of it getting back to Avraham, as Eliezer knew that his master would be most taken by such a refined character. And he figured as well that, on the contrary, Avraham would be disappointed when he heard that she grouped man and animal together (in accordance with Eliezer's own version).

Eliezer journeys homeward with this plan in mind. He was prepared to relate these events in the same manner when reporting back to Avraham himself, thereby securing the *shidduch* for his own daughter. But alas, Hashem had other plans. Unexpectedly, Yitzchak appeared before them in the field before Eliezer had a chance to make it to Avraham. Interestingly, in relating this development, the Torah itself draws a separation between man and beast:

- The *pasuk* first states: "וְיִצְחָק בָּא—**And Yitzchak was coming.**"[6]
- In the next *pasuk*, mention is made of the arrival of the camels: "וְהִנֵּה גְמַלִּים בָּאִים—**And behold, camels were arriving.**"[7]

The contrast certainly seems uncanny, as if underscoring to Eliezer the importance of such a separation. In any event, this unanticipated meeting seems to derail Eliezer's plan. We see that Rivkah herself was so overawed by Yitzchak's *kedushah* that "וַתִּפֹּל מֵעַל הַגָּמָל."[8] It appears that Eliezer was similarly overwhelmed by Yitzchak's radiance. He was so disarmed that he ended up revealing all: "וַיְסַפֵּר הָעֶבֶד לְיִצְחָק אֵת כָּל הַדְּבָרִים—And the servant related to Yitzchak all of the matters."[9] Thus we see that he told Yitzchak "כָּל הַדְּבָרִים"—everything as it actually happened: not his version, but the true superior level of Rivkah's character.

---

6   Ibid., v. 62
7   Ibid., v. 63
8   Ibid., v. 64.
9   Ibid., v. 66.

3

MOSHE ADDRESSES
THE FIGHTERS

וְהִנֵּה שְׁנֵי אֲנָשִׁים עִבְרִים נִצִּים וַיֹּאמֶר לָרָשָׁע לָמָּה תַכֶּה רֵעֶךָ.

*And behold, two Jewish men were fighting; and [Moshe] said
to the wicked one: "Why do you strike your fellow?"*

Shemos 2:13

THERE is a well-known incident in which Moshe tries to intervene
between two quarreling Jews. In his comments on this episode, *Rashi*
advances a fairly well-known *chiddush*. He takes note of the fact that the
Torah describes the individual addressed by Moshe as a *"rasha"*—even
though he had not yet actually struck his rival. Apparently, a person is
deemed a *rasha* for merely *lifting* his hand to strike a fellow Yid.

This is the "familiar" *chiddush*. But if we look further, we discover
what appears to be yet another (perhaps less well-known) *chiddush*. The
pasuk says: "וַיֹּאמֶר לָרָשָׁע לָמָּה תַכֶּה רֵעֶךָ—And [Moshe] said to the *rasha*,
'Why would you strike רֵעֶךָ (your fellow)?'" *Rashi* understands that this
term implies a measure of equality; and he thus explains Moshe's intent
in using this word: "רֵעֶךָ—רָשָׁע כְּמוֹתְךָ." The fellow you were poised to strike
is as much of a *rasha* as you.

10

This truly is a tremendous *chiddush* and requires some explanation. We can certainly understand how striking a Yid makes one a *rasha*, and it may also follow that simply raising a hand to strike makes one deserving of this label. But why would Moshe refer to the other individual as a *rasha*? What did *he* do? He didn't hit anyone, nor did he even lift his hand! On the contrary—if anything, he is merely the victim! Why is he being called a *rasha*? And not only that, but *Rashi* considers him as bad as the first one: "רָשָׁע כְּמוֹתְךָ"! How did it come to be that the victim is equated with his attacker?

The answer, it would seem, is that this attempted attack didn't simply come out of nowhere. Nothing justifies lifting one's hand against a fellow Jew, of course. But this was not a case where someone was about to pounce on a completely innocent person who was minding his own business. Rather, the *pasuk* states that the two were "נִצִּים," which *Rashi* explains to mean "מְרִיבִים" (quarreling). In other words, there was already a heated argument in progress; and it was this conflict that precipitated the near-attack. With his *chiddush*, then, *Rashi* is conveying another (most important) *yesod*; that, yes, the "victim" in such a case indeed bears much responsibility for the attack against him. It would have been one thing had he been going about his own affairs, uninvolved with the attacker. But that is not what happened here. Rather, they had both been engaged in a vicious confrontation. *Rashi* is thus teaching us that if one gets under the other's skin to the point that it comes to blows, the inciter is just as responsible as the attacker. After all, the "victim" wasn't just a victim. He did have a choice. He did not have to participate and prolong the confrontation, but could have walked away, or sought some other means to diffuse the situation. By reacting as he did—adding fuel to the fire instead of extinguishing it—he has committed a severe *aveirah*, of equal magnitude to the one he so antagonized. By leading his fellow to such a state of anger, he is properly branded as a "רָשָׁע כְּמוֹתְךָ."

We derive a most powerful and vital lesson from this episode, one that applies to situations in our own daily lives. When confronted with opposition, a person's natural inclination is to strike back and fight it out. But we are urged here to consider how different the outcome would be if we would choose the path of calm over escalation. Overcoming the urge to retaliate by maintaining our silence—or avoiding explosive situations in the first place—makes a tremendous impact in *Shamayim*. Rather than being labeled a *rasha*, we may be labeled a *tzaddik* instead.

4

BIRTH OF YOSEF

וְאַחַר יָלְדָה בַּת וַתִּקְרָא אֶת שְׁמָהּ דִּינָה.

And afterward she gave birth to a daughter, and she called her name Dinah.

Bereishis 30:21

THE name "Dinah," Chazal inform us, alludes to the rather intriguing circumstances of this child's birth. Apparently, Leah was actually pregnant with a boy; but the Matriarch conducted a deliberation ("*din*") with herself. She realized that giving birth to another boy would have severe consequences for her sister, Rachel. As things stood now, Leah had six sons, and each of the two *shefachos* had two sons each. Thus, a total of ten out of the twelve *shevatim* that Yaakov was destined to have had already been born, and now she was expecting again. If she would bear another son, that would leave Rachel the possibility of bearing only one of the remaining *shevatim* (Binyamin). Leah could not bear to see Rachel suffer such humiliation, as *Rashi* quotes her as saying: "אִם זֶה זָכָר לֹא תְהֵא רָחֵל אֲחוֹתִי כְּאַחַת הַשְּׁפָחוֹת—If this is a male, then my sister Rachel will not even be like one of the maidservants." Note that she was particular to refer to her as "רָחֵל אֲחוֹתִי," a sign of her tender affection and concern for her sister. And so, in what appears to be an act of supreme self-sacrifice,

Leah davened that Hashem adjust the baby's gender—which He proceeded to do! Instead of having Yosef, Leah gave birth to Dinah. She gave up the opportunity of producing another *shevet b'Yisrael* in order to save her sister from pain and disgrace. It certainly seems to be a tremendous gesture of selflessness.

However, was it really? Let us recall, for a moment, what Rachel had done on behalf of Leah. Originally, Rachel alone had been designated to marry Yaakov. Lavan engineered that Leah would take her place, but Yaakov—aware of Lavan's tendency toward trickery—had devised certain *simanim* to ensure he was getting the right bride. Rachel realized that her intended husband would thus discover the scam, and Leah would be disgraced for life. And so, to preserve her sister's dignity, Rachel gave her the *simanim*—essentially relinquishing her husband to her! And not only that, but she put herself in a most precarious position. For it seemed that while Rachel was destined to marry Yaakov, Leah was destined for Eisav; by agreeing to the "switch," Rachel would now potentially end up with Eisav herself. We see that she was even willing to forego her own eternity to protect her sister's feelings! In the final analysis, without Rachel, Leah would have had nothing—no Yaakov and no *shevatim*; the only thing she may indeed have had was Eisav. For all of this, she was greatly indebted to Rachel. What, then, did Leah seek to do for Rachel? Was she just making sure that she was not worse off than the *shefachos*? We do not wish to cast aspersions on one of the holy *Imahos*, of course, but Leah's actions seem perplexing. Was this really the best she could come up with? It would seem that Rachel deserved more!

A closer look will reveal that Leah indeed did much more for Rachel than simply put her on par with the *shefachos*. Yosef, as we know, bore two sons, Ephraim and Menasheh. And in *Parashas Vayechi*, Yaakov remarks to Yosef: "אֶפְרַיִם וּמְנַשֶּׁה כִּרְאוּבֵן וְשִׁמְעוֹן יִהְיוּ לִי"—Ephraim and Menasheh shall be to me like Reuven and Shimon."[1] As *Rashi* there explains, Yaakov Avinu was conferring on them the status of actual *shevatim*.

---

1   *Bereishis* 48:5.

What emerges, then, is that a total of three *shevatim*—two from Yosef, and one from Binyamin—emanated from Rachel Imeinu. Rachel was elevated to be not only the equal of the *shefachos*, but even beyond.

Such was the impact of Leah's gracious intervention. A great sister indeed.

5

NOACH, AVRAHAM, AND THE DIFFERENCE BETWEEN THEM

לֹא טוֹב הֱיוֹת הָאָדָם לְבַדּוֹ.

It is not good for man to be alone.

Bereishis 2:18

IT was in the context of creating a mate for Adam HaRishon that Hashem issued this declaration: "וַיֹּאמֶר ה׳ אֱלֹקִים לֹא טוֹב הֱיוֹת הָאָדָם לְבַדּוֹ אֶעֱשֶׂה לּוֹ עֵזֶר כְּנֶגְדּוֹ—And Hashem Elokim said: '**It is not good for man to be alone**; I shall fashion for him a helpmate opposite him.'" The statement certainly underscores the value and importance of marriage, and the interaction between spouses that enables them to grow together. Guidance, encouragement, and even constructive criticism (when necessary and appropriate) are all key ingredients for the strengthening of the bond between husband and wife.

Still, it appears that the statement can be understood in a much broader sense as well, encompassing the whole of society. The Torah here is conveying a simple and valuable lesson. "לֹא טוֹב הֱיוֹת הָאָדָם לְבַדּוֹ"—people need people. Being alone means missing the opportunity of strengthening the bond between ourselves and society. This idea is illustrated most dramatically through the famous incident involving Choni HaMaagil who, as the Gemara relates, fell asleep for seventy years.[1] When he awoke, he sought out his family, but they did not believe that he was the real Choni HaMaagil. He went to the *beis midrash*, but nobody there believed him either. He felt so alone in a world that had once appreciated and embraced him that he begged Hashem for mercy—and he died. To this point, Rava quotes the popular adage: "אוֹ חַבְרוּתָא אוֹ מִיתוּתָא—Either companionship or death." Disconnected as he was from society, Choni preferred death, and Hashem agreed.

At a more basic level, every parent is filled with pride and joy to see their children interacting with each other in a positive way, thereby strengthening the family bond. Similarly, we are Hashem's children and it gives Him much *nachas* when we interact with our fellow Jews. And by interacting with them, we can have a stronger impact not only on each other as individuals, but on society as a whole.

Noach and Avraham

A stark contrast can be drawn between Noach and Avraham in this area. Our Sages were highly critical of Noach for neglecting to interact with his generation. Had he reached out to them, his influence could have been considerable—so much so that the *mabul* may have been prevented. Chazal tell us that the *gezar din* for the *Dor Ha'mabul* was sealed on account of *gezel*.[2] By and large, people only steal from strangers—that is, people they don't really care about. Most people would be hesitant to cause harm to someone with whom they have a relationship. Noach, as we know, was a tremendous *tzaddik*; as such, his influence would have been all the more impactful. Had he interacted with society in a positive manner, it would have gone a long way toward strengthening the social bonds of his generation. This would have changed the overall culture of his society; it would have been a lot more difficult to steal, because people would have felt connected to each other. By

---

1   *Taanis* 23a.
2   *Sanhedrin* 108a.

engaging in even such simple gestures as greeting a neighbor, it would have become that much more difficult to harm another person. Had Noach reached out more to his generation, perhaps he would have fostered more harmony, minimized the occurrence of *gezel*, and prevented the destruction of the world.

A much different picture emerges when we examine the case of Avraham Avinu, who excelled in the area of social interaction. Chazal tell us that his tent was open on all four sides, serving as an open invitation to all to enter within and enjoy his hospitality. But it wasn't only Avraham's tent that was open for other people; his heart was, as well. Avraham was a very wealthy man, with a retinue of servants. But he himself was the first to greet visitors and offer them his personal service. The famous episode with the three *malachim* visiting him is a case in point. On the day of their arrival, Avraham was in tremendous pain; he had every excuse in the world to delegate his hosting responsibilities to his multitude of servants. But Avraham well understood the power of positive interaction, and he seized the moment. He didn't want to miss even a single opportunity to impart his goodness to the world.

It is noteworthy that a great calamity occurred at this time in the form of the destruction of Sodom. These people, as we know, were thoroughly evil, probably even more so than the *Dor Ha'mabul*. It is a wonder that such a pernicious influence stayed relatively local, not extending far beyond its borders. The fact that the destruction was indeed so localized is a credit to Avraham Avinu, whose conduct had a great impact on his surroundings. His drive to spread kindness to all created a positive culture that permeated throughout the world. And thus, we see clearly the great divide between Avraham and Noach. The former, due to his positive interaction, was able to perpetuate goodness and thereby minimize destruction. Noach was righteous enough that he himself was saved; but due to his lack of interaction and outreach, the greater world was wiped out.

The Three Pillars

The idea discussed above manifests itself in the well-known Mishnah that states: "עַל שְׁלֹשָׁה דְבָרִים הָעוֹלָם עוֹמֵד, עַל הַתּוֹרָה וְעַל הָעֲבוֹדָה וְעַל גְּמִילוּת

חֲסָדִים—The world stands upon three things: Torah, Divine service, and acts of kindness."[3] These three pillars are vital for the world's existence; and interestingly enough, it appears that the common denominator between them is the very notion of social interaction:

- Interaction with others is an essential component to Torah study on all levels, as indicated by Rebbi's declaration: "הַרְבֵּה תוֹרָה לְמַדְתִּי מֵרַבּוֹתַי, וּמֵחֲבֵירַי יוֹתֵר מֵהֶם, וּמִתַּלְמִידַי יוֹתֵר מִכּוּלָן—I have learned much Torah from my teachers, even more from my colleagues, but I learned the most from my students."[4]

- *Avodah* (davening) is a communal activity, of course. As we know, it is davening with a minyan that provides the optimal forum for *tefillos* to be accepted, for when a minyan assembles, it constitutes much more than just ten (or more) individuals who have gathered in one area and who pray at the same time. Rather, they join together and form a single, cohesive unit; and it is this powerful bond that strengthens the potency of the *tefillos*.

- The pillar of *chessed* also (obviously) relies on social interaction, as it inherently involves doing for and helping others. Furthermore, the *pasuk* says: "עוֹלָם חֶסֶד יִבָּנֶה—The world is built upon kindness."[5] When you perform a kind act for someone, you're not just helping that person; you are also helping his family, and perhaps even others who are associated with him.

Thus, we see again how positive interaction spreads beyond one's immediate vicinity and strengthens the world as a whole. Sharing *divrei Torah*, davening together, and improving another Jew's life are all examples of uplifting society as a whole and giving Hashem *nachas* from the world He created.

---

3   *Avos* 1:2.
4   *Makkos* 10a.
5   *Tehillim* 89:3.

6

LEAH AND RACHEL: SISTERLY CONCERN

וְעֵינֵי לֵאָה רַכּוֹת.

And the eyes of Leah were soft.

Bereishis 29:17

MOST of us are familiar with Rachel's legendary concern and self-sacrifice for her sister. This was manifest most especially in the matter of Leah's marriage to Yaakov, arranged due to the deception of Lavan. Yaakov had been intending to marry Rachel first, of course, and had even developed a "code" (*simanim*) with his bride to preempt any trickery on the part of his father-in-law. Realizing, however, the profound shame that would befall her sister, Rachel transmitted the *simanim* to Leah. She thereby relinquished her own husband just so that her sister would not suffer eternal disgrace.

As stated, this was an example of Rachel's exemplary care for her sister's well-being. But the truth is, as we shall see, that Leah likewise excelled in the same area.

The *pasuk* emphasizes the delicate nature of Leah's eyes—"וְעֵינֵי לֵאָה רַכּוֹת." Chazal tell us that this was a result of the many tears she shed in

response to the persistent reports about the sisters' destiny: "הָיוּ אוֹמְרִים
שְׁנֵי בָנִים יֵשׁ לָהּ לְרִבְקָה, שְׁתֵּי בָנוֹת יֵשׁ לוֹ לְלָבָן, גְּדוֹלָה לְגָדוֹל וּקְטַנָּה לְקָטָן—It was
being said that Rivkah had two sons [Eisav and Yaakov], and Lavan had
two daughters [Leah and Rachel]; the elder daughter [was to marry]
the elder son, and the younger daughter [was to marry] the younger
son."[1] What was the meaning of this "prediction"? According to the
simple understanding (brought down by *mefarshim*), the intent was
that Eisav, the firstborn, would marry Leah, and Rachel was designated
for Yaakov. Knowing the lowly and wicked character of Eisav, Leah cried
over her own fate.

Perhaps, however, we may suggest an alternate approach. Technically
speaking, it was really Yaakov who was the "older" brother. *Rashi* states
earlier that it was for this reason that Yaakov, during birth, was grasp-
ing Eisav's heel.[2] Yaakov rightfully wanted to be called the "firstborn,"
for it was he who was conceived first. And so, it was Yaakov who was
legitimately the *gadol* (elder). What emerges, then, is that the prediction stating "גְּדוֹלָה לְגָדוֹל" meant that it was *Leah* who would be wed to
Yaakov! If so, why was she crying? It would seem that she was distressed
not over her own blissful fate, but for the bitter one that awaited her
sister—who, it seemed, was destined for Eisav!

Indeed, we find that for some time Rachel herself was concerned that
she would fall to Eisav's lot. *Rashi* says explicitly that even after she was
married to Yaakov, Rachel feared she would be divorced on account of
her childlessness, and then Eisav would marry her.[3] *Rashi* also points
out that Eisav himself was hopeful that this possibility would come to
fruition (see below). In any event, this casts another of Leah's actions
in a new light. We had previously discussed the events surrounding the
birth of Yosef, whereby—as recorded by *Rashi*[4]—it was really Leah who
was initially pregnant with him. Not wanting to deprive her sister of
another *shevet*, however, she prayed to Hashem to switch the baby's

---

1   *Bava Basra* 123a.
2   *Bereishis* 25:26.
3   Ibid., 30:22.
4   Ibid., v. 21

gender. Her request was granted—Leah gave birth to Dinah, and Rachel had Yosef. With the birth of Yosef, Rachel's connection to her husband, Yaakov, was solidified. And so, we see that Leah had once again helped Rachel avoid the potential disaster of marrying Eisav. Significantly, it was at this time that Yaakov decided to return to his father's house in Eretz Yisrael. He turned to Lavan and declared: "תְּנָה אֶת נָשַׁי"—Allow me to take my wives."[5] Yaakov suddenly had the confidence to move on and face Eisav; he felt that now that Rachel had Yosef, she was safe from Eisav's clutches.

It appears, however, that an element of the danger still lingered. Thus, we find that when they eventually did meet up with Eisav, Yosef stepped in front to shield his mother. *Rashi* quotes Yosef's rationale: "שֶׁמָּא יִתְלֶה בָּהּ עֵינָיו אוֹתוֹ רָשָׁע, אֶעֱמֹד כְּנֶגְדָּהּ וְאֲעַכְּבֶנּוּ מִלְהִסְתַּכֵּל בָּהּ"—Perhaps this *rasha* will set his designs on her; I will stand and prevent him from gazing upon her."[6]

From all of the above, a most impressive picture emerges regarding the care and concern each sister displayed for the other. The great strength of Rachel's character becomes even more apparent. As we know, she was *moseres nefesh* so that Leah could marry Yaakov—despite the looming threat that she herself would fall to Eisav's lot. And we see how such care and concern was directed to Rachel, as Leah cried for her, davened for her, and also made tremendous personal sacrifices on her sister's behalf. Theirs was a level of fortitude and sisterly love that was truly befitting the *Imahos*, and that serves as a pristine model for all of Klal Yisrael.

---

5   Ibid., v. 26.
6   Ibid., 33:7.

7

GIVING—
AND RECEIVING—
TOCHACHAH

הוֹכֵחַ תּוֹכִיחַ אֶת עֲמִיתֶךָ.

You shall rebuke your friend.

Vayikra 19:17

CRITICISM tends not to be our most favorite thing. Nonetheless, the Torah instructs us to engage in rebuke: "הוֹכֵחַ תּוֹכִיחַ אֶת עֲמִיתֶךָ." It is noteworthy that the mitzvah is conveyed with the double *lashon* of "הוֹכֵחַ תּוֹכִיחַ." The intent may very well be to include the two aspects of *tochachah*—giving and receiving—as there is a proper way to do both. In any event, by gaining a healthier perspective on this matter, we may come to better appreciate (and more properly engage in) this important mitzvah.

Giving Tochachah

One dimension of this mitzvah is directed toward the individual giving the rebuke. The whole idea of giving *tochachah* may go against modern sensibilities, which favor a "mind your own business" attitude.

Many people today, then, would hesitate before offering criticism to someone else. The mitzvah of *tochachah*, however, reminds us that Klal Yisrael itself is really one unit. As such, when we see someone involved in sinful behavior, that blemish is really a part of ourselves. Therefore, it really is very much "our business;" in effect, correcting a fellow Yid is a form of self-improvement.

All that being said, there still is a correct way to go about it. In directing us to give rebuke, the *pasuk* uses the term *amisecha*, which means "your friend." This is quite purposeful; for as a number of commentators explain, the intent is to emphasize that the criticism must be done in a pleasant way, as one talking to a friend. When giving *tochachah*, one should deliver the rebuke in the same way he would want it told to him if he were on the receiving end. Thus, it should be thought out, so that it achieves its purpose. If done carelessly and improperly, the recipient will simply be resentful instead of actually improving his behavior.

Receiving Tochachah

Being on the receiving end of *mussar*, as noted, can be a challenge for many of us. Few people really enjoy being criticized. Rather than viewing it as beneficial, a common reaction people have (at least internally) is: "Who is he to tell me what to do?" Still, imagine if someone were getting ready to eat a certain dish, and another person would suddenly tell him that it contains poison! The diner would probably not start engaging in character analysis of the other person. More likely, he would immediately push away the plate, and probably offer his thanks. Unfortunately, when it comes to spiritual matters, many people have a different attitude. They first assess the character and motive of the person who is correcting them. However, if the receiver has clarity, he can feel genuine appreciation for the one giving the rebuke—even in the event it was not handled in the friendliest manner. In fact, he would be grateful—for he, as the recipient, was at least saved from ingesting poison.

The following scenario may serve to clarify the matter even further. A certain individual is granted a job interview for what promises to be a most lucrative position. The opportunity is so appealing that the candidate is hardly able to sleep the whole night before. He gets up in the morning with great eagerness, almost tasting the imminent turn of his fortune. His family wishes him well as he walks out the door, where he is picked up by a car full of familiar faces. These are friends of his who already work at the firm and who have offered him to join their carpool for the day. During the drive, they tell him how much they love their jobs and how lucky he is to have this opportunity. He arrives at the building with great pride and professional confidence. In the elevator he bumps into a few more acquaintances, and this makes him feel even more comfortable. They wish him well as he walks into the office. The secretary, who happens to be the boss' wife, greets him as he enters. It turns out that the two recognize each other as old neighbors from years back. At this point, the interviewee feels that, for all intents and purposes, the job is already his.

Finally, he sits down with the boss himself, and the interview gets underway. It goes by fairly quickly, and the boss thanks him for coming and says that he'll be in touch. Still brimming with an eager confidence, the candidate asks the boss when he can start working. At that point, the boss has to break the bad news, informing him that he did not get the job. Seeing the stunned look that suddenly appears on his face, the boss feels compelled to offer at least a brief explanation. "This is a very important job," he states, "that requires a very high level of professionalism." But from the unchanged expression on the interviewee's face, it is quite clear that he remains clueless. The boss plunges forward. "Let me ask you," he says, "did you have any chocolate this morning?" Finding his voice, the other man relates his astonishment. "Why, yes, in fact I did," he responds. "How did you know?" With a smirk, the boss answers: "You see, our company is looking for someone who takes pride in their appearance, maintaining it at all times. You should have checked the mirror before you left the house." Still reeling, the man leaves the office, finds the nearest restroom, looks in the mirror—and there discovers a smudge of chocolate on his cheek. Embarrassed and devastated, he cleans it off and leaves in a totally demoralized state.

What is the one thought uppermost in his mind on the way home? Most likely, he is completely bewildered over the fact that *no one said anything*—not his family, not the carpool, not his friends in the elevator. Not even the secretary who recognized him as an old neighbor. How could that happen? If only someone had pointed it out beforehand! Then, instead of suffering such humiliation and missing out on such a grand opportunity, his life could have taken a dramatic turn for the better! Now, if such is the sentiment a person would feel when it comes to material success, how much more so should it apply to spiritual matters, whose consequences are eternal.

Additionally, the man in this scenario would probably berate himself over his own oversight—the fact that he didn't look in a mirror before the interview. Had he done so, he could have avoided this whole disaster.

This is yet another way we may view our friends who offer critiques—in a sense, they are our mirrors, reflecting what needs *tikkun* and sparing us from hurting ourselves. Everyone checks a mirror before they leave their house in the morning, just to make sure they look appropriate. But if you check the mirror and see something you don't like, you don't get annoyed at the mirror! You immediately fix whatever is askew, look into the mirror again, and say, "Good thing I noticed this in time."

In truth, this is a much healthier perspective to take toward the *mussar* that is periodically given to us by our parents, teachers, and friends. Much like a mirror, they are saving us from going out into the world and behaving in a way that could prove detrimental to ourselves. If a person could thus understand the true value of constructive criticism, he may respond with genuine gratitude rather than annoyance.

8

CHOSHEID B'KESHEIRIM

וַיַּעַן מֹשֶׁה וַיֹּאמֶר וְהֵן לֹא יַאֲמִינוּ לִי וְלֹא יִשְׁמְעוּ בְּקֹלִי...וַיֹּאמֶר
אֵלָיו ה' מַזֶּה בְיָדֶךָ וַיֹּאמֶר מַטֶּה.

And Moshe answered, and he said: "But they will not believe me, nor will they listen to my voice..." And Hashem said to him: "What is this in your hand?" And he said: "A staff."

Shemos 4:1–2

WHEN appointing Moshe Rabbeinu as the redeemer of Yisrael, Hashem first had to persuade him to accept the mission. The Torah relates the extensive dialogue that took place between Hashem and Moshe, as the latter kept refusing for a variety of reasons. At one point, Moshe claims that his words would go unheeded by the people: "וַיַּעַן מֹשֶׁה וַיֹּאמֶר וְהֵן לֹא יַאֲמִינוּ לִי וְלֹא יִשְׁמְעוּ בְּקֹלִי—And Moshe answered, and he said: 'And they will not believe me, and will not listen to my voice.'"

True or False?

As it turns out, we find that Moshe was held to account for making this claim. Hashem responded by turning his attention to the staff: "וַיֹּאמֶר אֵלָיו ה' מַזֶּה בְיָדֶךָ וַיֹּאמֶר מַטֶּה—And Hashem said to him: 'What is that in your hand?' And he said: 'A staff.'" In doing so, *Rashi* explains,

Hashem was hinting to Moshe that he actually deserved to be punished: "מֶה שֶׁבְּיָדְךָ אַתָּה חַיָּב לִלְקוֹת, שֶׁחָשַׁדְתָּ בִּכְשֵׁרִים"—You really should be stricken with that which is in your hand [i.e., the staff]; for you have suspected the innocent."

As the narrative proceeds, Moshe is again reminded of his error. Hashem begins supplying Moshe with wonders to perform before the people, the first of which entails the transformation of his staff into a snake. *Rashi* clarifies the significance of this particular symbol. The *nachash* in Gan Eden engaged in slander. By turning the staff into a snake, Hashem was alluding to Moshe that he himself had followed the example of the *nachash* by speaking *lashon hara* against B'nei Yisrael.

These two messages, on the surface, seem to be conveying the same idea—Moshe is being reprimanded for alleging that B'nei Yisrael would not believe him. With a closer look, however, we see that they are actually quite different; in fact, they almost seem to contradict each other! As we know, while *lashon hara* is derogatory in nature and a grave *aveirah*, it does refer to a true report. (Had it been false, it would be classified as *motzi shem ra*, not *lashon hara*.) If Moshe's statement constituted *lashon hara*, that must mean that, in fact, he was correct; if not for the signs, the people would not believe him. And such indeed seems to be the case. The Torah states later on: "וַיַּעַשׂ הָאֹתֹת לְעֵינֵי הָעָם, וַיַּאֲמֵן הָעָם—And he performed the signs in front of the people's eyes; and the people believed."[1] The implication seems to be that it was only by seeing the signs that the people had *emunah*. The question, then, is how Moshe's statement could be characterized at the same time as an example of *chosheid b'kesheirim*.

Toward the beginning of *Sefer Shmuel*, the *Navi* relates how Eli saw Chanah moving her lips and suspected her of drunkenness. Chanah corrected the misimpression, explaining that she was really just davening her heart out to be blessed with a child. Eli apologizes and gives her a *berachah* that her request should be fulfilled—which is indeed what happened, as she gave birth to Shmuel Hanavi. The Gemara derives a

---

1   *Shemos* 4:30–31.

number of halachos from this story, including those relating to *cheshad* (suspicion).[2] As, for example, the Gemara concludes: "מִכַּאן לַחוֹשֵׁד אֶת חֲבֵרוֹ בְּדָבָר שֶׁאֵין בּוֹ שֶׁצָרִיךְ...לְבָרְכוֹ, שֶׁנֶּאֱמַר וֵאלֹקֵי יִשְׂרָאֵל יִתֵּן אֶת שֵׁלָתֵךְ—From here [we learn] that one who wrongly suspects his friend has to grant him a blessing; as it says: 'May the G-d of Yisrael grant your wish.'"[3] We see, in any event, that *chosheid b'kesheirim* refers to a case of wrongly suspecting someone—such as when Eli suspected that Chanah was drunk, when in reality she was sober.

How, then, can we reconcile these two statements of *Rashi*?

- On the one hand, he refers to Moshe's comments about B'nei Yisrael as a case of *chosheid b'kesheirim*, which would imply that they were being wrongly suspected.
- On the other, *Rashi* also calls it *lashon hara*, which would mean that Moshe's assertion was true; and as we have seen, the *pesukim* themselves intimate that B'nei Yisrael were not ready to simply take Moshe at his word.

Which was it, then? Was the claim true or false?

Chiddushim in the Laws of Chosheid B'Kesheirim

It seems we are compelled to follow the clear implication of the *pesukim*—namely, that Moshe's concern was indeed accurate, and the people were prone to disregard his message. As such, Moshe's comments rightly fall into the category of *lashon hara*—true statements of a derogatory nature. Nonetheless, it may still be possible to classify this as a case of *chosheid b'kesheirim*. To explain how, I would like to suggest a *chiddush* in the definition of *chosheid b'kesheirim*. It may very well be that there are times where even *correct* suppositions fall under the heading of this *din*. For "kesheirim" does not necessarily mean that they are "kasher" with regard to this specific suspicion, but rather that they are upstanding and reputable people—*kesheirim* overall. In other words, the *aveirah* of being *chosheid b'kesheirim* is to cast suspicion on reputable people—even if, in this specific instance, they are actually

---

3   *Shmuel I* 1:17.

guilty! Since they are inherently *kesheirim*, they must be given the benefit of the doubt. And so, it emerges that Moshe's comments could indeed be characterized as both *lashon hara* and a case of *chosheid b'kesheirim*. He happened to be correct that Yisrael would not believe him; nonetheless, as they were *kesheirim*, he was not authorized at the time to conclusively decide that they would act inappropriately.[4]

There is yet another *chiddush* pertaining to these halachos that emerges from the two cases of Moshe/Yisrael, and Eli/Chanah. As was mentioned above, Chazal derive from the narrative of Eli and Chanah that a person who is *chosheid b'kesheirim* has to subsequently grant a *berachah*. But while Eli did just that, we don't find that Moshe ended up giving a *berachah* to Klal Yisrael after being called to account for being *chosheid b'kesheirim*. As outlined above, there is a fundamental difference between these two examples: while both fall under the category of *chosheid b'kesheirim*, in Moshe's case the suspicion turned out to be true, while in Eli's it was unfounded. Apparently, then, a *berachah* must be granted only in an instance of *falsely* suspecting, but not for verified accusations. But why should that be? After all, we just showed that they are both examples of *chosheid b'kesheirim*!

Perhaps we may answer by going to the heart of the matter: why in the first place does one give a blessing after being *chosheid b'kesheirim*? What does one have to do with the other? The *inyan*, it would seem, is to repair the hurt that was caused; the *berachah* is an attempt to heal that pain. But the real pain occurs when a person is accused of something he did not (or would not) do; their reputation was unfairly damaged, and until they are eventually vindicated, the hurt is real and substantial. This would only apply if the suspicion was unfounded. If the individual is in fact guilty of the allegation, he doesn't experience that same level of hurt of being falsely and unfairly accused. This is why no *berachah* was called for in the case of Moshe and Yisrael.

---

4   As it relates to the episode of Eli and Chanah, that was an example of *chosheid b'kesheirim* in both senses of the term. She was in fact being wrongly suspected; she was completely sober, contrary to Eli's assertion. And furthermore, she of course was an inherently *kasher* individual in all of her dealings.

Background to Blessing

Regarding the blessing given by the *chosheid*, it seems that certain prerequisites apply. Eli's *berachah* to Chanah was obviously sincere, for it came to fruition with the birth of Shmuel. But as we shall see, delivering such a *berachah* is no simple matter and it requires a certain amount of background preparation.

To obtain greater clarity let us turn to the well-known episode in the Torah centering on the topic of *berachos*—namely, the blessing Yitzchak was to deliver to his first-born. Yitzchak, of course, was on the most exalted spiritual level, a *kadosh v'tahor* of the first order. And yet we find something most interesting in relation to his granting of the *berachos*. It seems that the blessing had to be preceded with some tasty delicacies; as Yitzchak declared: "וַעֲשֵׂה לִי מַטְעַמִּים כַּאֲשֶׁר אָהַבְתִּי וְהָבִיאָה לִי וְאֹכֵלָה בַּעֲבוּר תְּבָרֶכְךָ נַפְשִׁי—And prepare delicacies for me as I enjoy, bring them to me and I shall eat—so that my soul shall bless you."[5] Rivkah also appreciated the importance of these preliminaries, as she instructed Yaakov: "לֶךְ נָא אֶל הַצֹּאן וְקַח לִי מִשָּׁם שְׁנֵי גְּדָיֵי עִזִּים טֹבִים וְאֶעֱשֶׂה אֹתָם מַטְעַמִּים לְאָבִיךָ כַּאֲשֶׁר אָהֵב—Go now to the flock and take for me from there two goats; and I shall prepare them as delicacies for your father, in the manner he enjoys."[6]

Why all the focus on tasty food? Did a great *tzaddik* like Yitzhak really need all of this in order to give a *berachah*? The Rabbeinu Bachya offers a fascinating explanation. It is true, of course, that Yitzchak was an elevated soul, and that the *berachos* themselves were spiritual in nature. But in order for the *berachah* to be effective, the one offering the blessing must himself be in exceptionally good spirits. That is the reason that even *gashmiyusdike* "good food" played such a pivotal role in the *berachos*. This would generate the high spirits necessary for the *berachos* to have the maximum effect.

(In fact, this may even be the root of our practice to make a *kiddush* on the occasion of a *simchah*. Technically, we could just invite people over and they could wish mazel tov. However, we want these *berachos* to

---

5   *Bereishis* 27:4.
6   Ibid., v. 9.

be potent and come to fruition. A mazel tov on an empty stomach just isn't the same.)

What we see, in any event, is that both Yitzchak and Rivkah understood that for the *berachos* to take effect, the *mevarech* must be in high spirits and bear positive feelings toward the recipient of the *berachos*.

This is the challenge for the *chosheid b'kesheirim*. Why did he suspect this individual in the first place? After all, had he seen his parent or close friend take the same action, he would have been much quicker to give them the benefit of the doubt. Since he cares about them, his first reaction would be to see positive in them instead of negative. Thus, the fact that he indeed suspected this individual shows that his feelings toward him were not so friendly to begin with. This ill will, then, could severely weaken the power of whatever *berachah* he is about to give. And so, we learn from the case of Eli that measures must be taken to correct and transform these feelings. As Eli demonstrated, a two-step process must take place: The *chosheid* must:

1. regret having incorrectly suspected a decent person;
2. generate good feelings toward the other person.

A *berachah* delivered upon the fulfillment of these conditions will do much to heal the hurt experienced by the person who was suspected, as he will now detect the good will emanating from the *mevarech*. What is more—as in the case of Eli and Chanah—a heartfelt *berachah* given with good feelings has the power to turn great pain into real joy.

9

KAVOD RABO, THE POWER OF A YID, AND MOSHE SMITING THE MITZRI

> וְעָשׂוּ לִי מִקְדָּשׁ וְשָׁכַנְתִּי בְּתוֹכָם.
>
> *And they shall make for Me a Sanctuary, and I shall dwell within them.*
>
> *Shemos 25:8*

AS evidenced by various mourning practices we keep to this day, we are of course devastated by the loss of the Beis Hamikdash and the departure of Hashem's Presence from His dwelling place. There is, however, a slight consolation in that even today we are able to bring His Shechinah into our personal lives. The *pasuk* says: "וְעָשׂוּ לִי מִקְדָּשׁ וְשָׁכַנְתִּי בְּתוֹכָם—And they shall make for Me a Sanctuary, and I shall dwell within them," which Chazal interpret as "*b'socham mamash*—literally, within their very selves." We learn that through proper conduct and dedication we may fashion ourselves into a Mikdash in which Hashem's Presence will rest.

Respect for the Rebbi

By the same token, however, we find that there exists the possibility for Hashem's Presence to be chased away, *Rachmana litzlan.* For example, the Gemara lists a number of behaviors which are "גּוֹרֵם לַשְּׁכִינָה שֶׁתִּסְתַּלֵּק מִיִּשְׂרָאֵל—a causation for the Shechinah to depart from Yisrael."[1] Most of these items involve a lack of *derech eretz* displayed by the *talmid* toward his *rebbi*—such as greeting him in the same way one would greet his peers. Granted that one must show proper regard for his *rebbi*, but the question arises: Why, of all things, would this particular offense be responsible for chasing away the Shechinah? After all, there are any number of severe transgressions for which the Gemara never mentions that they are "גּוֹרֵם לַשְּׁכִינָה שֶׁתִּסְתַּלֵּק מִיִּשְׂרָאֵל"! What is it in particular about chutzpah toward a *rebbi* that it is singled out in this manner? And, for that matter, why are the effects so sweeping? We may have understood, perhaps, why the Shechinah would leave this specific offender. But the implication of Chazal's statement is that the Shechinah leaves *the entirety of the nation*: "גּוֹרֵם לַשְּׁכִינָה שֶׁתִּסְתַּלֵּק מִיִּשְׂרָאֵל." Why, indeed, does the punishment extend far beyond the individual sinner?

We may gain some insight from the Mishnah in *Avos*,[2] which underscores the level of awe and esteem in which one's *rebbi* should be held: "מוֹרָא רַבָּךְ כְּמוֹרָא שָׁמָיִם—Awe for your *rebbi* should be on the level of one's awe of Heaven." Thus we see that *kavod ha'rav* and *kavod Shamayim* are indeed connected. It is therefore understandable that chutzpah to a *rebbi* can push away the Shechinah, much as disrespect toward a *rebbi* is in effect directed at *Shamayim* as well.

Why, then, does it cause the Shechinah to depart from all of Yisrael? An episode in the Torah involving Moshe Rabbeinu should shed further light on this subject, as we shall see.

Moshe, the Mitzri, and Dasan and Aviram

The Torah relates how Moshe went out to behold the sufferings of his fellow Jews. He encountered a Mitzri mercilessly beating a Yisrael

---

1   *Berachos* 27b.
2   4:12.

and decided to intervene. The *pasuk* says: "וַיִּפֶן כֹּה וָכֹה וַיַּרְא כִּי אֵין אִישׁ וַיַּךְ אֶת הַמִּצְרִי—And he looked this way and that, and he saw that there was no man; and he smote the Egyptian."[3] According to its plain meaning, the *pasuk* is telling us that Moshe checked to make sure that no one was watching his deed. However, *Rashi* interprets it differently, explaining that Moshe was actually utilizing his *ruach ha'kodesh*. He peered into the future and saw "כִּי אֵין אִישׁ"—that he would have no worthy descendants. Only once Moshe was satisfied that no converts would emanate from this Mitzri did he proceed to dispatch him. This is quite noteworthy because, apparently, had Moshe seen that there would be a *ger*—even far into the future—he would have refrained from killing him. From this we learn about the inherent greatness of even an individual Jew. Moshe realized that each Jew has the potential to change the world for the better, and the ability to bring Hashem closer to the entire Jewish People. If there were to one day be a *ger* coming out of this Mitzri, that would translate into an increase in *kedushah* in the world; and this possibility was sufficient to spare this wicked Mitzri from death. Moshe determined that this was not to be, and so he killed him. Nonetheless, we may still derive from this episode the great power invested in every Yid.

The narrative continues, and on the next day Moshe Rabbeinu tried to stop Dasan and Aviram from fighting. The wicked pair were not particularly receptive to Moshe's message, and they felt no qualms about deriding Moshe for his efforts. Their negative response caused Moshe to experience a sense of fear: "וַיִּירָא מֹשֶׁה—And Moshe was afraid."[4] Citing the midrash, *Rashi* explains the source of his fear: "דָּאַג לוֹ עַל שֶׁרָאָה בְּיִשְׂרָאֵל רְשָׁעִים דֵּילָטוֹרִין, אָמַר מֵעַתָּה שֶׁמָּא אֵינָם רְאוּיִין לְהִגָּאֵל—He was worried over the fact that he saw there were some wicked gossipmongers among Yisrael, so he said: 'Perhaps they are no longer worthy of redemption.'" Now, this is likewise a noteworthy development. Of course, Dasan and Aviram were behaving wickedly, but after all, they are only two people. Why did Moshe think that this pair alone was capable of stopping the whole *geulah*? But we see, once again, the incredible potency attached

---

3   *Shemos* 2:12.
4   Ibid., v. 14.

to every single Yid—even in the negative sense. The power of a Jew is such that, yes, two Jews could have a negative impact on millions, and alter the course of Jewish history forever.

It is in this light that we may better understand the Gemara in *Berachos*. We had wondered why it is that chutzpah exhibited by one *talmid* toward his *rebbi* could cause the Shechinah to depart from all of Yisrael. But as we have seen above, this is indeed the case. The potency of a Yid is such that when one person doesn't act properly, it affects the whole nation. On the other hand, if one Jew has *derech eretz* for his *rebbi*—and certainly if we all do—then the Shechinah draws closer to us. In the final analysis, Hashem desires to dwell among Klal Yisrael as a unit, which may be why the *pasuk* uses the plural form: "וְשָׁכַנְתִּי בְּתוֹכָם—And I shall dwell **among them**." He therefore grants us the remarkable ability to affect the whole nation, so that through our deeds we can cause the Shechinah to rest among B'nei Yisrael.

10

CONNECTING TO HASHEM BY CONNECTING TO THE TZIBBUR

כִּי מִי גוֹי גָדוֹל אֲשֶׁר לוֹ אֱלֹקִים קְרֹבִים אֵלָיו כַּה׳ אֱלֹקֵינוּ בְּכָל
קָרְאֵנוּ אֵלָיו.

*For who else is a great nation that has G-d so close to it, as
Hashem our G-d is whenever we call out to Him.*

Devarim 4:7

WE live in a society that expects 24/7 accessibility. Whether in the form of an ATM, supermarket, or convenience store, the world wants it when they want it. Some even go so far as to hire lawyers and financial advisors in different time zones. This way, they'll always be covered—just in case they have a concern in the middle of the night.

Resolving the Contradiction

Now, as extreme as some may take it, the underlying sentiment is quite reasonable. Accessibility engenders a sense of security; knowing someone is always within reach gives one peace of mind. Even if these services aren't utilized, the mere fact that the access is available provides a person with a high level of confidence, the extra boost that pushes him to take risks for success.

Let us consider this idea as it relates to the spiritual realm. Imagine what a difference it would make if a Yid could have 24/7 access to Hakadosh Baruch Hu. Life would be so much less stressful, people would have more confidence, and the effects would spill over to their *avodas Hashem*. They would do more *chessed*, be more generous in giving *tzedakah*, and—best of all—could learn Torah without worries or distractions. All of this would be the result of knowing that any challenge that may surface could be solved by accessing Hashem at any time of the day or night.

The question is, is such a scenario a reality or fantasy? Is it really possible to attain such "round-the-clock" access to Hashem? Perhaps a true *tzaddik* enjoys such a privilege, but what about us "regular" Yidden? From these verses, however, it appears that Klal Yisrael is indeed privy to just such a phenomenon. As the *pasuk* states: "כִּי מִי גוֹי גָּדוֹל אֲשֶׁר לוֹ אֱלֹקִים קְרֹבִים אֵלָיו כַּה' אֱלֹקֵינוּ בְּכָל קָרְאֵנוּ אֵלָיו —For who else is a great nation that has G-d so close to it, as Hashem our G-d is whenever we call out to Him."

However, it appears that this matter must be qualified somewhat. The Gemara[1] notes that the above *pasuk* appears to be contradicted by another:

- On the one hand, this *pasuk* seems to be clearly expressing that Yisrael's prayers are always accepted: "בְּכָל קָרְאֵנוּ אֵלָיו."
- But the well-known *pasuk* from the *Navi* seems to imply otherwise: "דִּרְשׁוּ ה' בְּהִמָּצְאוֹ קְרָאֻהוּ בִּהְיוֹתוֹ קָרוֹב —Seek out Hashem when He is to be found, call out to Him while He is yet close."[2] The implication is that Hashem's closeness is restricted to certain times, and only during these limited periods is one guaranteed such access.

The Gemara resolves the issue by drawing a significant distinction: "הָתָם בְּיָחִיד הָכָא בְּצִבּוּר —[The subject] over there is the individual, while

---

1   *Rosh Hashanah* 18a.

2   *Yeshayah* 55:6.

over here it is the communal body." Thus we learn of the remarkable potency of the *ko'ach ha'tzibbur*. On his own, a *yachid* may be lacking the necessary *zechus* to be answered favorably. When he davens alone, the "microscope" of *Shamayim* is focused solely on him and his own merits. As such, it is much more difficult for an individual to be found worthy of special intervention, and it is only during *Aseres Yemei Teshuvah* that he enjoys special access. But the *achdus* provided by joining to a *tzibbur* is so powerful, it draws Hashem's attention at all times. Even if individuals may not deserve to have Hashem's ear, so to speak, they may be swept along by the *ko'ach ha'tzibbur*.

Part of One Whole

It may be possible, perhaps, to appreciate this difference even in relation to individuals themselves. For in truth, a lot may depend on how the *yachid* views himself. Some people see themselves as an island, completely separated from the "mainland" which is the community. They don't interact with other people, nor do they feel their pain. They don't teach Torah to others, because in their minds doing so detracts from their own personal growth. Of course, this type of mentality weakens one's bond with the *tzibbur* and ultimately with Hashem Himself. For this individual—an individual *mamash*—the opportunities to reach Hashem are indeed very limited.

Actually, this type of individual is functioning in a very unnatural way. The truth is that all Yidden are inherently part of one whole, a great, unified *"neshamah klalis"* of all of Klal Yisrael.

As all Yidden come from the same source, it serves like a magnet, a certain force that pulls us all toward each other; the natural state of things is that an individual Jewish soul tends to gravitate toward another.

One time, as my wife and I were shopping with our children in Costco, we were approached by an elderly couple. From the contents of their shopping cart, it certainly didn't seem that they were Jewish. But when they saw our children, they began speaking with them in Yiddish. They asked some questions, smiled at them, and continued on their way. After they left, my children were somewhat perplexed. They thought I must have known these people previously, but I clarified that I did not. "So why were they speaking to us in Yiddish?" they wondered. I gave it some thought, and then drew on the concept outlined above. Although they are not observant Jews, I explained, they still have a *Yiddishe neshamah* just like us. When one *Yiddishe neshamah* is in the proximity of another, they naturally gravitate toward each other. Sadly, it may very well be that for these people, the Yiddish language is their only connection to Yiddishkeit. But by speaking Yiddish to us, their *Yiddishe neshamah* was connecting with their fellow Jews.

Another time, someone asked me the following question: "Why is it that Jews always play 'Jewish geography'? When you mention a name, they immediately ask: 'Is he related to so-and-so?' and so forth." I explained to him similarly that Jews naturally love to connect with other Jews. Hashem created us with that natural feel of wanting to bond with each other. In fact, this may be why the well-known Mishnah in *Avos* employs the negative form when it states: "אַל תִּפְרֹשׁ מִן הַצִּבּוּר—Do not separate yourself from the community."[3] Why didn't the Mishnah simply instruct us in a positive fashion, something along the lines of, "*Hischaber la'tzibbur*—Join together with the community." The answer, it would seem, is that it was unnecessary to issue such a directive, because that indeed is the natural state. Instead, the Mishnah warns us against deviating from our innate tendency for *achdus*, and not to separate ourselves from the *tzibbur*.

We know, of course, that Hashem loves it when His children are united. We see this from *Matan Torah*; He would only give His most precious gift to His precious children when we displayed the highest level of unity. That is why the Torah describes this event in singular form: "וַיִּחַן שָׁם יִשְׂרָאֵל נֶגֶד הָהָר—And Yisrael **encamped** there, opposite the mountain."[4] As *Rashi* comments: "כְּאִישׁ אֶחָד בְּלֵב אֶחָד—As one man, with one heart." We may therefore understand that when a *yachid* views himself in this way—as part of the *tzibbur*—he merits constant closeness to Hashem. When a Yid cares about his fellow Jew, sharing in both his

---

3   *Avos* 2:4.
4   *Shemos* 19:2.

simchah and his pain, that *yachid* gains for himself the *ko'ach ha'tzibbur*. When that *yachid* davens, then, Hashem listens 24/7/365.

When a boy receives a bris, we make the following declaration: "זֶה הַקָּטֹן גָּדוֹל יִהְיֶה—This *katan* should become a *gadol*." Obviously, we express our desire that he grow up and become great; but it could be that this prayer also reflects the idea outlined above. A baby is concerned only with himself. Right now, this *katan* is a taker and not a giver, so we bless him that he should become a *gadol*—that is, to grow into the bigger picture. A *gadol* cares about others and is a giver. Someone who cares about others and connects with the *tzibbur* is indeed a true *gadol*, and one who—as we have seen—will have full and constant access to Hashem.

PART II

אמונה ובטחון

EMUNAH U'BITACHON

1

PACHIM KETANIM

וַיִּוָּתֵר יַעֲקֹב לְבַדּוֹ וַיֵּאָבֵק אִישׁ עִמּוֹ—שָׁכַח פַּכִּים קְטַנִּים וְחָזַר עֲלֵיהֶם.

"And Yaakov remained alone, and a man struggled with him"—He forgot the small vessels and returned for them.

Bereishis 32:25, Rashi

WE are all familiar with Chazal's teaching that, after bringing his family across the stream, Yaakov Avinu went back to retrieve the *pachim ketanim*—the small vessels that had been left behind. Yet, have we ever stopped to think about how mysterious this event was?

- Yaakov had become a very wealthy man in Lavan's house; surely, he could afford to replace these *pachim ketanim* one thousand times over.

- Yaakov was now facing the peril of his brother, Eisav, so by lingering behind, he was exposing himself to danger. Was it really worth risking his life for some fairly insignificant items? Even a poor person wouldn't go back to a crime-ridden area to reclaim his ninety-nine-cent pen that he had dropped. Why, then, would the prosperous Yaakov put himself in danger for the sake of these *pachim ketanim*?

Why did he deem them so special?

In truth, Yaakov's action demonstrates profound *emunah* and a clear understanding of the workings of the universe. A *tzaddik* recognizes that everything that Hashem does is purposeful, and that whatever he has comes directly from Him. As such, he realizes that any object he owns was given to him so that he could fulfill his purpose in this world. If a person is missing even one piece of a puzzle, it remains incomplete. Yes, it may be 99 percent of the way there, but there is no way to view it as perfect and whole. A true *tzaddik* is never satisfied with "almost," but instead strives for total perfection. This was the *cheshbon* that lay behind Yaakov's decision to pursue the *pachim ketanim*. If Hashem had bequeathed them to him, he knew that at some point in his life he would need them for his designated service of Hashem. In short, Yaakov understood that his *avodas Hashem* would be missing something without these *pachim ketanim*; it was only with them that he could attain true perfection. And for perfection, it was worth risking his life.

By applying a simple *kal v'chomer*, we can derive a tremendous lesson from this episode. Yaakov Avinu felt that his spiritual stature would suffer if he were missing something as seemingly insignificant as these *pachim ketanim*. How much greater would be the lack in our own *ruchniyus* if we fail to utilize our greatest strengths and abilities to serve Hashem.

2

PACHIM KETANIM II: VISUAL REMINDERS

וַיִּוָּתֵר יַעֲקֹב לְבַדּוֹ וַיֵּאָבֵק אִישׁ עִמּוֹ—שָׁכַח פַּכִּים קְטַנִּים וְחָזַר עֲלֵיהֶם.

"And Yaakov remained alone, and a man struggled with him"—He forgot the small vessels and returned for them.

Bereishis 32:25, Rashi

WE previously explored the issue of Yaakov Avinu's effort to retrieve his *pachim ketanim*. Why would he expose himself to potential danger for the sake of these (seemingly) insignificant items? This endeavor, as we explained, was actually an outgrowth of Yaakov's strong sense of *emunah*. He understood that if Hashem had given him these items, it must be for a very purposeful and significant reason. Recognizing that they were needed to perfect his *avodas Hashem* in some fashion, he felt it most important to reclaim them.

There remains, however, a matter that needs to be clarified: just how would these *pachim ketanim* affect his *avodah*? Let us revisit this topic to see if we may discover a possible approach.

The very first *middah* addressed in the *sefer Orchos Tzaddikim* is the *middah raah* of *gaavah*. He points to an idea that appears repeatedly in *Sefer Devarim*—namely, that *gaavah* causes a person to forget Hashem. As it states, for example: "פֶּן תֹּאכַל וְשָׂבָעְתָּ וּבָתִּים טֹבִים תִּבְנֶה וְיָשָׁבְתָּ...וּבְקָרְךָ וְצֹאנְךָ יִרְבְּיֻן וְכֶסֶף וְזָהָב יִרְבֶּה לָךְ...וְרָם לְבָבֶךָ וְשָׁכַחְתָּ אֶת ה' אֱלֹקֶיךָ..."—Lest you eat and become satisfied, and you build nice houses and become settled...And your cattle and sheep increase, and you increase for yourself silver and gold...**And your heart becomes haughty, and you forget Hashem your G-d...**"[1] On the other end of the spectrum, we know that Moshe Rabbeinu was the most humble of all men, yet the same time, he rose to the greatest level of prophecy ever; to the point that Hashem spoke with him "פָּנִים אֶל פָּנִים כַּאֲשֶׁר יְדַבֵּר אִישׁ אֶל רֵעֵהוּ—face to face, as a man speaks to his friend."[2] But this was no contradiction to Moshe's supreme humility; on the contrary, it was actually related to it. For Moshe understood that the humbler a person is, the closer to Hashem he can become. As we have seen, it is arrogance that makes a person distant, erecting an iron wall between Hashem and himself. *Gaavah* is completely antithetical to attaining closeness with Hashem, as the Gemara states: "כֹּל אָדָם שֶׁיֵּשׁ בּוֹ גַּסּוּת הָרוּחַ אָמַר הַקָּדוֹשׁ בָּרוּךְ הוּא אֵין אֲנִי וְהוּא יְכוֹלִין לָדוּר בָּעוֹלָם—[Regarding] anyone who has within him haughtiness of spirit, Hashem declares: 'I and he cannot dwell in the world together.'"[3]

This idea, in any event, may provide us with fresh insight into Yaakov's actions. In discussing what Yaakov left behind, *Rashi* uses the phrase "שָׁכַח פַּכִּים קְטַנִּים"—He **forgot** the small vessels." It could be that this itself is what alarmed Yaakov. As we have learned, a *tzaddik* like Yaakov Avinu views all that he has been given as instruments for serving Hashem. Yaakov thus perceived his forgetting of the *pachim* as if he had forgotten Hashem Himself, to some extent. In other words, Yaakov was worried that an element of *gaavah* may have crept in, and this is what caused him to forget. He was on an extremely lofty spiritual level, of course, but he had just recently devised a strategy for dealing with Eisav, and he feared

---

1   *Devarim* 8:12–14.

2   *Shemos* 33:11.

3   *Sotah* 5a.

he may have felt a trace of pride in this accomplishment. This is what made him so determined to retrieve his forgotten items. In exhorting a person to stay away from *gaavah*, the *Orchos Tzaddikim* states that one needs a constant reminder to maintain his focus on humility. It could very well be, then, that Yaakov saw the *pachim ketanim* as fulfilling this role. Significantly, they were, after all, not *pachim* **gedolim**, but **ketanim**. Yaakov thus felt that they would aid in banishing any residual trace of *gaavah* by calling his attention to lowliness and humility.

We thus learn an important lesson from the *pachim ketanim* about the substantial role that visual reminders can play in one's *avodas Hashem*.

On a personal note, this idea figured prominently in my own experience. Many years ago, after I had completed my post–high school learning in Eretz Yisrael, my *rebbi* took me to Rav Shach, *zt"l*, for a *berachah*. Given my imminent return to the States, my *rebbi* asked the *gadol* what I could do to protect my *ruchniyus*. Rav Shach looked at me for a few moments and then said that I should wear my tzitzis out. The advice appeared simple enough, yet at the same time, the actual task was intimidating. But the results were amazing. I later came to realize that the *eitzah* of the *gadol ha'dor* had a twofold effect:

- First, seeing my tzitzis out was a clear reminder to me that I was a different person now.
- Perhaps even more important, however, was the effect it had on my friends. When they saw my tzitzis out, *they* realized that I was a different person; and this made matters so much easier for me.

This was, in any event, a real-life example of what we learn from Yaakov Avinu. If a person really wants to strive for closeness to Hashem, visual reminders—no matter how small and insignificant they may seem—can offer a major *chizuk* as we develop our *ruchniyus*.

3

RIGHTEOUSNESS
OF NOACH:
FULL COMPLIANCE

וַיָּבֹא נֹחַ וּבָנָיו וְאִשְׁתּוֹ וּנְשֵׁי בָנָיו אִתּוֹ אֶל הַתֵּבָה מִפְּנֵי מֵי הַמַּבּוּל.

*And Noach came, with his sons, his wife, and his sons' wives
with him, to the ark because of the waters of the flood.*

Bereishis 7:7

THERE is something mystifying about Noach's entry into the *teivah*.
Early on in the Torah, Noach's qualities of righteousness and dedication to Hashem have been firmly established. He is referred to as a
tzaddik from the start—"נֹחַ אִישׁ צַדִּיק,"[1] and the Torah is particular to
highlight his adherence to Hashem's commands. Numerous instructions
are issued regarding the construction of the *teivah* and the preparations
for the sojourn within. The Torah makes explicit mention—twice—of
Noach's faithfulness in carrying them out: "וַיַּעַשׂ נֹחַ כְּכֹל אֲשֶׁר צִוָּה אֹתוֹ אֱלֹקִים"

---

1   *Bereishis* 6:9.

and "וַיַּעַשׂ נֹחַ כְּכֹל אֲשֶׁר צִוָּהוּ ה'."[2] Thus, his reputation as a loyal soldier in Hashem's service seems to be beyond question.

And then we arrive at the critical moment—entering the *teivah*. Of all matters, this must certainly have been one of the easiest with which to comply. Hashem had told Noach of the impending disaster—how He was to wipe out all existence by bringing the *mabul*. For 120 years, Noach labored on this great structure, according to all its specifications, which would save himself, his family, and the animals, and enable the rebuilding of the (new) world. The *teivah* was now fully complete, and the flood was about to arrive. The long-awaited moment was at hand.

However, Noach still didn't go into the *teivah*. From the *pasuk* we see that he delayed entry for as long as possible: "וַיָּבֹא נֹחַ וּבָנָיו וְאִשְׁתּוֹ וּנְשֵׁי בָנָיו אִתּוֹ אֶל הַתֵּבָה מִפְּנֵי מֵי הַמַּבּוּל—And Noach came, with his sons, his wife, and his sons' wives with him, to the *teivah* **because of the waters of the flood**." As *Rashi* explains, the encroaching waters eventually left him no choice: "לֹא נִכְנַס לַתֵּיבָה עַד שֶׁדְּחָקוּהוּ הַמַּיִם—He did not enter the *teivah* until he was forced to by the water." How exactly does this correspond with Noach's overall loyalty to Hashem's commands? For years and years, he faithfully carried out Hashem's will to the last detail; and then, when it came to what should have been the simplest thing—avoiding a catastrophic flood—Noach had to be cajoled? What exactly was he thinking?

When we look a bit more closely, however, we discover that there really is no contradiction to Noach's stellar record of obedience. Noach never disregarded Hashem's word—not even in this instance. For the truth of the matter is that Hashem never actually told Noach to go *into* the *teivah*. He was told repeatedly to come to the *teivah*'s vicinity, "*Bo el ha'teivah*—Come to the *Teivah*," and this he did, together with his family and the animals and provisions. We don't find an actual command, however, instructing him to be "*nichnas*" (to enter) the *teivah*; he indeed loyally executed all directives: "וַיַּעַשׂ נֹחַ כְּכֹל אֲשֶׁר צִוָּהוּ ה'."

In this respect, Noach's situation is comparable to that which occurred in connection with the episode of *Akeidas Yitzchak*. There, of

---

2   Ibid., 7:5.

course, Avraham was given a most severe trial, as he was told to bring his son as a sacrifice: "קַח נָא אֶת בִּנְךָ אֶת יְחִידְךָ אֲשֶׁר אָהַבְתָּ אֶת יִצְחָק וְלֶךְ לְךָ אֶל אֶרֶץ הַמֹּרִיָּה וְהַעֲלֵהוּ שָׁם לְעֹלָה—Take your son, your only one, whom you love, Yitzchak; and go for yourself to the Land of the Moriah, and bring him up there as a burnt-offering."[3] As we know, when Avraham displayed his unshakeable *emunah* and passed the test, he was prevented from slaughtering his son: "וַיֹּאמֶר אַל תִּשְׁלַח יָדְךָ אֶל הַנַּעַר...כִּי עַתָּה יָדַעְתִּי כִּי יְרֵא אֱלֹקִים אַתָּה...—And [the angel] said: 'Do not send forth your hand against the lad...for now I know that you are G-d–fearing...'"[4]

The *Me'am Lo'ez* points out something quite remarkable. It asserts that Avraham was actually quite perplexed at this point; he couldn't understand how Hashem had initially instructed him to sacrifice his son, and now seemed to be rescinding that command. Hashem answered that there indeed was no contradiction: He had never actually stated that Yitzchak should be slaughtered. Hashem initially only said "וְהַעֲלֵהוּ שָׁם לְעֹלָה," which technically just means that Yitzchak was to be elevated *in the manner* of an olah. Had He intended there to be an actual sacrifice, Hashem would have stated "וְהַעֲלֵהוּ עֹלָה—Offer him as an *olah*."

What emerges, in any event, is that Avraham in fact did exactly as Hashem instructed, making all the necessary preparations as told and elevating Yitzchak. And in Noach's case, as well, Hashem's commands were all faithfully and completely observed.

---

3   Ibid., 22:2.
4   Ibid., v. 12.

4

YOSEF'S RESPONSE
TO PHARAOH

וַיַּעַן יוֹסֵף אֶת פַּרְעֹה לֵאמֹר בִּלְעָדָי אֱלֹקִים יַעֲנֶה אֶת שְׁלוֹם פַּרְעֹה.

*And Yosef answered Pharaoh, saying: "It is aside from me. It is
G-d Who shall restore the well-being of Pharaoh."*

Bereishis 41:16

𝒜N answer almost always comes in response to a question. That may
be patently obvious; except that in this verse, we seem to have an exception to the rule. Pharaoh has his mysterious dreams, in which seven fat
cows are swallowed by seven emaciated ones, and later seven full ears
of corn are likewise swallowed by lean ones. None of his wise men are
able to offer a satisfying interpretation. Finally, Yosef is summoned to
appear before Pharaoh, with his reputation as an interpreter preceding
him. As Pharaoh remarks: "חֲלוֹם חָלַמְתִּי וּפֹתֵר אֵין אֹתוֹ וַאֲנִי שָׁמַעְתִּי עָלֶיךָ לֵאמֹר
תִּשְׁמַע חֲלוֹם לִפְתֹּר אֹתוֹ—I have dreamed a dream, and none can interpret
it; but I have heard it said about you that you listen to dreams and interpret them."[1]

---

1   *Bereishis* 41:16.

It was in response to these comments that Yosef "answers" Pharaoh: "וַיַּעַן יוֹסֵף אֶת פַּרְעֹה לֵאמֹר בִּלְעָדָי אֱלֹקִים יַעֲנֶה אֶת שְׁלוֹם פַּרְעֹה"—And Yosef answered Pharaoh, saying: 'It is aside from me. It is G-d Who shall restore the well-being of Pharaoh.'" Note, however, that Pharaoh had not expressed anything in question form. He had merely mentioned to Yosef that his enigmatic dreams had not yet been interpreted, and that he had heard of Yosef's success in this area. It was perfectly in order, of course, for Yosef to clarify that the power to interpret emanates from Hashem. But why would the Torah phrase this in these terms: "וַיַּעַן יוֹסֵף"—And Yosef **answered**," when something like "he stated" or "he remarked" would seem to be more appropriate descriptions? What question had been posed that warranted an "answer"? Furthermore, "וַיַּעַן" implies that Yosef is already in the mode of offering solutions. This is also difficult to understand. After all, Pharaoh had not even told him yet what the dreams were; how could Yosef already be providing solutions?

However, a closer look at Yosef's response reveals that he was conveying to Pharaoh a fundamental *yesod*—one which was the ultimate solution to this and indeed all problems. As he declared: "בִּלְעָדָי אֱלֹקִים יַעֲנֶה אֶת שְׁלוֹם פַּרְעֹה." True, Pharaoh had not yet informed Yosef of the particulars of his dream. It was clear, however, that he was in a state of anguished bewilderment; he had a disturbing dream, and to this point, no one could provide any guidance or clarity. This was the situation Yosef sought to address. He was letting Pharaoh know that he and everyone around him had left out the key factor—Hashem—and this omission was ultimately the source of all of their confusion. It was this *chiddush* that formed the essence of Yosef's response. He was relaying to Pharaoh that, in the final analysis, it doesn't make a difference what the problem is, for the answer will always be the same. And that answer is that Hashem is in charge.

This was the reason Pharaoh's advisors couldn't provide him even the slightest bit of clarity, for they lacked an understanding of how the world really operates. If Hashem isn't in the equation, then *takeh*, nothing makes sense. When Hashem *is* in the equation, as Yosef educated Pharaoh, it is a different matter entirely. Suddenly, even the most perplexing issues—like the weak devouring the strong—are seen in a totally different light. With the knowledge that Hashem is in charge, everything indeed makes perfect sense.

5

AKEIDAS YITZCHAK AND EMUNAH

וַעֲקֵידַת יִצְחָק לְזַרְעוֹ הַיּוֹם בְּרַחֲמִים תִּזְכּוֹר.

And remember Akeidas Yitzchak today for his offspring, with mercy.

Mussaf of Rosh Hashanah

AKEIDAS *Yitzchak* plays a most significant role in our *avodah* on Rosh Hashanah. It is the subject of the Torah reading on the second day, and it figures quite prominently in our *tefillos*. The reason for this seems obvious. After all, it is the *Yom Ha'din*, the day on which we are judged and our fate is determined. As we know, *Akeidas Yitzchak* generated tremendous merit for Klal Yisrael, lasting for generations. We need all the merit we can summon at this solemn time, when so much hangs in the balance, so we beseech Hashem: "וַעֲקֵידַת יִצְחָק לְזַרְעוֹ הַיּוֹם בְּרַחֲמִים תִּזְכּוֹר—And remember *Akeidas Yitzchak* today for his offspring, with mercy." It would be worthwhile, in any event, to spend some moments contemplating the nature of this *zechus* that Yitzchak Avinu provided for us.

Of course, a central quality of this event is the self-sacrifice that Yitzchak displayed. It behooves us, however, to fully appreciate the extent of Yitzchak's dedication. It is not simply that he agreed to go along with Avraham. One can picture the scenario whereby Yitzchak is awoken early to set out with his father on a journey. He can't help but notice that his father has brought along a knife. Surely, at the very least, this item would arouse Yitzchak's curiosity. From our point of view, it would seem to have been perfectly in order for Yitzchak to ask his father what this whole matter with the knife was all about. If Yitzchak would have been told and still agreed to continue the journey, this itself would have constituted a high level of self-sacrifice and devotion. But not only did he accept the situation, he rose to an even higher level—he didn't even feel the need to question his father. Yitzchak may have realized that even a subtle intimation of second-guessing would have somewhat diminished the great *zechus* Klal Yisrael would ultimately derive from the *Akeidah*. By placing his complete trust in Avraham Avinu, displaying not the slightest hesitation, Yitzchak elevated the *zechus* of the *Akeidah* to a whole new level. We thus invoke the memory of this event on Rosh Hashanah, such that the *zechus* of Yitzchak's supreme level of *emunah* will stand us in good stead at this time of judgment.

Now, there is a tremendous lesson we can take out of Yitzchak's example. We ourselves have an opportunity, every Rosh Hashanah, to walk in his footsteps and actually perform an *Akeidah* of sorts. The year has just passed, but its memories still linger; there were some successes, but also things that did not always go the way we had wished. There is a temptation to reflect and perhaps even wonder why things ended up the way they did. The *yetzer hara* may cause one to think: *Why did Hashem do such and such? It doesn't seem to make sense!* In reality, this mode of thinking turns the whole nature of the day on its head; Rosh Hashanah is a *Yom Ha'din*, a Day of Judgment, because Hashem is judging *us*—not because a person should be judging Hashem! Ideally, then, a person should adopt the same attitude displayed by Yitzchak. As we have seen, the hallmark of *Akeidas Yitzchak* was the fact that Yitzchak did not question or even hesitate in the least. In a similar vein, it is most important for us to put our complete faith and trust in Hashem. A person may feel that he has the total picture of the previous year and, in his estimation, he is justified to ask questions. But the truth is that our whole lifetime—let alone an individual year—is not even a drop in the ocean of the big picture of history. Only Hashem knows the whole past, present, and future, and how it all fits together. By acknowledging and internalizing this vital fact, we have the ability to generate the *zechus* of our own form of *Akeidah*—in the manner of Yitzchak, who opted for trust instead of questions.

6

MAKKAS DAM: HITTING THE WATER

וַיֹּאמֶר ה׳ אֶל מֹשֶׁה אֱמֹר אֶל אַהֲרֹן קַח מַטְּךָ וּנְטֵה יָדְךָ עַל מֵימֵי
מִצְרַיִם עַל נַהֲרֹתָם עַל יְאֹרֵיהֶם וְעַל אַגְמֵיהֶם וְעַל כָּל מִקְוֵה
מֵימֵיהֶם וְיִהְיוּ דָם...וַיַּעֲשׂוּ כֵן מֹשֶׁה וְאַהֲרֹן כַּאֲשֶׁר צִוָּה ה׳ וַיָּרֶם
בַּמַּטֶּה וַיַּךְ אֶת הַמַּיִם אֲשֶׁר בַּיְאֹר לְעֵינֵי פַרְעֹה וּלְעֵינֵי עֲבָדָיו וַיֵּהָפְכוּ
כָּל הַמַּיִם אֲשֶׁר בַּיְאֹר לְדָם.

*And Hashem said to Moshe: "Say to Aharon: 'Take your staff
and stretch out your hand over the waters of Egypt—over
their rivers, canals, lakes, and all bodies of water—and they
shall become blood...'" And Moshe and Aharon did as Hashem
commanded; and he raised the staff and struck the waters of
the river before the eyes of Pharaoh and the eyes of his servants,
and all of the water that was in the river turned into blood.*

Shemos 7:19–20

THERE is a common thread that runs between the first two
makkos of *dam* and *tzfardei'a*: both emanated from the water and were
summoned with the *mateh*. Still, we do find some curious distinctions
between them:

- The instructions regarding the *makkah* of *dam* included an explicit command to "take" the *mateh*: "קַח מַטְּךָ וּנְטֵה יָדְךָ עַל מֵימֵי מִצְרַיִם...וְיִהְיוּ דָם...—**Take your staff** and stretch out your hand over the waters of Egypt...and they shall become blood..." When it came to the *makkah* of *tzfardei'a*, however, no such mention is made; rather, they are simply told: "נְטֵה אֶת יָדְךָ בְּמַטֶּךָ עַל הַנְּהָרֹת עַל הַיְאֹרִים וְעַל הָאֲגַמִּים וְהַעַל אֶת הַצְפַרְדְעִים—**Stretch out your hand with your staff** over the rivers, canals, and lakes, and bring up the frogs."[1]

- Furthermore, we find that the onset of the *makkah* of *dam* took place specifically in front of Pharaoh and his advisors: "וַיָּרֶם בַּמַּטֶּה וַיַּךְ אֶת הַמַּיִם אֲשֶׁר בַּיְאֹר לְעֵינֵי פַרְעֹה וּלְעֵינֵי עֲבָדָיו—And he raised the staff and struck the waters of the river **before the eyes of Pharaoh and the eyes of his servants**." This feature was likewise absent by the *makkah* of *tzfardei'a*.

What accounts for these differences?

There is yet another intriguing aspect of how the *makkah* of *dam* came about. We see that Aharon struck the water with the *mateh*: "וַיָּרֶם בַּמַּטֶּה וַיַּךְ אֶת הַמַּיִם אֲשֶׁר בַּיְאֹר." But when we look back at the instructions Moshe was to relay to Aharon, they include no mention of any "hitting." Rather, as we have seen, he was simply told to "take" the *mateh* and stretch forth his hand: "וַיֹּאמֶר ה' אֶל מֹשֶׁה אֱמֹר אֶל אַהֲרֹן קַח מַטְּךָ וּנְטֵה יָדְךָ עַל מֵימֵי מִצְרַיִם...וְיִהְיוּ דָם..." So Aharon was never told to strike the water, but he proceeded to do so anyway. And not only that, but the *pasuk* characterizes his deed as a fulfillment of Hashem's command: "וַיַּעֲשׂוּ כֵן מֹשֶׁה וְאַהֲרֹן כַּאֲשֶׁר צִוָּה ה' וַיָּרֶם בַּמַּטֶּה וַיַּךְ אֶת הַמַּיִם...—And Moshe and Aharon did so, **as Hashem commanded**, and he raised the staff and **struck the waters**." How could hitting the water legitimately be considered "כַּאֲשֶׁר צִוָּה ה'," when Hashem only said to "take" the *mateh*?

We may draw some insight into this matter from an earlier *pasuk*. Initially, Hashem instructed Moshe to perform certain signs before the nation. One of these resembled the (future) first *makkah*, involving the

---

1   *Shemos* 8:1.

transformation of water to blood: "וְלָקַחְתָּ מִמֵּימֵי הַיְאֹר וְשָׁפַכְתָּ הַיַּבָּשָׁה...וְהָיוּ לְדָם—בַּיַּבֶּשֶׁת—And you shall take from the waters of the river and pour them upon the land...and they shall become blood upon the land."[2] Now, the sign itself entailed pouring water upon the ground, while in the first *makkah*, the entire river was turned to blood. There was a real connection, however, as *Rashi* there explains that the sign foreshadowed the first *makkah*. "רָמַז לָהֶם שֶׁבְּמַכָּה רִאשׁוֹנָה נִפְרַע מֵאֱלֹהוּתָם—[With this sign, Hashem] was hinting to them that in the first plague, He would exact punishment from the god [of the Mitzrim; i.e., the Nile, which they worshipped]."

Based on this, we may now begin to understand how Aharon derived the fact that he was to strike the water to bring about *makkas dam*. The wording associated with the sign is noteworthy. Rather than stating merely that water should be poured on the ground, the instructions include a specific directive to first "take" it, "וְלָקַחְתָּ מִמֵּימֵי הַיְאֹר וְשָׁפַכְתָּ הַיַּבָּשָׁה," implying a need for real action. And so it stands to reason. After all, the idea here is to punish the god worshipped by the Egyptians; by employing a term of action, Hashem was conveying that He would be directing a major "*potch*" against that false deity. In the case of the sign, the action involved the actual "taking" of the water, followed by its pouring upon the ground. When it came to the *makkah* of *dam*, however, the water itself was to remain in place and turn to blood; no "taking" was involved here. And yet, the same term surfaces in connection with the *makkah*: "קַח מַטְּךָ וּנְטֵה יָדְךָ עַל מֵימֵי מִצְרַיִם." Knowing that this term refers to action, and that Hashem intended to deliver a major *potch* against the Nile, Aharon understood that a forceful action was called for. He therefore struck the water, which was fully in accordance with Hashem's wishes: "וַיַּעֲשׂוּ כֵן מֹשֶׁה וְאַהֲרֹן כַּאֲשֶׁר צִוָּה ה׳ וַיָּרֶם בַּמַּטֶּה וַיַּךְ אֶת הַמַּיִם."

It is for this reason, as well, that the *pasuk* emphasizes that all of this occurred "לְעֵינֵי פַרְעֹה וּלְעֵינֵי עֲבָדָיו." For the whole point was for them to see it with their own eyes. Hashem was delivering a message to them that their god is powerless: He will be hit, you will witness it, and you

---

2   Ibid., 4:9.

won't be able to do anything to stop it. And we may also understand why these particulars applied only to the *makkah* of *dam*, but not to the *makkah* of *tzfardei'a*. It was the *makkah* of *dam* that was designated to send this message against the Egyptian god. The message wasn't needed again by the second *makkah*—that had its own message, which we will not discuss here.

We see how breaking down the *makkah* into its parts and paying attention to the details gives us unique insight into the lessons contained within.

7

CHEIT HA'EIGEL:
DANGER OF DISTANCE

וּמֹשֶׁה יִקַּח אֶת הָאֹהֶל וְנָטָה לוֹ מִחוּץ לַמַּחֲנֶה הַרְחֵק מִן הַמַּחֲנֶה
וְקָרָא לוֹ אֹהֶל מוֹעֵד וְהָיָה כָּל מְבַקֵּשׁ ה׳ יֵצֵא אֶל אֹהֶל מוֹעֵד אֲשֶׁר
מִחוּץ לַמַּחֲנֶה.

*And Moshe took the tent and erected it outside the camp—far
away from the camp—and he called it the "Tent of Meeting";
and it would be, that anyone who sought Hashem would go out
to the Tent of Meeting, which was outside the camp.*

Shemos 33:7

HOW could they do it? How could a nation—after witnessing
such spectacular miracles and rising so high—fall so low and commit a
transgression of such a colossal magnitude?

One of the outcomes of this episode was Moshe's relocation of the
ohel. But the change went beyond the mere fact that it used to be inside
the camp and was now removed to the outside. Rather, the Torah makes
a point of stating that it moved quite a distance: "וּמֹשֶׁה יִקַּח אֶת הָאֹהֶל וְנָטָה
לוֹ מִחוּץ לַמַּחֲנֶה הַרְחֵק מִן הַמַּחֲנֶה—And Moshe took the tent and erected it

outside the camp, **far away from the camp**." As we shall see, it appears that this emphasis on "distance" reflects the origins of this grave sin.

As we will discuss in a later chapter, Klal Yisrael on their own did not initiate the movement to fashion the *eigel*; it was the *eirav rav* who were the instigators. We know that it was Moshe's own idea to allow the *eirav rav* to join Klal Yisrael in the first place. *Rashi* relates that Hashem reminded Moshe of this fact: "עֵרֶב רַב שֶׁקִּבַּלְתָּ מֵעַצְמְךָ וְגִיַּירְתָּם וְלֹא נִמְלַכְתָּ בִּי...הֵם שִׁחֵתוּ וְהִשְׁחִיתוּ—The *eirav rav* that you accepted and converted of your own accord, without having consulted Me—it is they who have corrupted themselves, and corrupted others."[1] As such, it was only on account of Moshe that this group had any connection with Hashem. The Satan saw here an opening to bring about this great downfall; when Moshe's arrival seemed to be delayed, the Satan staged a spectacle purporting to show that Moshe had passed away. Deprived of Moshe, any connection the *eirev rav* had with Hashem was completely dissolved. And without a connection to Hashem, the making of an *eigel* was possible.

The notion of "distance" was not limited just to the *eirev rav*, however. The *eirev rav*'s conduct—their constant complaining and agitation—had a negative impact on Klal Yisrael, taking a toll on their high spiritual level. This *hashpaah* may not have completely severed Yisrael's connection with Hashem, but it certainly caused them to become more distant. And it was this distance that figured so prominently in the whole episode of the *eigel*. The *eirev rav* were the principle participants, while Yisrael's main responsibility lay in the fact that they failed to protest. But it was the distance from Hashem that had dulled their sensitivities and served as the basis for this failure.

Think of it this way: it is very difficult to cause pain to someone you feel close to, or even to tolerate seeing them in pain. People hurt those who are or seem to be far away: Consider the whole modern phenomenon of technology and digital communication. It allows people to express themselves in ways they would be too uncomfortable to do had the other person been standing right in front of them. With the click of

---

1   *Shemos* 32:7.

a button it is possible to offend millions of people. Distance gives people this sense of "courage," enabling them to behave and communicate in a manner they would otherwise never dream of. Thus freed from inhibitions, the most quiet, introverted person can act like the greatest extrovert. In any event, it was this sense of distance that played such a significant role in the *cheit ha'eigel*. Due to the influence of the *eirev rav*, Yisrael had drifted farther from Hashem. Had they remained close to Him, they would not have been able to sit idly by while this egregious activity was taking place. The fact that they did not protest was a direct result of their distance from Hashem.

This was the message Moshe sought to convey by moving the *ohel* not only outside the camp, but "הַרְחֵק מִן הַמַּחֲנֶה." He was demonstrating to the people what the *shoresh* of their *cheit* was, highlighting the fact that distance makes one callous to all that should be precious to him. As part of the *teshuvah* process, the focus had to be on closing this distance and thereby rebuilding that once beautiful relationship.

8

SENSITIVITY

וַיִּקַּח אַבְרָהָם אֶת עֲצֵי הָעֹלָה וַיָּשֶׂם עַל יִצְחָק בְּנוֹ וַיִּקַּח בְּיָדוֹ אֶת הָאֵשׁ וְאֶת הַמַּאֲכֶלֶת וַיֵּלְכוּ שְׁנֵיהֶם יַחְדָּו, וַיֹּאמֶר יִצְחָק אֶל אַבְרָהָם אָבִיו...הִנֵּה הָאֵשׁ וְהָעֵצִים וְאַיֵּה הַשֶּׂה לְעֹלָה.

And Avraham took the wood for the burnt-offering, and he placed it upon Yitzchak, his son; and he took in his hand the fire and the knife, and the two of them went together. And Yitzchak said to Avraham his father: "...Here is the fire and the wood, but where is the sheep for the burnt-offering?"

Bereishis 22:6–7

To all appearances, the tone of Klal Yisrael's departure from Mitzrayim was a triumphant one. As the *pasuk* itself attests: "וּבְנֵי יִשְׂרָאֵל יֹצְאִים בְּיָד רָמָה—And B'nei Yisrael left with an upraised arm."[1] And it stands to reason that they were brimming with confidence at this time; after all, they had just witnessed all the great *nissim* that were performed on their behalf through the *Makkos*, which decimated Mitzrayim and led to their freedom. They were also going out of the country laden with all of its riches, and they were on their way to the grand event of *Matan*

---

1   *Shemos* 14:8.

Torah at Har Sinai. Their *emunah* at this point, one would imagine, must have reached the greatest of levels.

However, as stated, this was only the appearance of things. There were elements among the people whose confidence was somewhat shaky. And so it was that Hashem had to lead Yisrael on a circuitous route: "וַיְהִי בְּשַׁלַּח פַּרְעֹה אֶת הָעָם וְלֹא נָחָם אֱלֹקִים דֶּרֶךְ אֶרֶץ פְּלִשְׁתִּים כִּי קָרוֹב הוּא כִּי אָמַר אֱלֹקִים פֶּן יִנָּחֵם הָעָם בִּרְאֹתָם מִלְחָמָה וְשָׁבוּ מִצְרָיְמָה—And it was, as Pharaoh sent away the nation, and G-d did not lead them by way of the land of the Pelishtim, for it was nearby; for G-d said: '**Perhaps the nation may undergo a change of heart upon seeing war, inducing them to return to Egypt.**'"[2] What should we make of this development? How come the feelings of the people didn't seem to square with the reality? For as outlined above, they indeed should all have had supreme confidence. Why, then, was there a concern that they would panic and run at the first sign of trouble?

This situation seems to speak to the delicate side of human nature. Hashem understood that people can be very sensitive and may be easily rattled when things don't go their way. As confident as the people should have been, they could nonetheless easily have second thoughts when encountering bumps in the road. And we see from later events that this concern was indeed borne out. As *Rashi* here notes, even after taking the longer route, their reaction upon meeting up with trouble was: "נִתְּנָה רֹאשׁ וְנָשׁוּבָה מִצְרָיְמָה—Let us appoint a leader and return to Egypt."[3]

This quality of sensitivity can also be channeled in a positive direction. As we shall see, it appears that Avraham and Yitzchak did just that during the monumental event of the *Akeidah*.

We have previously discussed the nature of the greatness displayed during the *Akeidah*: It was not only that Yitzchak showed a willingness to be *moser nefesh*, but that he did so unquestioningly. His level of *emunah* was such that he trusted completely in his father's guidance, without challenging him on a single aspect. Let us focus now on a certain detail in which this idea is very pronounced.

---

2   Ibid., 13:17.

3   *Bamidbar* 14:4.

At one point, as the two are on their way to their destination, Yitzchak does pose a question to his father about the particulars of the *korban*. But if we look closely, it appears that he asks this question in a curious manner. The *pasuk* first relates that Avraham took along various items they would be needing: "וַיִּקַּח אַבְרָהָם אֶת עֲצֵי הָעֹלָה וַיָּשֶׂם עַל יִצְחָק בְּנוֹ וַיִּקַּח בְּיָדוֹ אֶת הָאֵשׁ וְאֶת הַמַּאֲכֶלֶת—And Avraham took the wood for the burnt-offering, and he placed it upon Yitzchak, his son; and he took in his hand the fire and the knife." In Yitzchak's question, however, he makes mention of only some of these items: "וַיֹּאמֶר יִצְחָק אֶל אַבְרָהָם אָבִיו...הִנֵּה הָאֵשׁ וְהָעֵצִים וְאַיֵּה הַשֶּׂה לְעֹלָה—And Yitzchak said to Avraham his father: '...Here is the **fire** and the **wood**; but where is the sheep for the burnt-offering?'" Avraham had brought wood, fire, and the knife; for some reason, however, Yitzchak only refers to the fire and the wood. Why did he omit the knife?

The answer, it appears, is that Yitzchak was being mindful of the sensitivity that his father may have been experiencing. Yitzchak was asking about the whereabouts of the sheep; but it seems that he was already beginning to get an inkling of the real answer (as the *Malbim* indeed points out). Aware of the distinct possibility that he himself would be the sacrifice, he realized how difficult this must be for his father, and it was for this reason he did not bring up the matter of the knife. He thereby sought to avoid the possibility of causing any hesitation on the part of Avraham, so that the will of Hashem would be carried out without even the slightest room for second-guessing.

There is another possible approach to explaining Yitzchak's omission of the knife along the lines of the above, but with one significant distinction. Perhaps it was actually Avraham who was being mindful of sensitivity here. That is, it may be that the reason Yitzchak did not mention the knife was because, in truth, he didn't know it was there. And the reason for this is because Avraham purposefully hid it from view. In fact, this seems to be the implication of the *pasuk* itself. As mentioned, Avraham took along three main items: wood, fire, and the knife. But he did not carry them all the same way. Rather, the Torah relates that he placed the wood on Yitzchak, and carried the other two items himself: "וַיִּקַּח אַבְרָהָם אֶת עֲצֵי הָעֹלָה וַיָּשֶׂם עַל יִצְחָק בְּנוֹ וַיִּקַּח בְּיָדוֹ אֶת הָאֵשׁ וְאֶת הַמַּאֲכֶלֶת.

What was the purpose of this arrangement? It could be that Avraham placed the wood upon Yitzchak in order to distract him from detecting the knife, which he held discreetly by himself. Avraham took such pains to hide the knife because he knew that seeing this item may have been too traumatic for Yitzchak. According to this approach, Avraham was the one who was cautious over Yitzchak's potential sensitivity, acting in a way to minimize the possibility of even the slightest hesitation on the part of his son.

Either way, we see that both father and son were concerned about the other's ability to pass this monumental *nisayon* in the most perfect manner. In the same fashion as Hakadosh Baruch Hu's dealings with Yisrael, Avraham and Yitzchak were each concerned that the other not become rattled and perhaps develop even momentary second thoughts. Perhaps that is why the *pasuk* concludes with the phrase "וַיֵּלְכוּ שְׁנֵיהֶם יַחְדָּו—And the two walked together." This shows that ultimately there was no hesitation—neither on the part of Avraham or Yitzchak. They were both of the same mindset, working together to fulfill Hashem's will to perfection.

9

EISHES OVADIAH AND THE MIRACLE OF THE OIL

וַיֹּאמֶר אֵלֶיהָ אֱלִישָׁע...מַה יֶּשׁ לָךְ בַּבָּיִת וַתֹּאמֶר אֵין לְשִׁפְחָתְךָ כֹל בַּבַּיִת כִּי אִם אָסוּךְ שָׁמֶן, וַיֹּאמֶר לְכִי שַׁאֲלִי לָךְ כֵּלִים מִן הַחוּץ מֵאֵת כָּל שְׁכֵנָיִךְ כֵּלִים רֵקִים אַל תַּמְעִיטִי.

And Elisha said to her: "...What do you have in the house?" And she said: "Your maidservant has nothing in the house, except for a flask of oil." And he said: "Go borrow for yourself vessels from the outside, from all of your neighbors—empty vessels, do not be sparing."

Melachim II 4:2–3

$\mathcal{SEFER}$ Melachim II relates the wondrous miracle wrought through Elisha HaNavi, involving the oil flask of Ovadiah's wife.[1] She had told Elisha of her troubles, how she was left destitute and alone after the death of her G-d-fearing husband. She had no money with which to pay her debt, and there loomed a real threat that the creditor would instead take her children away as slaves. "What do you have in the

---

1   *Melachim II*, ch. 4.

house?" Elisha asks her, to which she responds that her sole possession is a single flask of oil. Elisha instructs her to borrow from her neighbors as many *keilim* as she can—"אַל תַּמְעִיטִי—Do not be sparing"—into which she should pour her existing oil. The woman followed through and, lo and behold, the original flask kept dispensing oil until all of the *keilim* were filled. Elisha then told her to use the new-found bounty to pay off her creditor and to support her family with the rest.

Increasing Emunah

It is certainly a moving narrative which, as we shall see, *b'ezras Hashem*, can be understood on a number of levels. What, indeed, is the significance of these *keilim*, which the woman was encouraged to gather in great quantity? The passage seems to be imparting a most important lesson about *emunah*. *Emunah* may sometimes dictate that we minimize our efforts. Such is the case when it comes to *Shabbos Kodesh*, for example. By working only six days a week instead of seven, a Yid thereby demonstrates a higher level of faith in Hashem; he conquers the urge to engage in more *hishtadlus*, trusting that refraining from work on Shabbos will actually benefit him. But in the instance of Ovadiah's wife, it appears that the opposite was true; the more *keilim* she collected, the greater show of *emunah* she demonstrated. A great man inspired by a G-dly spirit of prophecy had given her instructions. Following these instructions revealed her belief in Hashem; as such, every additional *kli* she collected represented a higher level of *emunah*.

From this we learn that one can elicit Hashem's generosity by increasing our *emunah*. The converse is also true: A person with a "כֹּחִי וְעֹצֶם יָדִי" attitude, who thinks that success is determined by his own efforts, will end up working much harder—and have less to show for it. A story is told of a certain *chassid* who came to the Satmar Rebbe for advice. His financial situation was challenging, and he wanted to know whether or not he should purchase a home. The Rebbe took hold of the *chassid*'s hand and made the following remark: "If you have money, buy a house; if you don't have money, buy two houses." Seeing the *chassid*'s perplexed look, the Rebbe proceeded to explain. There is a certain danger to having money; a person may begin to think that his money is his power, instead of Hashem. With such an attitude and lack of *emunah*, it will end up being difficult to afford even one house. If someone doesn't have money, however, it is much less likely that he will rely so heavily on his own efforts. Rather, he realizes that without Hashem, nothing is possible. "Once a person has such trust in Hashem," the Satmar Rebbe concluded, "he might as well purchase two houses."

Basis for Nissim

The bottom line is that Hashem so desires and, of course, has the unmitigated ability to provide our needs—even in a most miraculous fashion. But one's level of *emunah* can either maximize or minimize the miracles that Hashem would love to perform on our behalf. This thought adds yet another dimension of meaning to the episode of the oil flask, as the matter of increasing the volume of *keilim* can be understood in this light. *Nissim* can happen, but they require a certain basis from which to develop; and that basis—the *kli* holding the capacity for the performance of miracles—is, of course, *emunah baHashem*. This is what the *Navi* was encouraging the woman to do—to increase her *keilim* of *emunah*.

There are many ways to enlarge and further solidify this essential *kli*: not undermining our fellow Jew in business, avoiding discussion of business matters on Shabbos, giving generously to *tzedakah*, and, of course, increasing our Torah learning on a daily basis. These are some examples of building our *emunas Hashem* so that the *nissim* will indeed have a firm basis.

The well-known narrative involving Rabbi Shimon Bar Yochai further highlights this idea. The Gemara in *Shabbos* (33b) relates how he had to flee from the wicked Roman government who had decreed his execution. His wife would bring food and drink as he and his son hid from the authorities. But he realized this set-up was too dangerous, as the Romans might force his wife to reveal their whereabouts, so the two concealed themselves further; they went into a cave and hid in this undisclosed location for thirteen years, wholly immersed in Torah the entire time.

This was an act of supreme *Emunah*; they had not included his wife in the plan and had thus entered the cave with no source of sustenance. All they had was their reliance on Hashem, and He indeed performed a miracle for them. A carob tree bearing fruit appeared in the cave, as well as a running brook of fresh water. The *Maharsha* goes a step further, characterizing this as a *"neis b'soch neis."* The first *neis* was the simple fact that the carob tree appeared in the first place. The second *neis* was related to the fruit itself because a carob tree usually requires seventy years to start bearing fruit—but in this case it was ready right away! Now, imagine if Rabbi Shimon Bar Yochai had entered the cave having taken along a sandwich (or the like) "just in case." In a miniscule way, this may have detracted somewhat from his high level of *emunah*—and perhaps the miracle wouldn't have happened. But he didn't do that, and instead entered the cave with 100 percent reliance on Hashem alone. And thus, it was that by the strength of his *emunah* this great *"neis b'soch neis"* was wrought on his behalf. Despite having entered without even a morsel of food, Hashem supplied Rabbi Shimon Bar Yochai and his son with provisions that were ready to eat that very moment. Rabbi Shimon Bar Yochai's *kli* of *emunah* was so formidable that he and his son were *zocheh* to this *neis* for thirteen years.

We see from the above how Hashem is ready to shower His children with the most amazing blessings and miracles, as long as we prepare the necessary basis. Much like Eishes Ovadiah, we need to supply the *keilim* of *emunah* into which Hashem may pour the "oil" and blessings.

10

CHEIT HA'MERAGLIM

תָּנָא מִשְׁמֵיהּ דְּר׳ עֲקִיבָא לְעוֹלָם יְהֵא אָדָם רָגִיל לוֹמַר כָּל דְּעָבִיד רַחֲמָנָא לְטַב עָבִיד.

It was taught in the name of Rabbi Akiva: A person should always be accustomed to declare: "All that the Merciful One does, He does for the good."

Berachos 60b

THE consequences of the *Cheit Ha'meraglim* are really quite astounding. The *Meraglim* denigrated Eretz Yisrael with their negative report, thereby disheartening the people and causing them to cry out. As the *pasuk* states: "וַתִּשָּׂא כָּל הָעֵדָה וַיִּתְּנוּ אֶת קוֹלָם וַיִּבְכּוּ הָעָם בַּלַּיְלָה הַהוּא"—And the entire congregation raised up their voices, and the nation cried on that night."[1] As we know, as a result, that generation forfeited their right to enter Eretz Yisrael; they had to wander in the *midbar* for forty years, corresponding to the forty days the *Meraglim* spied out the Land. But the effects extended even beyond this. The crying out took place on Tishah B'Av, and as a result, that date became associated with tragedy for years to come. Chazal relate that Hashem announced: "אַתֶּם בְּכִיתֶם

---

1   *Bamidbar* 14:1.

בְּכִיָה שֶׁל חִנָם, וַאֲנִי קוֹבֵעַ לָכֶם בְּכִיָה לְדוֹרוֹת—You issued a cry for nothing; I shall set for you crying for generations."[2] What emerges, then, is that the *Cheit Ha'meraglim* was the catalyst for so much suffering, including the destruction of both the First and Second Beis Hamikdash.

But the question may be asked: Does the punishment really fit the crime? What did they do, after all, other than give vent to their disappointment? We know complaining isn't proper, of course; but should it really carry such dire consequences? It is essential, then, that we delve more deeply into the *Cheit Ha'meraglim*, for it certainly seems that such colossal tragedies could only have resulted from a more serious crime.

Everything for the Good

We may gain more insight into the nature of their deed by contrasting their behavior with that of the great sage, Rabbi Akiva. The Gemara in *Berachos* (60b) relates a well-known incident in which Rabbi Akiva's repeatedly declared: "כֹּל דְּעָבִיד רַחֲמָנָא לְטַב עָבִיד—Whatever Hashem does is for the best." He had been traveling and wanted to lodge for the night in the town. No one offered him a place, however, and he was forced to spend the night in the forest. Rabbi Akiva reacted to this development by expressing: "כֹּל דְּעָבִיד רַחֲמָנָא לְטַב." He had with him a lamp, a rooster, and a donkey. As the night went on, a wind blew out his lamp, a cat ate his rooster, and a lion devoured his donkey. Still, Rabbi Akiva's response to all of these events was: "כֹּל דְּעָבִיד רַחֲמָנָא לְטַב." That very night, as Rabbi Akiva slept in the forest, a group of thugs set upon the town and carried away all of the inhabitants into captivity. Rabbi Akiva turned to his companions and said: "Don't you see—it is as I have said: All that Hashem does is for the best." As *Rashi* explains, had the lamp remained lit—or had the donkey brayed or the rooster crowed—the thugs would have been alerted to Rabbi Akiva's presence. It was thus plain to see how all of the "misfortunes" of that night had actually spared him from a most unhappy fate.

---

2   *Taanis* 29a.

Significantly, the very next Gemara deals with the topic of complaining.[3] Quoting Rabbi Meir, the Gemara says: "לְעוֹלָם יִהְיוּ דְּבָרָיו שֶׁל אָדָם מוּעָטִין לִפְנֵי הַקָּדוֹשׁ בָּרוּךְ הוּא—A person's words before Hashem should always be minimized." This statement of Rabbi Meir, explains the *Maharsha*, refers to a person who wants to complain. Instead of just airing all his grievances, he should minimize his complaints to Hashem. After all, we don't always understand what's happening. And as demonstrated by the incident with Rabbi Akiva, whatever does happen is ultimately for the best: "כֹּל דְּעָבִיד רַחֲמָנָא לְטַב עָבִיד"—**Everything** is good, whether we understand it at the time or not. The classic example given is of a person about to make a business trip to seal the deal of a lifetime. He has to catch a 7:00 AM plane, so he sets his alarm to go off at 5:00. Somehow, the alarm doesn't go off until 7:00, at which point the man realizes that he missed his flight. He literally cries and complains how life isn't fair. A short time later, he hears that this very plane was in a tragic accident which left no survivors. In retrospect, of course, he should have been dancing in the street when the alarm didn't go off.

Of course, we are not always privy to see the "*kol*" (of "כֹּל דְּעָבִיד רַחֲמָנָא לְטַב עָבִיד"), but it is there nonetheless. Sometimes we see it, sometimes we don't. However, in Hashem's world, that's the rule and not the exception. That's the *derech Hashem* and a most fundamental aspect of *emunah*.

Misinterpretation of Events

We have seen the stark contrast between the attitude of the *Meraglim* and that of Rabbi Akiva. In truth, a sentiment very similar to that of Rabbi Akiva was expressed by the legendary Nachum Ish Gamzu, who would proclaim about his misfortunes: "גַּם זוּ לְטוֹבָה—This, too, is for the good."[4] In fact, Rabbi Akiva was a *talmid* of Nachum, and it is most likely that he cultivated this attitude as a result. Rabbi Chaim Shmuelevitz points out that Nachum was accorded a title of the utmost prestige, such as we find in the case of Hillel: the fact that he is called by his

---

3   *Berachos* 61a.

4   *Ta'anis* 21a.

own name without it being preceded by "Rav" (or the like) is a sign of supreme *chashivus*. We therefore see, on the one hand, the attitude exemplified by the likes of Rabbi Akiva and Nachum Ish Gamzu, which is highly regarded because it reflects a firm belief in Hashem's unmitigated goodness. On the other hand, we see the attitude displayed by the *Meraglim* and those who listened to them—that is, those who complained against Hashem. The mindset of complainers is the exact opposite of those who recognize that "גַּם זוּ לְטוֹבָה." Such people focus only on the negative, and in so doing display a lack of basic *emunah*.

With this in mind, we may better appreciate the gravity of the *Cheit Ha'meraglim* and Yisrael's response to their report. It wasn't just that they spoke badly of Eretz Yisrael and stirred up the Yidden. What so distressed Hashem was the fact that after all He did for us, the response was a glaring lack of basic *emunah*. As Hashem Himself said to Moshe: "עַד אָנָה יְנַאֲצֻנִי הָעָם הַזֶּה וְעַד אָנָה לֹא יַאֲמִינוּ בִי בְּכֹל הָאֹתוֹת אֲשֶׁר עָשִׂיתִי בְּקִרְבּוֹ—For how long shall this nation provoke Me, and for how long shall they fail to believe in Me, given all of the miracles I have performed in their midst?"[5] This, then, was the major cause of the *Meraglim*'s downfall: their tendency to interpret what they saw as bad instead of trusting and believing in Hashem that it is good.

Actually, the *Meraglim* and their followers had things exactly reversed. We see what their idea of "good" was, when they declared: "הֲלוֹא טוֹב לָנוּ שׁוּב מִצְרָיְמָה—Wouldn't it be **good** for us to return to Egypt."[6] With their warped view, they took something as horrific as the ordeal in Mitzrayim and saw it as "טוֹב." By contrast, *tzaddikim* such as Kaleiv and Yehoshua are able to perceive what is truly good, as they proclaimed: "טוֹבָה הָאָרֶץ מְאֹד מְאֹד—The Land is very, very **good**."[7] It is noteworthy that the *Meraglim* used the word טוֹב while Yehoshua and Kaleiv selected a term with an added letter *hei*: טוֹבָה. The *hei* can be seen as alluding to Hashem, for it is *emunah* in Hashem that marks the fundamental difference between these two attitudes. Only a person who views life without *emunas*

---

5   *Bamidbar* 14:11.
6   Ibid., v. 3.
7   Ibid., v. 7.

Hashem can look upon 210 years of excruciating slavery in Mitzrayim and consider it preferable to entering the *eretz zavas chalav u'devash*. It is only when we truly apply *emunas Hashem* to our lives that we will fully appreciate that everything Hashem does for us is "לְטוֹבָה."

11

LESSONS OF LIGHT

נֵר ה׳ נִשְׁמַת אָדָם.

The candle of Hashem is the soul of man.

Mishlei 20:27

WHILE yahrzeit candles used to come only in glass containers, nowadays, tin holders have become increasingly prevalent. From a purely halachic standpoint, there's not much difference, but I've always preferred the old glass holders, as their usage is so much more meaningful. With the current tin holders, as the candle burns and lowers, the flame tends to sink out of sight. But the glass containers allow one to continually view the flame, and thereby better appreciate its intended message. After all, we find that a person's soul is likened to a *ner*: "נֵר ה׳ נִשְׁמַת אָדָם—The candle of Hashem is the soul of man." In the spiritual realm, the *ner* affords much benefit to the *neshamah* of the *niftar*. But it also highlights the immortal nature of the soul, reminding the living that although their loved one is no longer physically present, their *neshamah* continues to live on and "illuminate." Taken as a whole, the *ner* actually serves to remind each person of his own makeup and nature. The ever-diminishing wax reminds a person of his own mortality, but the flame—"נֵר ה׳ נִשְׁמַת אָדָם"—provides a visual picture, enabling one to focus on the immortal nature of the *neshamah*, his true essence. Especially during this solemn time of contemplation, a person is thereby able to concentrate on those entities that sustain and elevate the soul—that is, Torah, mitzvos, and good deeds.

There is yet another meaningful lesson the *ner* conveys in this regard. The candle begins as a full and solid entity, but over time—as the wax progressively melts—the body of the candle becomes smaller and smaller. Throughout, however, the flame itself maintains its size, as well as its ability to ignite further. This symbolizes the fact that—whether at the beginning of one's sojourn on this earth, or toward the end—the *neshamah* itself is never diminished. And so, no matter what point one is at in life, the *neshamah* always possesses the ability to reignite a person and lead him to *teshuvah*.

Now, we find that Torah is also associated with light: "כִּי נֵר מִצְוָה וְתוֹרָה אוֹר—For a mitzvah is a candle, and Torah is light."[1] I had a personal experience that, I feel, enabled me to better appreciate this idea. In the *beis midrash* where I daven, people had been remarking that the light near the front seemed too dim. My mother, *a"h*, had recently passed away, and I offered to sponsor an upgrade of the lighting *l'iluy nishmasah*. The lighting was improved, the room seemed much brighter, and everyone was very pleased—initially, at least.

Not long after, I heard someone make the following comment: "The front looks good, but in the back it's like reading in a cave." To take care of this problem, new lights were installed in the back. Now the *beis midrash* was really glowing. Not a few months passed before someone asked: "Are these the brightest lights available? We could really use some more…"

I think this experience really reflects the true nature of light. At first it feels good; then you grow accustomed to it, and soon you are pining for more. This could be why Torah is compared to light, for, in a real and positive sense, our approach to Torah should mirror the process outlined above. Torah uplifts one's soul. After a person learns Torah, he

---

1   *Mishlei* 6:23.

feels great! But as time goes by, his *neshamah* should feel as if it's due for another upgrade. And at some point—hopefully sooner rather than later—a person should be asking: "Is there any more Torah available? I really need some more!"

There is another facet to the light of a flame that would seem to relate to both the *neshamah* and to Torah. This is the phenomenon of a flame's ability to maintain its potency. A person can use one candle to light another, and the flame of the first does not diminish. In fact, not only is the light not reduced, but now—given the additional burning candles—an *increase* in light has been achieved. When Hashem imbues a person with a *neshamah*, He imparts to him a "portion," as it were, from His own *kedushah*; the *neshamah* is considered a "חֵלֶק אֱלוֹקַ מִמָּעַל—G-dly portion from Above."[2] Of course, the *kedushah* of Hashem is boundless and eternal, so this in no way diminishes from His own *kedushah*. A Yid therefore possesses within himself an entity of supreme *kedushah*, but he can increase *kedushah* in this mundane world through *kiddush Hashem* and by inspiring others. So too with the "flame" of Torah. One never loses out by spreading Torah and helping another Jew learn and grow. On the surface, it may seem that by taking from his own time, he will lose out and stunt his own growth. But the truth is that one's own level actually increases as a result; by elevating the spiritual level of a fellow Yid, one's own *neshamah* is elevated further.

Each week at the close of Shabbos, we all gather around a flame during the recital of Havdalah. During this time, we proclaim aloud in unison: "לַיְּהוּדִים הָיְתָה אוֹרָה..." Here we have another visual reminder coupled with a reinforced message. What a powerful way to begin each week anew! We thereby further instill within us the important lessons of light, as they relate to Torah and our *neshamos*.

---

2   *Iyov* 31:2.

12

MOSHE'S HANDS
WERE HEAVY

וִידֵי מֹשֶׁה כְּבֵדִים וַיִּקְחוּ אֶבֶן וַיָּשִׂימוּ תַחְתָּיו וַיֵּשֶׁב עָלֶיהָ וְאַהֲרֹן וְחוּר
תָּמְכוּ בְיָדָיו מִזֶּה אֶחָד וּמִזֶּה אֶחָד וַיְהִי יָדָיו אֱמוּנָה עַד בֹּא הַשָּׁמֶשׁ.

*And Moshe's hands were heavy, and they took a stone and
set it beneath him, and he sat upon it; and Aharon and
Chur supported his hands—one on this side, and one on the
other—and his hands were [stretched out in] faithfulness until
the sun set.*

Shemos 17:12

SHORTLY after *yetzias Mitzrayim*, Klal Yisrael was faced with one of the most significant battles of their history—the war with Amalek. It was the aftermath of *k'rias Yam Suf*, in which Hashem's unparalleled power had been displayed for all to see. The whole world was quaking in fright—and then the wicked nation of Amalek attacked. Defeating them, obviously, was a matter of prime importance.

Yehoshua's Appointment

And yet, interestingly enough, Moshe Rabbeinu himself did not take center stage. Instead, he ceded the primary role to Yehoshua: "וַיֹּאמֶר מֹשֶׁה אֶל יְהוֹשֻׁעַ בְּחַר לָנוּ אֲנָשִׁים וְצֵא הִלָּחֵם בַּעֲמָלֵק...—And Moshe said to Yehoshua: 'Choose men for us, and go out to fight against Amalek...'"[1]

Now, it appears he indeed had a solid calculation in doing so. We find in *Parashas Vayeitzei* that Yaakov Avinu was not prepared to leave Lavan's house until Yosef was born: "וַיְהִי כַּאֲשֶׁר יָלְדָה רָחֵל אֶת יוֹסֵף וַיֹּאמֶר יַעֲקֹב אֶל לָבָן שַׁלְּחֵנִי וְאֵלְכָה אֶל מְקוֹמִי וּלְאַרְצִי—And it was, when Rachel gave birth to Yosef, Yaakov said to Lavan: 'Send me away, and I shall go to my place and my land.'"[2] *Rashi* there explains the timing. Yaakov knew that upon leaving Lavan's house, he faced the difficult prospect of confronting Eisav. But this became more doable with the birth of Yosef, for Yosef is the adversary and counterweight to Eisav. As the Navi declares: "וְהָיָה...בֵית יוֹסֵף לֶהָבָה וּבֵית עֵשָׂו לְקַשׁ—And the House of Yosef shall be a flame, while the House of Eisav is straw."[3] It was for this very reason, asserts the *Me'am Lo'ez*, that Moshe sought to appoint Yehoshua. As a descendant of Yosef, Yehoshua was imbued with this *ko'ach* of "לֶהָבָה" with which he could overcome the "קַשׁ" of Amalek, descendant of Eisav.

It seemed like Yehoshua was the perfect choice to go head to head with Amalek. But in *Parashas Beshalach*, we find that Moshe was criticized for making the appointment! The *pasuk* states that Moshe's hands were heavy—"וִידֵי מֹשֶׁה כְּבֵדִים"—and *Rashi* explains why: "בִּשְׁבִיל שֶׁנִּתְעַצֵּל בְּמִצְוָה וּמָנָה אַחֵר תַּחְתָּיו נִתְיַקְּרוּ יָדָיו—Because he had been lax in the mitzvah [of fighting Amalek] and appointed someone else in his place, his hands became heavy." In regular circumstances, of course, we apply the general rule that "מִצְוָה בּוֹ יוֹתֵר מִבִּשְׁלוּחוֹ"—it is preferable to perform the mitzvah oneself, rather than through a proxy.[4] But, as the *Me'am Lo'ez* laid out, Moshe had a very sound reason for specifically appointing Yehoshua. Why, then, did he deserve to be criticized?

1   *Shemos* 17:9.
2   *Bereishis* 30:25.
3   *Ovadiah* 1:18.
4   *Kiddushin* 41a.

There is yet another curious aspect of this episode. The same *pasuk* that refers to Moshe's hands as *"keveidim"* provides an additional description of his hands: "וִידֵי מֹשֶׁה כְּבֵדִים...וַיְהִי יָדָיו אֱמוּנָה עַד בֹּא הַשָּׁמֶשׁ"—And Moshe's hands were **heavy**...and his hands were [stretched out in] **faithfulness** until the sun set." What is the connection between these entities of *keveidim* and *emunah*?

As mentioned, *milchemes Amalek* occurred shortly after *k'rias Yam Suf*; as we shall see, analyzing that latter event should shed much light on the issues outlined above.

Glory of Hashem

K'rias Yam Suf was the culmination of yet another epic battle—that of the Mitzrim against Klal Yisrael. This was effectively Pharaoh's last stand, the last chance for Mitzrayim to subdue Yisrael. Pharaoh did not delegate the task of choosing officers to an underling, but in fact led the charge into battle himself. Now, this was no act of heroism on his part, nor was it even a symptom of his hatred for Yisrael. Rather, he had little choice in the matter, as Hashem was directing his actions. The Torah makes clear the objective of Hashem's plan in this regard: "וְחִזַּקְתִּי אֶת לֵב פַּרְעֹה וְרָדַף אַחֲרֵיהֶם וְאִכָּבְדָה בְּפַרְעֹה וּבְכָל חֵילוֹ וְיָדְעוּ מִצְרַיִם כִּי אֲנִי ה'—And I shall harden the heart of Pharaoh, and he shall pursue them; and I shall be glorified through Pharaoh and all of his army, and Egypt shall know that I am Hashem."[5] Hashem was orchestrating matters such that a great *kiddush Hashem* would result. As *Rashi* explains: "כְּשֶׁהַקָּדוֹשׁ בָּרוּךְ הוּא מִתְנַקֵּם בָּרְשָׁעִים שְׁמוֹ מִתְגַּדֵּל וּמִתְכַּבֵּד—When Hashem exacts vengeance from the wicked, His Name becomes great and glorified." And it was for this reason that He arranged for Pharaoh himself to lead the charge. In this way, the *kiddush Hashem* was increased all the more, as the whole world saw that the most powerful king in the world met defeat at the hands of Hashem. As Moshe proclaimed to Yisrael: "ה' יִלָּחֵם לָכֶם וְאַתֶּם תַּחֲרִשׁוּן—Hashem shall fight on your behalf, while you [need only] remain silent."[6]

---

5   *Shemos* 14:4.
6   Ibid., v. 14.

Hence, we may begin to understand why Moshe—according to his exalted level—was somewhat faulted for having delegated the task of fighting the war to Yehoshua. True, he had a very reasonable *cheshbon* of drawing on the power of Yosef's *lehavah* to fight the *kash* of Eisav. But there was a great lesson to be learned from the recent event of *k'rias Yam Suf*, which was specifically arranged to maximize the aspect of *kiddush Hashem*. Moshe had a similar opportunity to create a tremendous *kiddush Hashem* through the *milchamah* of Amalek, and this *neis* would likewise have been maximized had he himself, Klal Yisrael's principle leader, led the actual battle. It appears, as well, that it was for this reason that Moshe's hands became heavy—"וִידֵי מֹשֶׁה כְּבֵדִים." It is noteworthy that the *shoresh* of the word כְּבֵדִים is כבד, the same as that of "וְאִכָּבְדָה בְּפַרְעֹה." Hashem was thereby signaling to Moshe that the optimal choice would have been for Moshe himself to be more personally involved. Doing so would have maximized the *kiddush Hashem* even further—as occurred in the case of Pharaoh's defeat.

Just Do It

It seems that there is yet another lesson from *k'rias Yam Suf* that Moshe could have applied to the war with Amalek. At one point, with Pharaoh and his forces coming ever closer, Klal Yisrael appeared to be frozen with fear. But Moshe himself responded to the people by encouraging them to fortify their *emunah*. They were given the message that, in fact, it was not even the time to pray: "וַיֹּאמֶר ה' אֶל מֹשֶׁה מַה תִּצְעַק אֵלָי דַּבֵּר אֶל בְּנֵי יִשְׂרָאֵל וְיִסָּעוּ—And Hashem said to Moshe: 'Why cry out to Me? Speak to B'nei Yisrael, and they should travel on.'"[7] What Hashem was conveying to them, as *Rashi* explains, was that the sea will split for them in the *zechus* of their *emunah*. For their part, then, now was not the time to daven or to make any *cheshbonos*; all they had to do was—go!

We see, then, that there are times when a *cheshbon* may actually reflect a certain *chisaron* in *emunah*. This is a vital lesson to be gleaned from *k'rias Yam Suf*. At its highest level, *emunah* may entail going against logic and calculations; when *emunah* is solid, one simply goes forward. Take

---

7   Ibid., v. 15.

Shabbos, for example. From a logical standpoint, does it really make sense that by working only six days of the week, one will make the same amount as if he had worked all seven? Similarly, it doesn't seem rational that by giving generously to *tzedakah* one will actually become wealthier! On paper it *takeh* doesn't make sense; but *emunah* is the great equalizer. The math begins to work once *emunah* is part of the equation. Moshe indeed had a very good *cheshbon* for appointing Yehoshua, but as *k'rias Yam Suf* demonstrated, a higher level of *emunah* was called for here; one that transcended the regular order of logic and calculations.

This idea may be reflected by the two descriptions in the *pasuk* of Moshe's hands—"*keveidim*" and "*emunah*." There is indeed a connection, for when a person lacks real *emunah*, a certain heaviness descends over his life. Fear, stress, and worry are all the result of a *chisaron* in *emunah*. But a person who works on his *emunah* becomes unburdened and will feel much more relaxed. He will no longer be subject to overthinking things through logic, a tendency which could distract a person from making the correct choice. By placing one's full trust in Hashem, life will no longer be so stressful and heavy; instead, he will be able to focus clearly and serenely on simply serving Hashem "עַד בֹּא הַשֶּׁמֶשׁ."

PART III

תְּשׁוּבָה, תְּפִילָה, צְדָקָה

TESHUVAH, TEFILLAH, TZEDAKAH

1

BLESSING FOR WEALTH

הֱוֵה גְבִיר לְאַחֶיךָ וְיִשְׁתַּחֲווּ לְךָ בְּנֵי אִמֶּךָ.

You shall be a gevir over your brother, and the sons of your mother shall bow to you.

Bereishis 27:29

WHO doesn't want to be rich? Many people assume that being a *gevir* is *mamash* "the life." They picture an existence surrounded by luxury and comfort, involving only smooth sailing and catching every green light.

The reality, however, is often much different. History has proven that many people with wealth struggle with a whole host of challenges: familial problems, societal pressures, and even emotional issues such as depression. Hillel famously sums up the situation when he states: "מַרְבֶּה נְכָסִים, מַרְבֶּה דְאָגָה"[1]—An increase in wealth causes an increase of worries."[1] A materially wealthy person can never really be secure about his friendships. *What do people* really *think about me?* he wonders. *Perhaps they only like me because of my money?* And, of course, he worries about maintaining his financial status: *Is my wealth secure? Am I managing it*

---

1   *Avos 2:7.*

wisely and making good deals? Will I eventually suffer a reversal and lose everything?

Given the Torah's true perspective on wealth, it is somewhat hard to understand the blessing Yitzchak gives to his son—a blessing that seems to focus on material riches: "וְיִתֶּן לְךָ הָאֱלֹקִים מִטַּל הַשָּׁמַיִם וּמִשְׁמַנֵּי הָאָרֶץ וְרֹב דָּגָן וְתִירֹשׁ—G-d should grant you [blessing] from the dew of the heavens and the fat of the land, abundant grain and wine."[2] Yitzchak even goes on to state: "הֱוֵה גְבִיר לְאַחֶיךָ—You shall be a *gevir* over your brother"![3] How could any parent—let alone one of the *Avos ha'kedoshim*—give a *berachah* like this to their child, knowing the challenges it would bring?

The truth is that this word carries another meaning, as many *mefarshim* translate it as "*sar*" or "*adon*"—a reference to leadership. However, it is clear that power and responsibility likewise pose their own serious trials. How, indeed, are we to understand Yitzchak's *berachah* of "הֱוֵה גְבִיר לְאַחֶיךָ"?

It seems that the key word here is actually "לְאַחֶיךָ—to your brother." Of course, Yitzchak wasn't giving a *berachah* about *stam* being rich and powerful for its own sake. Rather, he was conveying that these qualities can only be considered a *berachah* if they are utilized "לְאַחֶיךָ"—to take care of your brother and help a fellow Jew. A true leader is one who uses his wealth and abilities for the sake of helping others.

Now, in truth, this may be no simple task. No matter how much money a person has, he may find it very hard to part with it! Yitzchak's *berachah* addresses this point as well, as the term גְבִיר relates to the word גִּבּוֹר; it takes real might and strength to let go of one's money in a generous fashion. If a person doesn't overcome this *yetzer hara* and keeps his resources for his own usage, there is no greater *kelalah*. But if he acts like a real *gibor*, using his wealth and influence to help his brother, there is no greater *berachah*.

---

2   *Bereishis* 27:28.
3   Ibid., v. 29.

2

OLAM HABA
THROUGH ASHREI

אַשְׁרֵי יוֹשְׁבֵי בֵיתֶךָ עוֹד יְהַלְלוּךָ סֶּלָה.

*Fortunate are those who sit in Your house, they will praise You
again, forever.*

Tehillim 84:5

WE are all familiar with Chazal's teaching that one is assured a
portion in *Olam Haba* by saying *Ashrei* three times a day.[1] It definitely
sounds like a good deal: three times a day, set aside a few moments—and
you have it made. But is this really possible? It doesn't sound like it's
much of a challenge to make it to *Olam Haba*!

Of course, it doesn't seem to make sense that it should be so easy.
By taking a look at where *Ashrei* is situated in the *tefillos*, we may be
able to uncover Chazal's true intent. At *Minchah*, we recite *Ashrei* right
at the beginning. In *Shacharis*, it occurs in the middle of the davening,
and then again toward the end: beginning, middle, end. What emerges,
then, is that to fulfill Chazal's directive and merit *Olam Haba*, a person

---

1   *Berachos* 4b.

has to be present *for the entirety of* davening. He has to come on time and remain until the end. And, of course, he can't disappear in the middle.

This is the true essence of *Ashrei*. "אַשְׁרֵי יוֹשְׁבֵי בֵיתֶךָ—Fortunate are those who sit in **Your house**": not in the lobby, not in the hallway, and certainly not at home. When a person is consistent with his shul attendance, he shows Hashem that he truly values the privilege of sitting in Hashem's house. And that person is surely deserving of *Olam Haba*.

3

PERSPECTIVES
ON GIVING

וְיִקְחוּ לִי תְּרוּמָה מֵאֵת כָּל אִישׁ אֲשֶׁר יִדְּבֶנּוּ לִבּוֹ תִּקְחוּ אֶת תְּרוּמָתִי.

And they shall take for Me a gift; from every man whose heart motivated him you shall take My gift.

Shemos 25:2

WHEN it comes to giving charity, there are, *baruch Hashem*, a number of very generous *baalei tzedakah* around. At the same time, however, it is not uncommon for this mitzvah to pose a challenge to many people, even those who have been blessed with great wealth. After all, it's not so easy to part with one's hard-earned money, so the attitudes in this regard tend to run the gamut:

- There are those, as stated, who give quite freely.
- There are those who may feel generous at the moment of commitment—but when the credit card bill comes in, the second-guessing begins.
- Others simply make themselves immune, able to ignore those in need.

What, indeed, is the ideal *mehalech*? What does the Torah demand of us in this area? At first glance, it may seem like a lot. The Torah reveals its sentiments on the matter of giving when discussing the donations for the *Mishkan*, as it states: "דַּבֵּר אֶל בְּנֵי יִשְׂרָאֵל וְיִקְחוּ לִי תְּרוּמָה מֵאֵת כָּל אִישׁ אֲשֶׁר יִדְּבֶנּוּ לִבּוֹ תִּקְחוּ אֶת תְּרוּמָתִי—Speak to B'nei Yisrael, and they shall take for Me a gift; from every man whose heart motivates him you shall take My gift." Regarding the curious expression of "יִדְּבֶנּוּ לִבּוֹ," *Rashi* explains it as a *lashon* that connotes *ratzon tov*, "good will." We see, then, that the Torah expects us not only to give generously, but to do so with a full and willing heart. This may, however, appear as something of a tall order. After all, many people have "worked on themselves" to the point where they can say no with a smile; how does one get himself to say yes with a smile? If the Torah demands this level of us, it must be that it is reachable. But the question is, how?

The key, it would seem, lies in gaining a true understanding of the mechanics of *tzedakah*; an awareness of the underlying ramifications may motivate us to indeed rise to the occasion. Suppose, for example, a friend offers you a thousand dollars on one condition: you have to give a hundred to *tzedakah*. Would anyone say "One hundred dollars is a lot to give away; sorry, no deal"? Of course not! We would take such a deal any day of the week. Knowing that by doing so we're pocketing most of the thousand, we'd be thrilled to give away a small percentage. We would indeed give this one hundred dollars to *tzedakah* with a smile and a *ratzon tov*.

And in fact, this is the Torah's real perspective on *tzedakah*: Hashem offers us this very deal. On the words, "עַשֵּׂר תְּעַשֵּׂר,"[1] we are familiar with Chazal's *derashah*: "עַשֵּׂר בִּשְׁבִיל שֶׁתִּתְעַשֵּׁר—Give away a tenth so that you will become wealthy."[2] We therefore see from a practical standpoint that *tzedakah* is quite a serious matter—our *parnassah* depends on it. Wouldn't we then want to do it in the most optimal way, in the manner of *ratzon tov* that Hashem favors most? Imagine what an impact our *tzedakah* would make then! And that is truly a deal that could make anyone smile.

---

1   *Devarim* 14:22.
2   *Shabbos* 119a.

4

"A GUT YOR!"

לְשָׁנָה טוֹבָה תִּכָּתֵב וְתֵחָתֵם לְאַלְתַּר לְחַיִּים טוֹבִים וּלְשָׁלוֹם.

May you be inscribed and sealed for a good year, immediately, for good life and peace.

Rosh Hashanah machzor

WE are all familiar with the beautiful Rosh Hashanah *minhag* (mentioned by the *Rama*[1]) to wish one another a favorable judgment and a good year. In actual practice, in a more casual sense, people begin offering such blessings even before Rosh Hashanah arrives. As the year nears its end, it is not at all uncommon for one colleague to mention to another something along the lines of, "Next year, may you be blessed with..." It surely sounds appropriate, and it is certainly well-intentioned. However, I feel that this latter aspect is actually problematic. It seems, in fact, to be a well-disguised ploy of the Satan, intended to rob Yidden of some of the blessings they were otherwise slated to receive.

As we know, the Satan plays a substantial role in the whole judgment process of the *yemei ha'din*. Chazal tell us, of course, that Rosh Hashanah is the time when Hashem apportions all of one's needs for the coming

---

1   *Orach Chaim* 582:9.

year, providing health, wealth, and *nachas*. The Satan, however, is not at all pleased to see Yisrael showered with blessing and does everything in his power to prevent them from receiving it. He thus inserts himself in the process, voicing his various *kitrugim* (accusations) in an attempt to sway the judgment in an unfavorable direction. He is very tenacious and determined in this regard, fighting against us every step of the way. Even when he sees that certain blessings will be decreed for this or that person, he still does not give up. If the decree is unavoidable, he will work it out that some of the bounty be delayed until the final moments of the year.

But even then, he is not satisfied. He proceeds to implement an ingenious and devious plan to ensure that this Yid will lose out on those blessings altogether. And so, toward the end of the year, he convinces a person that, for all intents and purposes, the year is already over. In reality, there may be a few days remaining, but through the Satan's machinations, a person's mindset is already on the year ahead. We start thinking to ourselves: *With only three more days to go, what are the chances of something good happening this late in the game? Hopefully, next year will be better.* With our focus thus directed solely on the future, we stop davening for the blessings of *this* year. And it is from this attitude that people start extending their good wishes to others. They do so with a full heart, but in offering such blessings for next year, they are essentially oblivious to the treasures that still await one in the current year. In our innocence, we allow ourselves to be duped by the Satan's scam to cheat us out of those blessings reserved for the end of the year.

This idea has been borne out in my personal experience. I remember an incident from my dating years. It was a few days before Rosh Hashanah; a certain well-meaning individual put his hand on my shoulder, and said, "Maybe next year you will meet your *bashert*." A few days later—the very last night of the year—I went out with my wife-to-be. Many people were blessing me for next year, but Hashem said, "No! It was decreed last Rosh Hashanah that *this* would be the year; it may be the last day of the year, but it's going to be this year." In truth, the last days of the year are priceless. The Satan conspires for us to "leave money on the table," but we must not allow him to succeed. We have to make sure to daven for each day of the year, until the very last moment. After that point, we can begin wishing each other beautiful blessings for the coming year.

5

HARCHEV PICHA: YESODOS OF TEFILLAH

> אָנֹכִי ה׳ אֱלֹקֶיךָ הַמַּעַלְךָ מֵאֶרֶץ מִצְרָיִם הַרְחֶב פִּיךָ וַאֲמַלְאֵהוּ׃
>
> *I am Hashem your G-d Who has brought you up from the land of Egypt; open wide your mouth, and I shall fill it.*
>
> Tehillim 81:11

THE initial phase of *yetzias Mitzrayim* begins to unfold as Moshe is appointed by Hashem to administer the *geulah*.

For Lack of Prayer

However, the arrangement by which this mission was to be carried out was somewhat curious. The issue—as Moshe made clear during his extensive "negotiations" with Hashem on the matter—was that Moshe had a speech problem. Hashem had instructed him to travel to Mitzrayim, inform the people of the coming *geulah*, and tell Pharaoh to release the nation. In his great humility, Moshe tried to decline, advancing numerous arguments to buttress his position. It was in this context that he brings up his speech impediment, pointing to it as a disqualifying factor: "לֹא אִישׁ דְּבָרִים אָנֹכִי...כִּי כְבַד פֶּה וּכְבַד לָשׁוֹן אָנֹכִי"—I am not a person of words...for I am heavy of mouth and of tongue."[1] Because of Moshe's persistent reluctance, Hashem eventually decides to send Aharon to accompany and assist him in his task, and the arrangement was finalized: Hashem would communicate to Moshe what needed to be said, Moshe would relay the message to Aharon, and Aharon would serve as the actual spokesman.

The obvious question, of course, is why such an elaborate solution was adopted. Hashem can do anything, of course, and there seems to have been a much "simpler" *eitzah*. Why didn't Hashem merely heal Moshe's condition? With the impediment removed, it would seem, the problem would be completely solved.

In addressing this question, the *Ramban* offers some telling remarks. He asserts that this would indeed seem to have been the most straight-forward course of action. But it didn't happen for one simple reason: Moshe never asked for it. As he writes: "וְהַקָּדוֹשׁ בָּרוּךְ הוּא, כֵּיוָן שֶׁלֹּא הִתְפַּלֵּל בְּכָךְ לֹא רָצָה לְרַפְּאוֹתוֹ—And as for Hakadosh Baruch Hu, being that Moshe didn't pray for it, He did not want to heal him."

Moshe, for his part, was not simply neglectful; he had his own reasons why he didn't pray for healing: "הִנֵּה מֹשֶׁה מֵרֹב חֶפְצוֹ שֶׁלֹּא יֵלֵךְ לֹא הִתְפַּלֵּל לְפָנָיו יִתְבָּרַךְ שֶׁיָּסִיר כְּבֵדוּת פִּיו—For Moshe, given his intense desire not to go [on the mission], did not pray before [Hashem] blessed is His Name that the heaviness of his mouth should be removed." Basically, Moshe didn't want to go and therefore didn't pray that he should be made able to go. Still, the simple fact remains that the only reason Moshe wasn't cured was because of a lack of davening. Had he done so, he indeed would have been healed.

Thus, the *Ramban* reveals a simple but powerful illustration of the es-sential nature of *tefillah*. Hashem may desire to bestow a certain bless-ing upon a person—something from which he would greatly benefit, and from which possibly countless Jews would benefit as well. But if the individual does not daven for it, it won't happen. This is actually quite a sobering thought. Imagine what would happen if, after 120 years, a

---

1   *Shemos* 4:10.

person goes up to *Shamayim* and is presented with a revelation: he is shown just how beautiful his whole life could have been had he only davened for it. It is so important that we constantly bear this idea in mind. Hashem, of course, is the *Tov U'Meitiv* and only wants the best for us. But He has set up the *beriah* in such a way that, to receive all of this bounty, a person must be willing to simply ask Hashem first.

Davening and Yetzias Mitzrayim

On the topic of asking Hashem, there is another key element to the *avodah* of davening that can help us maximize its potential. The *pasuk* states: "אָנֹכִי ה׳ אֱלֹקֶיךָ הַמַּעַלְךָ מֵאֶרֶץ מִצְרָיִם הַרְחֶב פִּיךָ וַאֲמַלְאֵהוּ—I am Hashem your G-d Who has brought you up from the land of Egypt; open wide your mouth, and I shall fill it." Now, we recite this *pasuk* every day toward the end of *Hodu*. But as familiar as it may be to us, did we ever stop to fully consider its meaning? In fact, at first glance it may appear perplexing. The first half of the *pasuk* mentions *yetzias Mitzrayim*; the second half is about making requests of Hashem. What does one have to do with the other?

Herein lies another important lesson about the *ko'ach* of *tefillah*, for which *yetzias Mitzrayim* was the prototype. The truth is that no one could really even dream about leaving Mitzrayim. The place was a virtual prison from which not a single slave had ever escaped. Certainly, there was no prospect at all for an entire people to exit the land. And yet it happened. How? Because Klal Yisrael davened: "וַיֵּאָנְחוּ בְנֵי יִשְׂרָאֵל מִן הָעֲבֹדָה וַיִּזְעָקוּ וַתַּעַל שַׁוְעָתָם אֶל הָאֱלֹקִים מִן הָעֲבֹדָה...וַיֵּדַע אֱלֹקִים—And B'nei Yisrael moaned from the labor, and they cried out, and their call emanating from the labor arose to G-d...And G-d knew."[2] This, of course, was not just any "regular" request; by davening to leave Mitzrayim, they were essentially asking for the impossible. And yet, that is exactly what happened. And so, Hashem points to *yetzias Mitzrayim* to show us what davening is supposed to be like. Don't just "ask," Hashem is saying; but "הַרְחֶב פִּיךָ—open your mouth wide." Even when it comes to something seemingly impossible, Hashem declares: "וַאֲמַלְאֵהוּ—I will fill it."

---

2   Ibid., 2:23–25.

Children have big *hasagos*. If you call a child over and offer to give him candy, he will immediately open both hands wide. You may only be intending to give him a morsel, but it doesn't matter; even before seeing the candy, both his hands will be out. If you offer soda, he won't come with a small schnapps cup, but a sixteen-ounce glass. As surprising as it may seem, the *pasuk* is conveying to us that this should be our model when it comes to davening. A person may otherwise have shied away from asking too much of Hashem, but in limiting the scope of his requests, he is actually restricting the quality of his physical and spiritual life. The bottom line is that we must never underestimate the *ko'ach* of *tefillah*. From the episode of Moshe's *keveidus peh* we learn just how important it is to daven. And "הַרְחֶב פִּיךָ" exhorts us to daven big.

6

NATURE OF THE SHOFAR

כֵּן הוּא הַטֶּבַע שֶׁל הַשּׁוֹפָר, לְעוֹרֵר וּלְהַחֲרִיד.

Such is the nature of the shofar—to awaken and instill awe.

Kitzur Shulchan Aruch 128:2

THE sounding of the shofar, as any child knows, is closely intertwined with the notion of *teshuvah*. The *Rambam* refers to it as a "wake-up call" arousing us to search out and improve our deeds, and return to Hashem.[1] The *Kitzur Shulchan Aruch* adds that "כֵּן הוּא הַטֶּבַע שֶׁל הַשּׁוֹפָר, לְעוֹרֵר וּלְהַחֲרִיד—Such is the nature of the shofar—to awaken and instill awe." This is a most significant assertion, for natural properties function automatically. Take water, for example. If you dip your hand in a bucket of water, it will get wet. It makes no difference whether you want it to get wet or not; such is the nature of water—it happens automatically. And so, when the *Kitzur Shulchan Aruch* states that the "nature" of the shofar is to awaken us to *teshuvah*, that means it should happen automatically—even if someone is not so interested. And here arises the obvious question: does this really happen? How many of us, in reality, are thinking of taking a break or making Kiddush around the

---

1   *Hilchos Teshuvah* 3:4.

time we hear the shofar? And yet, according to the *Kitzur*, this should be the last thing on our minds. Upon hearing the shofar blasts, we should be filled with immediate inspiration to repent. Why doesn't it always happen this way?

It appears that the answer lies in a *pasuk* in the Torah, which exhorts us: "וּמַלְתֶּם אֵת עָרְלַת לְבַבְכֶם—You shall circumcise the covering of your heart."[2] We see, then, that our *aveiros* have given rise to a covering over our hearts, and it is this covering that obstructs the true power of the shofar. We spoke above of the nature of water to make one's hand wet. If, however, the hand is covered with a waterproof glove, it will remain totally dry even if immersed in a bucket of water. As long as the glove remains on the hand, not even a drop of water will penetrate. And so it is, unfortunately, with the feelings of our heart. It is true that the "nature" of the shofar is to arouse the heart to *teshuvah*. But as long as the heart is covered with a "glove" resulting from our *aveiros*, the inherent power of the shofar cannot reach it.

What, then, is the solution? How can a person remove the glove that rests on his heart? The operative factor, it would seem, is *ratzon*; a person has to truly *want* to take off that glove. It may sometimes seem as if it is cemented on. But in truth, it is not irremovable—much to the dismay of the *yetzer hara*. A person who is a real *mevakeish* poses the greatest threat to the *yetzer hara*. His powerful desire to do what is right can melt the glove away. With this obstacle removed, the nature of the shofar will yield its full effect upon his heart, and thus pave the way for a full and complete *teshuvah*.

---

2   *Devarim* 10:16.

7

AVODAH OF ASERES YEMEI TESHUVAH

דְּרְשׁוּ ה' בְּהִמָּצְאוֹ...אֵלּוּ עֲשָׂרָה יָמִים שֶׁבֵּין רֹאשׁ הַשָּׁנָה לְיוֹם
הַכִּפּוּרִים.

"Seek out Hashem when He is to be found" (Yeshayah 55:6)...
These are the ten days between Rosh Hashanah and Yom
Kippur.

Rosh Hashanah 18a

WHILE the goal of a Yid is to serve Hashem as best as he can, we all have ups and downs in our *avodas Hashem*. Whatever the reason for our lapses, we always have the ability at any time to make amends through *teshuvah*.

But as we know, there is one period of the year that stands out in this regard. The ten days beginning with Rosh Hashanah and culminating with Yom Kippur, known as the *Aseres Yemei Teshuvah*, are designated especially for *teshuvah* and good deeds. Reflecting the elevated nature of this time, the halachah encourages us not only to rectify what needs to be fixed, but even to take upon ourselves added stringencies. For example, the *Shulchan Aruch* states that one should refrain from *pas akum*

104

during *Aseres Yemei Teshuvah*, even if he eats it the rest of the year.[1] In short, we see that this ten-day window turns us into "model Jews."

But here, any honest person must be moved to ask: Who are we kidding? What are we trying to prove with this "extra *frumkeit*"? In fact, perhaps we should worry that such conduct could backfire, *Rachmana litzlan*. Instead of generating *zechuyos* for us, Hashem may view our newfound piety as a form of *sheker*. He may feel that we're using the *Aseres Yemei Teshuvah* as an excuse—we can waste the whole year and then rely on this time period to suddenly become model Jews. Certainly, we can't fool Hashem with this ruse. What, then, is this really all about?

Actually, something happened in my own experience that I believe offers much insight on this issue. In order to get hired as a *rebbi* or teacher, a potential candidate has to first give a "model lesson." With the principal in attendance (and watching closely), the applicant "auditions" by giving a lesson to the class. I had always wondered about this practice; and many years ago, at the beginning of my teaching career, I asked my principal what the purpose is. After all, the candidate prepares ahead of time for hours and hours; he perfects his lesson down to the last detail and rehearses it over and over again. It's obviously unrealistic to expect that, if hired, he'll make the same investment of time and energy for every class, every single day of school. Basically, then, the whole thing is a show. So what's the point? My principal agreed with the sentiment, but he gave two answers—the second of which was truly eye-opening. First, he said: "I want to see how good he can be when he gives his best effort." Then he added: "I want *him* to see how good he can be when he gives his best effort."

Our approach to *Aseres Yemei Teshuvah* may be understood in a similar fashion. Obviously, there is a lot more at stake when we conduct ourselves as model Jews during this judgment period than when someone applying for a job gives a model lesson. Nonetheless, the same principle may apply. Of course we are not trying to fool Hashem. Rather, Chazal were interested that we give it our best shot so that we don't

---

1   *Orach Chaim* 603:1.

fool *ourselves*—by overlooking the great potential that every Yid really has. In general, the *yetzer hara* wants a person to sell himself short. He hopes a person will not strive to improve, thinking—through misplaced humility—that he's not so great anyhow and so there's no use in trying. But Chazal recognized that the greatest obstacle to real progress is fear of failure. And so, our conduct during *Aseres Yemei Teshuvah* is not a ruse; it is rooted in the true idea that success breeds confidence—if you can do it once, the next time will be easier. During this period, then, we show ourselves how great we can be when we indeed give it our best.

8

TZADDIK AND CHACHAM:
THE DIFFERENCE

שְׁלֹשָׁה סְפָרִים נִפְתָּחִין בְּרֹאשׁ הַשָּׁנָה, אֶחָד שֶׁל רְשָׁעִים גְּמוּרִין,
וְאֶחָד שֶׁל צַדִּיקִים גְּמוּרִין, וְאֶחָד שֶׁל בֵּינוֹנִיִּים. צַדִּיקִים גְּמוּרִין
נִכְתָּבִין וְנֶחְתָּמִין לְאַלְתַּר לְחַיִּים...

*Three books are opened on Rosh Hashanah: One for the
completely wicked, one for the completely righteous, and
one for those in the middle. The completely righteous are
immediately inscribed and sealed for life...*

Rosh Hashanah 16b

𝕐OSEF was a renowned and elevated figure. How could he best
be characterized? For his part, we see that Pharaoh referred to him as
a *chacham* of the highest order: "וַיֹּאמֶר פַּרְעֹה אֶל יוֹסֵף אַחֲרֵי הוֹדִיעַ אֱלֹקִים אוֹתְךָ
אֶת כָּל זֹאת אֵין נָבוֹן וְחָכָם כָּמוֹךָ—And Pharaoh said to Yosef: 'After G-d has
revealed all of this to you, there is none so astute and wise as you!'"[1]
Indeed, a strong case can be made to confer such a title on Yosef. He displayed tremendous foresight in this episode with his strategic planning,

---

1   *Bereishis* 41:39.

the consequences of which helped save Mitzrayim and the world at large from starvation. The power of foresight is a hallmark of a *chacham*, as Chazal proclaim: "אֵיזֶהוּ חָכָם, הָרוֹאֶה אֶת הַנּוֹלָד—Who is wise? One who anticipates the future."[2] Another example of Yosef's great foresight occurred in the episode involving Eishes Potiphar. Chazal relate that at the height of temptation, Yosef divined the consequence of succumbing to sin: his name would be erased from the stones of the *ephod*.[3] As a result of this foresight, he was able to overcome his inclination and restrain himself from committing this transgression.

In short, we see numerous examples of Yosef's great *chochmah*. When Shlomo HaMelech was offered any form of Heavenly gift, he felt that *chochmah* was the most valuable. It would certainly seem, then, that "Yosef HaChacham" would be a most fitting and appropriate title.

And yet—that is not how he is known! His great wisdom notwithstanding, Yosef is referred to as "Yosef HaTzaddik—Yosef the Righteous." It is true, of course, that Yosef was outstanding in his righteousness. The very act of restraint was a demonstration of his high level of piety. But as we have seen, it demonstrates foresight and *chochmah* as well. Why, then, was the characterization of Yosef **HaTzaddik** favored over that of Yosef **HaChacham**?

Course of Action

The answer, it would seem, lies in the precise definition of these terms. What, indeed, is the significant difference between a *tzaddik* and a *chacham*? A *chacham*, as we have seen, excels in the area of foresight. Pharaoh saw Yosef as brilliant for his insights on the affairs of Mitzrayim further down the road. But while a *chacham* is impressive for his intellectual abilities and his skillful planning, a *tzaddik* is distinguished for taking real action. Although Yosef showed great foresight in the episode of Eishes Potiphar, he earned his title of "Yosef HaTzaddik" for *acting* upon that foresight: "וַיַּעֲזֹב בִּגְדוֹ בְּיָדָהּ וַיָּנָס וַיֵּצֵא הַחוּצָה—And he

---

2   *Tamid* 32a.

3   *Sotah* 36b.

left his garment in her hand, and he fled and exited to the outside."[4] Physically running away from the *aveirah* is what made him forever known as Yosef **HaTzaddik**.

An interesting manifestation of this idea surfaces in the topic of the *Yamim Nora'im*. At the end of *Hilchos Yom Kippur*,[5] the *Rama* brings the following halachah: "הַמְדַקְדְקִים מַתְחִילִים מִיַד בְּמוֹצָאֵי יוֹם כִּפּוּר בַּעֲשִׂיַת הַסוּכָּה כְּדֵי לָצֵאת מִמִּצְוָה אֶל מִצְוָה—Those who are scrupulous [about mitzvos] begin to construct the sukkah immediately upon the conclusion of Yom Kippur, so as to go from one mitzvah [Yom Kippur] to the next [sukkah]." It is curious that the *Rama* includes this halachah in *Hilchos Yom Kippur*. Wouldn't it have been more appropriate to mention it instead in the next *siman*,[6] which discusses the actual *halachos* of Sukkos? But as we shall see, it appears that the *Rama*'s intention here is to underscore what the *avodah* of the *Yamim Nora'im* is all about.

The Gemara in *Rosh Hashanah* (16b) cites the well-known *Beraisa*: "שְׁלֹשָׁה סְפָרִים נִפְתָּחִין בְּרֹאשׁ הַשָׁנָה, אֶחָד שֶׁל רְשָׁעִים גְמוּרִין, וְאֶחָד שֶׁל צַדִיקִים גְמוּרִין, וְאֶחָד שֶׁל בֵּינוֹנִיִים. צַדִיקִים גְמוּרִין נִכְתָּבִין וְנֶחְתָּמִין לְאַלְתַּר לְחַיִים...—Three books are opened on Rosh Hashanah: one for the completely wicked, one for the completely righteous, and one for those in the middle. The completely righteous are immediately inscribed and sealed for life..." Everyone, of course, wants to be a *tzaddik* and merit a favorable judgment. And so, we spend the *Yamim Nora'im* beseeching Hashem to inscribe us in the *sefer ha'chaim*, and we strategize how to be better Jews. This is, of course, a sign of good planning; but as Yom Kippur draws to a close, it still remains only a "great idea." We are wise to the nature and purpose of the *Yamim Nora'im*, but what about putting these plans into action? After all, as we have learned, that is the hallmark of a true *tzaddik*. It could be for this very reason, then, that the *Rama* instructs one to begin building the sukkah *mi'yad* (immediately) after Yom Kippur. Doing so demonstrates to Hashem that we are taking our wisdom of the *Yamim Nora'im* and immediately translating it into real action—thereby warranting

---

4   *Bereishis* 39:12.

5   *Orach Chayim* 624:5.

6   Ibid., §625.

inclusion in the *sefer* of *tzaddikim*. Therefore, the halachah of building a sukkah is indeed incorporated into the halachos of Yom Kippur, for the notion is very much connected to the *avodah* of this period.

The Mishnah in *Avos* reflects this idea when it states: "כֹּל שֶׁמַּעֲשָׂיו מְרֻבִּין מֵחָכְמָתוֹ, חָכְמָתוֹ מִתְקַיֶּמֶת—[Regarding] anyone whose actions exceed his wisdom, his wisdom will endure."[7]

Wisdom is impressive, but if not acted upon it has very little meaning. Being a *chacham* alone is not sufficient to merit a sealed verdict of life. From Yosef **HaTzaddik** we learned the importance of converting our wisdom into action.

---

7   *Avos* 3:9.

9

INCARCERATION OF YOSEF

וַיֹּאמֶר לוֹ יוֹסֵף...כִּי אִם זְכַרְתַּנִי אִתְּךָ כַּאֲשֶׁר יִיטַב לָךְ וְעָשִׂיתָ נָּא עִמָּדִי חָסֶד וְהִזְכַּרְתַּנִי אֶל פַּרְעֹה וְהוֹצֵאתַנִי מִן הַבַּיִת הַזֶּה, כִּי גֻנֹּב גֻּנַּבְתִּי מֵאֶרֶץ הָעִבְרִים וְגַם פֹּה לֹא עָשִׂיתִי מְאוּמָה כִּי שָׂמוּ אֹתִי בַּבּוֹר.

And Yosef said to him: "…But may you bear my memory in mind when goodness befalls you, and perform kindness for me and mention me to Pharaoh, thereby extricating me from this place. For I have been stolen away from the land of the Jews; and here, as well, I have done nothing to warrant their placing me in this pit."

Bereishis 40:12–15

YOSEF'S confinement to an Egyptian jail by his former master was yet one more chapter in a long list of tribulations he had to endure. Yet, at one point, it appeared that things were beginning to look up. The warden was greatly impressed by Yosef and granted him privileges and raised his profile even in the confines of prison. Then came the encounter with the *sar ha'mashkim*, whose dream Yosef interpreted in a most favorable fashion. Seeing that the *sar ha'mashkim* was destined to be freed and quite pleased at the prospect, Yosef saw this as a golden opportunity. He requested that the official return the favor, and petition Pharaoh upon his release to free Yosef as well.

Playing a Part

But it was not to be—at least not right away. "אֶת הַמַּשְׁקִים שַׂר זָכַר וְלֹא וַיִּשְׁכָּחֵהוּ יוֹסֵף—And the Chief Cupbearer did not remember Yosef, and he forgot about him."[1] A full two years were to pass before Yosef would be released from jail: "...יָמִים שְׁנָתַיִם מִקֵּץ וַיְהִי."[2]

What happened here, exactly? Why indeed did Yosef deserve this additional two-year sentence? Of course, we must bear in mind in any discussion of the great *tzaddikim* that they are held to a completely different standard. Given their supremely elevated stature, a certain action or attitude may be deemed as a shortcoming, even though for us the same action or attitude may be considered praiseworthy. By analyzing Yosef's comments to the *Sar Ha'mashkim*, we may be able to identify a potential cause of Yosef's extended ordeal.

Yosef related a bit of his history to the *Sar Ha'mashkim*: "גֻּנַּבְתִּי גֻנֹּב כִּי בַּבּוֹר אֹתִי שָׂמוּ כִּי מְאוּמָה עָשִׂיתִי לֹא פֹּה וְגַם הָעִבְרִים מֵאֶרֶץ—For I have been stolen away from the land of the Jews; and here, as well, I have done nothing to warrant their placing me in this pit."[3] We see that Yosef decried the mistreatment he suffered in both of these instances; back in Eretz Yisrael at the hand of his brothers, and here in Mitzrayim in the wake of the episode with Eishes Potiphar. Clearly, Yosef considered himself completely blameless, the innocent victim of petty persecution.

And herein may lay the answer—it was this attitude that seems to be the issue. Yosef was certainly justified to claim that he had been treated unfairly and had suffered much misfortune, but it seems he overlooked whatever role he himself may have played. When it came to his brothers, for example, it appears that Yosef's conduct contributed to their envy

---

1   *Bereishis* 40:23.
2   Ibid., 41:1.
3   Ibid., 40:23.

and resentment. After all, the Torah in this episode describes Yosef as a "נַעַר"; for, as *Rashi* explains, "הָיָה עוֹשֶׂה מַעֲשֵׂה נַעֲרוּת—He engaged in immature behavior."[4]

On a certain level, his current circumstance in the Egyptian jail may be traced back to his own indiscretion as well. True, he had been repeatedly tempted and badgered by Eishes Potiphar, culminating in the false accusation that landed him in prison. But had he really done all that he could to avoid the prospect of sin? The *pasuk* states about the fateful day: "וַיְהִי כְּהַיּוֹם הַזֶּה וַיָּבֹא הַבַּיְתָה לַעֲשׂוֹת מְלַאכְתּוֹ וְאֵין אִישׁ מֵאַנְשֵׁי הַבַּיִת שָׁם בַּבָּיִת—And it was on this day, and he came to the house to perform his *melachah* [literally, "work"], and no man from the members of the household were there in the house."[5] What work is referred to here?

- According to one opinion in the Gemara, the term *melachah* here is a euphemism, conveying that he had decided to succumb to temptation![6]
- The other view maintains that the literal translation is the correct meaning, and Yosef intended merely to do his work.

Even according to the second view, how could he have placed himself in such a compromising position in the first place? Yosef was well aware of the history of this temptress and the danger she presented—how could he have allowed himself to remain alone with her in the house? This is all aside from the point that *Rashi* makes at the beginning of the episode. Yosef had originally gained favor and prestige in Potiphar's house for so deftly managing his master's affairs. But *Rashi* depicts how this success affected him: "כֵּיוָן שֶׁרָאָה עַצְמוֹ מוֹשֵׁל הִתְחִיל אוֹכֵל וְשׁוֹתֶה וּמְסַלְסֵל בִּשְׂעָרוֹ, אָמַר הקב"ה...אֲנִי מְגָרֶה בְּךָ אֶת הַדּוֹב. מִיַד—וַתִּשָּׂא אֵשֶׁת אֲדֹנָיו [אֶת עֵינֶיהָ אֶל יוֹסֵף...]—Once [Yosef] saw of himself that he was granted a position of authority, he began to eat, drink, and fiddle with his hair. Hakadosh Baruch Hu said: '...I shall incite the bear against you.' Immediately—'The wife of his master lifted her eyes toward Yosef...'"[7]

---

4   Ibid., 37:2.
5   Ibid., 39:11.
6   *Sotah* 36b.
7   *Bereishis* 39:6–7.

What emerges is that Yosef himself seems to have had some hand in both of the circumstances mentioned above—his transfer into slavery at the hands of his brothers, and his present incarceration in an Egyptian jail. While certainly a victim, he was *not* completely blameless. Yet, as he bemoans his fate to the *Sar Ha'mashkim*, Yosef omits any hint of his own blame: "וְגַם פֹּה לֹא עָשִׂיתִי מְאוּמָה‎—Here also **I have not done a thing**." We can now begin to appreciate the severity (in accordance with Yosef's high level) of his misstep, which may be responsible for his extended stay in jail. Yosef bore some responsibility for all that occurred, and for this, he had to do *teshuvah*. As with any *aveirah*, however, the first step to doing *teshuvah* is acknowledging one's guilt. But Yosef was adamant that he had done nothing wrong! The denial of his participation in these two events—being sold into slavery and Potiphar's wife—thus necessitated the extended sentence—one extra year for each denial.

Time to Contemplate

To illustrate further, let us look at some other well-known incidents of incarceration in the Torah. When B'nei Yisrael were in the *midbar*, there were two individuals who committed *aveiros*, for which they were held in prison while Moshe awaited further instruction from Hashem. One of these was the *mekalel* (in *Parashas Emor*) who blasphemed the Name of Hashem, and the other was the *mekoshesh* (in *Parashas Shelach*) who desecrated Shabbos. *Rashi* mentions that although these incidents occurred at the same time, the perpetrators were not placed together in the same cell.[8] Why were they kept separate? It stands to reason that this was done purposefully to elicit their remorse. When perpetrators are caught, their natural reaction is to claim innocence. If they are kept together, the likelihood is that they will persist in their denial, for each will encourage the other to maintain their stance. They will blame the system, or even the victim—anybody but themselves. With all of this mutual support, it will be very difficult for them to repent. Why should they admit their guilt if they're being told all the time that they're innocent? Therefore, the ideal circumstance for such individuals is for

---

8   *Vayikra* 24:12.

them to be placed in isolation. This gives the sinner the opportunity to think more honestly, reach the proper conclusions, and recognize his own guilt. And thus, he will finally be able to do *teshuvah*.

We see, then, that a primary purpose of imprisonment, in the eyes of the Torah, is contemplation; the sinner is afforded an opportunity to reflect on his deeds and begin the *teshuvah* process. Yosef, of course, was in jail, but the manner in which his conditions are described is quite illuminating. From Yosef's own words, it appears that he was not overly distressed by his surroundings. Certainly, he preferred to be freed, but when asking the *Sar Ha'mashkim* for help, he said: "וְהוֹצֵאתַנִי מִן הַבַּיִת הַזֶּה—Take me out of this **house**." House? Yosef was in a prison, and he's calling it a בַּיִת? Recall, however, that Yosef received preferential treatment even in his incarceration. The warden recognized that he was no typical prisoner; he valued Yosef's leadership qualities and granted him a measure of authority and autonomy. In a sense, then, Yosef was afforded a comfortable stay in prison—almost like being in a house. This itself became problematic; to a large extent, it undermined the very purpose of his imprisonment. For as we saw from the *mekalel* and *mekoshesh*, the real function of incarceration is to lead a person to contemplate his actions. The comfortable surroundings Yosef enjoyed served as a distraction, preventing him from recognizing and reflecting on his own guilt. He felt he was in a בַּיִת, which contributed to the mindset that he had done nothing wrong.

For the situation to change, something had to occur that would awaken his sensibilities and focus his mind on the underlying causes. And so it was that his jail term was extended for a prolonged period. Hashem wanted Yosef to spend two more years of introspection—corresponding to the two "denials." In this way, he could identify where his own responsibility lay, come to a full repentance, and then leave prison with a clean slate.

10

BEFORE OUR EYES

יִתְחָרֵט עַל מַעֲשָׂיו הָרָעִים, וְיֹאמַר בְּלִבָבוֹ מֶה עָשִׂיתִי, אֵיךְ לֹא הָיָה
פַּחַד אֱלֹקִים לְנֶגֶד עֵינַי...

He should regret his wicked deeds, and say in his heart: "How could I have failed to place fear of G-d before my eyes?"

Shaarei Teshuvah 1:10

CHARATAH—sincere regret—is one of the key aspects of the *avodah* of *teshuvah*. In discussing this quality, Rabbeinu Yonah lays forth a most fundamental *yesod*. He explains that a person must feel remorse from the depth of his heart, and ask himself the following question: "אֵיךְ לֹא הָיָה פַּחַד אֱלֹקִים לְנֶגֶד עֵינַי—How could I have failed to place fear of G-d **before my eyes**?" With these words, Rabbeinu Yonah underscores the importance of maintaining a clear connection with Hashem and with *emes*, and to do so even in the visual sense. The *yetzer hara* tries to place all manner of obstacles in the face of this connection, but here Rabbeinu Yonah reveals that these obstacles may be overcome by placing "פַּחַד אֱלֹקִים לְנֶגֶד עֵינַי."

In truth, we already see such an idea promoted by *Avos*, which likewise encourages a person to increase his *yiras Hashem* by means of "visual contemplation." As conveyed by the Mishnah: "הִסְתַּכֵּל בִּשְׁלֹשָׁה דְבָרִים וְאֵין אַתָּה

116

בָּא לִידֵי עֲבֵרָה, דַּע מֵאַיִן בָּאתָ, וּלְאָן אַתָּה הוֹלֵךְ, וְלִפְנֵי מִי אַתָּה עָתִיד לִתֵּן דִּין וְחֶשְׁבּוֹן —**Look** at three things and you will not fall into the hands of sin: Know from where you came, to where you are going, and before Whom you will have to give an account and reckoning in the future."[1] It may be said that the common denominator of these three ideas is Hashem. We came from Hashem, we are going back to Hashem, and we are ultimately going to have to answer to Hashem. If this is a person's focus, and he pictures Hashem in front of him, he will have a much easier time making the right decisions and rectifying whatever may need improvement.

A Parent's Image

Yosef HaTzaddik serves as a classic example of how this notion can be put into action. The Torah tells us that Yosef was subjected to relentless temptation at the hands of Eishes Potiphar.[2] There finally came a moment when, seeing that no one else was in the house, Eishes Potiphar made a final and desperate attempt. It almost seemed as if her efforts would succeed and Yosef would succumb to temptation. But his moment of weakness became a moment of strength—Yosef overcame his desires and fled the house. What gave him this burst of strength, *Rashi* explains, is that the image of his righteous father appeared before his eyes.

Chazal provide further insight into the turning point of this episode. As stated, Eishes Potiphar picked this time because no one was home. Where was everyone? According to one opinion in the midrash, the entire household had gone away for an idolatrous celebration.[3] This was the day that the Nile would overflow its banks, and the Mitzrim (who worshipped the Nile) conducted an elaborate ceremony surrounding the event. But while Eishes Potiphar assumed this was the ideal opportunity, in truth it may have been the very worst time for her purposes. It was actually Yaakov Avinu who in large part was responsible for the bounty afforded by the Nile, and one of the blessings resulting from

---

1   *Avos* 3:1.
2   *Bereishis*, ch. 39.
3   *Bereishis Rabbah* 87:7.

his arrival in Mitzrayim was the tendency for the Nile to overflow.[4] And so, while the Mitzrim foolishly associated the Nile's bounty with idolatry, Yosef was well aware of the true reason. Ironically, then, while the Mitzrim all vacated the house to celebrate the rising of the Nile, Yosef was reminded of his father's greatness. Perhaps it was this that gave him the strength to conjure up his father's likeness in his moment of weakness and be spared from sin. In any event, we see that at the critical time, Yosef utilized the power of "לְנֶגֶד עֵינַי"; thereby, he was able to connect with *emes* and make the right decision.

Interestingly enough, this same idea may relate to the customary practice of blessing the children on Shabbos night. The *berachah* itself is quite powerful—a blessing delivered from a parent to a child is always potent—but the power is magnified all the more by the special *ko'ach* of Shabbos. Yet, there very well may be an additional benefit to this practice—namely, it may have a significant, long-term impact on the children's behavior. Just the knowledge that they will be looking their parents in the eyes at this time can help them maintain their focus and make better decisions throughout the week. Furthermore, there are children who unfortunately get upset and may want to avoid their parents for extended periods of time. The realization that come Friday night they will have to "face" their parents may help soften their anger as Shabbos approaches.

Desire to See

As potent a force as visuals may be, we find there are times that they may not be sufficient. Such seems to have been the case during the episode of the *Meraglim*. Chazal intimate that Moshe was aware of the potential danger connected to the *Meraglim*'s mission. It appears that he sought to address this, at least in part, by placing an emphasis on "seeing." His very first instructions centered on this very idea: "וַעֲלִיתֶם אֶת הָהָר, וּרְאִיתֶם אֶת הָאָרֶץ...—Ascend the mountain, **and see** the land..."[5] Moshe hoped that they would gain a favorable first impression by viewing the

---

4   Cf. *Rashi, Bereishis* 47:10.
5   *Bamidbar* 13:17–18.

beauty of Eretz Yisrael, and thus would establish a positive connection. Things worked out differently, however. The *Meraglim* indeed punctuated their report with numerous references to seeing: "וְגַם יְלְדֵי הָעֲנָק רָאִינוּ שָׁם—And also **we saw** there the children of the Giants,"[6] "וְכָל הָעָם אֲשֶׁר רָאִינוּ בְתוֹכָהּ אַנְשֵׁי מִדּוֹת—And all of the nation **we saw** therein were men of stature,"[7] "וְשָׁם רָאִינוּ אֶת הַנְּפִילִים—And there **we saw** the Nefilim."[8] They made it quite clear that they "saw"—but with an eye toward negativity.

What happened here? Why didn't the visuals in this instance produce the desired result, and enable them to connect with the *emes*? We may perhaps gain some insight on this issue from a remarkable teaching of the Kotzker Rebbe. The Torah relates how Moshe Rabbeinu beheld an amazing phenomenon—a bush was burning with fire but was not consumed. This is truly an incredible sight, but the Kotzker Rebbe asserts that Moshe was actually not the first one to encounter it. Many others had seen it before him, but they had a much different reaction. "That's very interesting," they said, and then went on with their lives. What was different about Moshe? His reaction to the spectacle is very revealing: "וַיֹּאמֶר מֹשֶׁה אָסֻרָה נָּא וְאֶרְאֶה אֶת הַמַּרְאֶה הַגָּדֹל הַזֶּה מַדּוּעַ לֹא יִבְעַר הַסְּנֶה"—And Moshe said: 'Let me turn now and see this great sight—why does the bush not burn?'"[9] Moshe, apparently, made an extra effort to take in the sight. Hashem responded to his determined effort: "וַיַּרְא ה' כִּי סָר לִרְאוֹת וַיִּקְרָא אֵלָיו אֱלֹקִים מִתּוֹךְ הַסְּנֶה—And Hashem saw that he had turned to see; and G-d called to him from the midst of the bush."[10] Being that Moshe had a real desire to see, the connection was forged and cemented for eternity. And it was this element that the *Meraglim* were so obviously lacking.

Moshe and Yosef taught us what it means to connect with Hashem by forming a clear picture in front of us. They demonstrated how the power of לְנֶגֶד עֵינַי can enable a person to withstand even those *nisyonos* beyond human ability, and to ascend to the highest levels of greatness.

---

6 Ibid., v. 28.
7 Ibid., v. 32.
8 Ibid., v. 33.
9 *Shemos* 3:3.
10 Ibid., v. 4.

PART IV

שלום בית, חינוך

SHALOM BAYIS, CHINUCH

1

THE TALMIDIM
OF RABBI AKIVA

אָמַר לְהוּ, שַׁבְקוּהָ, שֶׁלִּי וְשֶׁלָּכֶם שֶׁלָּה הוּא.

He said to them: "Leave her be—what is mine and what is yours, is really hers.

Kesubos 63a

THERE are a few well-known episodes involving the experiences of Rabbi Akiva. One of these is the tragic tale of the loss of his many *talmidim*, the twelve thousand pairs who died because "לֹא נָהֲגוּ כָּבוֹד זֶה לָזֶה—They didn't treat each other with the proper level of respect."[1]

It is somewhat difficult to understand why it is that they received such a harsh punishment. Of course, it would have been much better had they showed more dignity to their colleagues. But were they really deserving of such a massive punishment just because their *bein adam l'chaveiro* was somewhat lacking?

Perhaps we may understand this better based on another well-known event involving Rabbi Akiva. As Chazal relate, Rabbi Akiva started out

---

1   *Yevamos 62b.*

as a shepherd whose wife sent him off to learn Torah.[2] He learned so diligently and intensely that he came back after twenty-four years accompanied by his twenty-four thousand *talmidim*. When his wife came out to greet him, the *talmidim* tried to hold her back, not realizing who this poverty-stricken woman was. But Rabbi Akiva intervened and issued his classic declaration: "שֶׁבְּכוּחָ, שֶׁלִּי וְשֶׁלָּכֶם שֶׁלָּהּ הוּא"—"Leave her be—what is mine and what is yours, is really hers." All of our learning, he was saying, is on account of her initiative and support.

What Rabbi Akiva said to his *talmidim* was quite telling. He could have stated something along the lines of, "You should know, all of us are really equal partners here." That itself would really have been something. But instead, he attributed *everything* to her: "שֶׁלִּי וְשֶׁלָּכֶם שֶׁלָּהּ"—My learning and your learning—it is all hers." Rabbi Akiva was a great sage, of course, and certainly very astute; most likely, he was aware of his students' shortcomings and knew that they could yet grow in the arena of *bein adam l'chaveiro*. With this statement he was imparting to them a most powerful lesson: the key to gaining perfection in this area is to understand that *it's all about the other person*. Each *chavrusa* needs to view his partner in this way—to truly hear their opinion and understand their position. Rabbi Akiva knew that if they would adopt such an attitude and internalize this important message, their whole *bein adam l'chaveiro* would vastly improve.

Unfortunately, they did not make use of Rabbi Akiva's teaching to the fullest extent. Indeed, Rabbi Akiva himself was the embodiment of this ideal, as we see from the episode in *Kesubos*. We see this as well from the fact that he would constantly emphasize the importance of properly regarding one's fellow. The midrash relates that this was Rabbi Akiva's classic teaching: "וְאָהַבְתָּ לְרֵעֲךָ כָּמוֹךָ, ר׳ עֲקִיבָא אוֹמֵר זֶה כְּלָל גָּדוֹל בַּתּוֹרָה"—'You shall love your fellow as yourself,'[3] Rabbi Akiva says: This is a great, encompassing principle of the Torah."[4] We can now begin to understand how such a colossal tragedy came about. They were hearing Rabbi

---

2   *Kesubos* 62b–63a.

3   *Vayikra* 19:18.

4   *Toras Kohanim, Parashas Kedoshim.*

Akiva promoting this great ideal every day—and yet they failed to fully absorb the message. This was indeed a grave error, and for this they were severely punished.

We ourselves can learn from this tragic event how important it is to heed Rabbi Akiva's message, which provides us with the key for our own interpersonal relations. In order for any partnership to succeed at the highest level, one must recognize about his partner—whether a spouse, *chavrusa*, or *stam* a fellow Jew—that it's all about the other person.

2

AVRAHAM AND SARAH: MODELS OF SHALOM BAYIS

> וַתִּצְחַק שָׂרָה בְּקִרְבָּהּ לֵאמֹר אַחֲרֵי בְלֹתִי הָיְתָה לִי עֶדְנָה וַאדֹנִי זָקֵן,
> וַיֹּאמֶר ה' אֶל אַבְרָהָם לָמָּה זֶּה צָחֲקָה שָׂרָה לֵאמֹר הַאַף אֻמְנָם אֵלֵד
> וַאֲנִי זָקַנְתִּי.
>
> *And Sarah laughed inwardly, saying: "After I have aged, shall I regain youth, while my husband is elderly?" And Hashem said to Avraham: "Why is it that Sarah laughed, saying: 'Is it even true that I shall give birth, while I have become elderly?'"*
>
> Bereishis 18:12–13

𝒜VRAHAM and Sarah provide us with a fundamental example of *shalom*. When Sarah overheard that she was going to have a baby, her initial reaction was one of disbelief. She laughed internally, wondering how such a thing could be possible; after all, "וַאדֹנִי זָקֵן—And my husband is old." Hashem was not pleased with Sarah's doubtfulness, and in the next *pasuk* relays His displeasure to Avraham: "וַיֹּאמֶר ה' אֶל אַבְרָהָם לָמָּה זֶּה צָחֲקָה שָׂרָה לֵאמֹר הַאַף אֻמְנָם אֵלֵד וַאֲנִי זָקַנְתִּי—Why is this that Sarah has

126

laughed, saying: 'Could it really be that I would give birth, while I have grown old?'"

Rashi notes that Hashem actually changed the quotation:

- Sarah had really commented about her *husband's* age: "וַאדֹנִי זָקֵן."
- Hashem reported that she had said it about herself: "וַאֲנִי זָקַנְתִּי."

The reason for this shift, explains *Rashi*, was to prevent hard feelings and maintain the peace: "שָׂנָה...מִפְּנֵי הַשָּׁלוֹם." We therefore learn from this episode just how important *shalom bayis* is and what we may do to preserve it.

At least, this is how many of us regarded the matter until this point. But if we take a step back, we discover a major issue: Why did Hashem say anything at all? Of course, He was interested in preserving the peace; and once He said something, He said it in a way that would minimize strife. But it seems that there was a much simpler way of avoiding any issues: if nothing at all had been said, nothing would have had to be changed. Why, then, did Hashem seem to go out of His way to relate Sarah's words to Avraham at all, thereby necessitating a change in the phrasing? Why not just let the whole matter drop?

Actually, the question gets even stronger; for it seems that even with the change, a certain level of tension was aroused between the spouses. The Torah goes on to relate that upon hearing the report, Avraham actually confronted Sarah about her doubting attitude. This caused Sarah to deny the matter, which in turn led Avraham to deny the denial: "וַתְּכַחֵשׁ שָׂרָה לֵאמֹר לֹא צָחַקְתִּי כִּי יָרֵאָה וַיֹּאמֶר לֹא כִּי צָחָקְתְּ"—And Sarah denied it, saying: 'I did not laugh'—for she was afraid; and he said: 'No, but you did laugh.'"[1]

Hashem was *meshaneh mipnei ha'shalom*. But was this really *shalom*?

By way of explanation, we may say that Hashem felt it was absolutely necessary to convey this information to Avraham. Why? Sarah's reaction to the news of the impending birth had betrayed a certain lack of *emunah*. In relating her sentiments to Avraham, Hashem even used the *lashon* of "אֻמְנָם," the *shoresh* of which is *emunah*. It seems that this was

---

1   *Bereishis* 18:15.

a precondition for the occurrence of the miracle; if Sarah's *emunah* was not absolute, she would not have a child at all. Thus, it was vital that Hashem convey this to Avraham, who had to "reprimand" his spouse so that she could rectify the issue, and they could have their child.

While we may now understand the need for Hashem to inform Avraham of Sarah's sentiments, there yet remains the issue of *shalom bayis*. The implication of *Rashi* was that Hashem was acting in the interests of *shalom*. But as we have seen, it appears that some form of confrontation ensued. In what way does that represent *shalom*?

The truth of the matter is that even this aspect may fall within the category of *shalom bayis*—if we really understand what *shalom bayis* is all about. Of course, the Torah demands of everyone in a household to take care of each other. But doing so may at times involve a willingness to enter into a somewhat uncomfortable situation: part of being a true *eizer k'negdo* is to aid one's spouse, in an appropriate way, in areas needing improvement.

When it came to the issue of Avraham's age, there was obviously nothing that he could do about that. Mentioning that matter to Avraham would only have caused painful feelings, and so Hashem avoided doing so to preserve the *shalom*. But in the case of Sarah's doubtfulness, this was something that needed to be addressed and rectified. As such, it was imperative to inform Avraham and have him urge her to improve and perfect her *emunah*. And this is precisely what she did, as evidenced by the fact that the miracle of Yitzchak's birth did in fact occur. In short, then, the interaction between Avraham and Sarah on this matter should not be viewed as a detraction from *shalom bayis*. On the contrary—it led to the most wonderful blessings, and ultimately was the greatest manifestation of *shalom bayis* between them.

3

GUIDING B'NEI YISRAEL

וַיְדַבֵּר ה׳ אֶל מֹשֶׁה וְאֶל אַהֲרֹן וַיְצַוֵּם אֶל בְּנֵי יִשְׂרָאֵל וְאֶל פַּרְעֹה
מֶלֶךְ מִצְרָיִם לְהוֹצִיא אֶת בְּנֵי יִשְׂרָאֵל מֵאֶרֶץ מִצְרָיִם.

And Hashem spoke to Moshe and Aharon, and He commanded
them regarding B'nei Yisrael and Pharaoh the king of
Egypt—to take out B'nei Yisrael from the Land of Egypt.

Shemos 6:13

THE Torah here recounts how Hashem gives the leaders of Klal Yisrael instructions about how to deal with the people. But the nature of these instructions, at first glance, seems somewhat cryptic. For the *pasuk* merely states: "...וַיְדַבֵּר ה׳ אֶל מֹשֶׁה וְאֶל אַהֲרֹן וַיְצַוֵּם אֶל בְּנֵי יִשְׂרָאֵל"—And Hashem spoke to Moshe and Aharon, and He commanded them regarding B'nei Yisrael..." What does this phrase mean, exactly? And what indeed were these special instructions?

Filling in some key details, *Rashi* explains: "צִוָּה עֲלֵיהֶם לְהַנְהִיגָם בְּנַחַת וְלִסְבּוֹל אוֹתָם—He commanded, regarding [Yisrael], that they should lead them gently, and bear them with patience." But this itself needs some explanation. As we know, Moshe was the humblest individual; surely, he epitomized gentleness and patience. It is safe to assume that Moshe appreciated the importance of these *middos* and already used them in

129

his dealings with Klal Yisrael. So why did he need to be told to "lead them gently, and bear them with patience"? What is the *chiddush* of *Rashi*?

It is important to look at the greater context of this statement. Hashem delivers (through Moshe) an announcement of the coming *geulah*. But Moshe found that B'nei Yisrael were not receptive to his message: "וְלֹא שָׁמְעוּ אֶל מֹשֶׁה מִקֹּצֶר רוּחַ וּמֵעֲבֹדָה קָשָׁה—They did not listen to Moshe, from a troubled spirit and harsh labor."[1] When Hashem then told Moshe to appear before Pharaoh and demand Yisrael's release, Moshe expressed his reluctance: "הֵן בְּנֵי יִשְׂרָאֵל לֹא שָׁמְעוּ אֵלַי וְאֵיךְ יִשְׁמָעֵנִי פַרְעֹה"—Behold, B'nei Yisrael has not listened to me; how will Pharaoh listen to me?"[2] It is in the following *pasuk* that Hashem provided the instructions outlined above—"וַיְצַוֵּם אֶל בְּנֵי יִשְׂרָאֵל"—which, as *Rashi* explained, refers to leading with gentleness and patience.[3]

From all of the above, it certainly seems that Moshe Rabbeinu was experiencing a certain amount of frustration with the people; no matter how much guidance he provided, it was met with stubbornness and lack of appreciation. It goes without saying that this was not the simple, petty type of frustration that you or I may feel. Rather, Moshe was pained because he felt he was not getting through to the people he loved so much. But in any event, such a situation did indeed call for an extraordinary measure of patience.

This, then, is the essence of what Hashem was instructing Moshe at this time. Of course, Moshe was well aware of the importance of being gentle and patient, and he used these traits in leading the people. But Hashem sought to underscore that it was not enough to be patient while leading them gently and everything was running smoothly. It is possible, Hashem was telling Moshe, that you may take care of them, guide them, feed them, clothe them, and teach them, all in the gentlest way, and instead of gratitude or even passivity, they will respond with bitter complaints. A truly frustrating situation, indeed; but that is precisely when patience is needed most. *Rashi's chiddush* is that Hashem provided

---

1   *Shemos* 6:9.
2   Ibid., v. 12.
3   Ibid., v. 13.

the leaders of Klal Yisrael fresh insight on how to best deal with them. What is most important is to exercise patience at all times—before, during, and especially after. That is the key to true success, and the sign of real leadership.

4

BLESSING THE SONS OF YOSEF

וַיְבָרֲכֵם בַּיּוֹם הַהוּא לֵאמוֹר בְּךָ יְבָרֵךְ יִשְׂרָאֵל לֵאמֹר יְשִׂמְךָ אֱלֹקִים
כְּאֶפְרַיִם וְכִמְנַשֶּׁה.

*And he blessed them on that day, saying: "By you shall
Yisrael bless, saying: 'May G-d make you like Ephraim and
Menasheh.'"*

Bereishis 48:20

THERE is something curious about the phrasing of Yaakov Avinu's
berachah to Yosef's sons. He was speaking, of course, to Ephraim and
Menasheh, relating to them that they would be featured in the blessings
fathers give to their children for all time: "בְּךָ יְבָרֵךְ יִשְׂרָאֵל לֵאמֹר יְשִׂמְךָ אֱלֹקִים
כְּאֶפְרַיִם וְכִמְנַשֶּׁה—By you shall Yisrael bless, saying: 'May G-d make you
like Ephraim and Menasheh.'" Why, then, did he employ the *singular*
form, stating, "בְּךָ יְבָרֵךְ יִשְׂרָאֵל"? Seemingly, it would be more correct to
say, "בָּכֶם יְבָרֵךְ יִשְׂרָאֵל"!

Of course, the very fact that Ephraim and Menasheh were the subject
of this blessing is itself a cause of wonderment. It is true that they were
upstanding Jews, even rising to the level of the rest of the *Shevatim*,

132

as Yaakov told Yosef: "אֶפְרַיִם וּמְנַשֶּׁה כִּרְאוּבֵן וְשִׁמְעוֹן יִהְיוּ לִי"—Ephraim and Menasheh shall be to me as Reuven and Shimon."[1] We don't necessarily see, however, that their level *surpassed* that of the *Shevatim*. Why, then, were these two singled out *more* than any of Yaakov's other offspring?

Actually, there is a factor that distinguishes them from the rest, the environment of their upbringing:

- The other *Shevatim* were *zocheh* to grow up in the household of Yaakov Avinu, located in the Holy Land. This was an extremely pristine atmosphere, essentially a yeshiva-style setting. They davened together, learned together, and were always available to give each other *chizuk*—truly the optimal environment for growing and developing into the holy *Shevatim* of Yisrael.
- In stark contrast, Ephraim and Menasheh grew up far away from such a Torah-friendly atmosphere. They had nothing resembling a minyan for davening or a bustling *beis midrash* for learning. On the contrary, Mitzrayim was notorious for its spiritual contamination. The environment was exceedingly hostile to growth, as they were surrounded by elements seeking to pull them away from Torah and everything holy. Nevertheless, they remained strong and withstood all of these pressures, even reaching the level of the *Shevatim* while in the heart of this spiritual wasteland.

Therefore, it was quite deliberate that they are held up as the paradigm for all Jewish children for generations to come. In this way, the blessing conferred on Yisrael applies not only to those fortunate enough to be blessed with a rich spiritual upbringing, but even to those who find themselves in challenging surroundings and situations.

We may therefore appreciate why it is that Ephraim and Menasheh were singled out—they overcame great disadvantages to become great people. Still, this itself requires some clarification: how, indeed, did they manage this great feat? After all, they were surrounded by the lowliest elements on earth, forced to grow up among a nation steeped in the

---

1   *Bereishis* 48:4.

depths of immorality. What was the secret of their success in the face of such overwhelming odds?

The answer, it would seem, comes down to their father, Yosef. He was the only one they could learn from, the sole beacon of light in the midst of such profound darkness. He himself had to face numerous trials and challenges, yet he showed his children that it was possible, through it all, to retain one's purity. Yosef remained a tremendous *tzaddik* and even grew spiritually throughout his stay in the depraved land of Mitzrayim. Apparently, he succeeded in imparting this vital lesson to his children, and they followed in his footsteps.

Now we may better understand the essence of Yaakov's blessing. We had wondered why he spoke in singular form, stating "בְּךָ" instead of "בָּכֶם." But in light of the above, it appears that in doing so he was actually addressing a single person at this point—he was referring to Yosef himself. Of course, every *ehrliche Yid* desires for his children to grow up to be *b'nei Torah*. In giving this *berachah*, Yaakov was conveying to Yosef that the key to fulfilling this dream lies "בְּךָ," with *you*. You, the father, are your children's real and only hope; and as such, it is crucial that you serve as a pristine role model for them. It is by setting such an example for your children that you will exert the most positive influence; and in this way they will grow up to be an Ephraim and Menasheh.

This is the central message of Yaakov's blessing. When we bless our own children on Shabbos night, we must realize that their success depends on the kind of example we set for them as parents. Just like Yosef HaTzaddik, we have to be the beacon of light in a world that—especially for children—can often seem quite dark. If we truly want Hashem to fulfill the *berachah* for our children to be like Ephraim and Menasheh, then it is up to us to be true paradigms of Torah, following in the ways of Yosef HaTzaddik.

5

RIGHTEOUSNESS
OF NOACH II

נֹחַ אִישׁ צַדִּיק תָּמִים הָיָה בְּדֹרֹתָיו. אֶת הָאֱלֹקִים הִתְהַלֶּךְ נֹחַ.

Noach was a perfectly righteous man in his generation; it was with G-d that Noach walked.

Bereishis 6:9

FROM the *pasuk* itself one comes away with a most favorable impression of Noach. He was a *tzaddik*, close to Hashem, and was deemed the only one worthy of being saved and perpetuating the human race. But then, as we know, *Rashi* complicates the issue:

- The first *p'shat*, of course, upholds Noach's sterling reputation: if he was able to maintain his righteousness even in such a wicked generation, he most certainly would have been even greater had he been surrounded by *tzaddikim*.

- *Rashi* proceeds, however, to cite the alternate interpretation: יֵשׁ שֶׁדּוֹרְשִׁים אוֹתוֹ לִגְנַאי, לְפִי דוֹרוֹ הָיָה צַדִּיק וְאִילוּ הָיָה בְּדוֹרוֹ שֶׁל אַבְרָהָם לֹא הָיָה נֶחְשָׁב לִכְלוּם—There are those who expound this critically: He was only righteous in comparison with his own generation;

had he been in Avraham's generation, he would not have been considered as anything."

The question, however, is—why do this to Noach? Does he really deserve to be criticized? At the end of the day, he surely achieved a substantial level of greatness in his own right. Hashem gives each person strengths and weaknesses to succeed in their specific purpose in this world. Every generation has its particular challenges, and Noach was (purposely, of course!) placed into the generation of the Flood to fulfill his mission. Hashem is completely fair and judges each person in relation to his own self, based on his circumstances, generation, and overall environment. Surely such was the case with Noach, as well. Why, then, would we hold up Noach to such a standard, comparing him to the generation of Avraham? Almost anyone would get a low rating if evaluated in such a manner. After all, we don't compare one child to another, or one student to another. So why is Noach being judged in comparison to Avraham Avinu's generation, thereby casting him in a negative light?

We may glean some insight into this issue from the Mishnah in *Avos* that states: "רְ מַתְיָא בֶן חָרָשׁ אוֹמֵר, הֱוֵי מַקְדִּים בִּשְׁלוֹם כָּל אָדָם; וֶהֱוֵי זָנָב לָאֲרָיוֹת, וְאַל תְּהִי רֹאשׁ לַשּׁוּעָלִים—Rabbi Masya ben Charash says: Initiate a greeting to every person. And make yourself as a tail to lions, and not a head to foxes."[1] From the beginning of the Mishnah, we see that Rabbi Masya's teaching bears particular relevance to Noach. It appears that Noach was not accustomed to act in this manner. Rather than approaching others, he took a more passive stance; it was not exactly his style to reach out to passersby. This posed a significant challenge, for how was he to induce people to repent? And so, Hashem arranged matters so that others would come to him. He ordered Noach to build a *teivah*—an endeavor that took 120 years and became a great public spectacle. The hope was that people would see this and approach Noach, asking what was going on. Noach would have to respond to their questions, and a potential conversation would ensue. Thus, Noach was effectively *forced* to interact with society; in explaining his behavior, there arose an opportunity

---

1   *Avos* 4:15.

to inspire others to do *teshuvah*. Rabbi Masya suggests, however, that the proactive approach is the preferred path. One can't always wait for outside factors to further his outreach efforts; rather, a person should aim to be "מַקְדִּים בִּשְׁלוֹם כָּל אָדָם."

The end of the Mishnah may be applied to Noach, as well—and in this way, we may answer the original question. The truth is, the second *p'shat* in *Rashi* may not even have been insinuating anything negative at all: The phrase "יֵשׁ שֶׁדּוֹרְשִׁים אוֹתוֹ לִגְנַאי" can be read in question form: "יֵשׁ שֶׁדּוֹרְשִׁים אוֹתוֹ לִגְנַאי—Is this really considered an insult?" On the contrary; as we see from the Mishnah, it can actually be a compliment to suggest that Noach would not have been so regarded in Avraham's generation. After all, it is more honorable to be a "C" student in the highest class than an "A" student in the lowest class. Therefore, it may have been that in Avraham's generation, Noach would rank much lower—but Avraham's generation was most lofty, while Noach's own generation was deplorable. We have seen that the Mishnah values the "זָנָב לָאֲרָיוֹת" over the "רֹאשׁ לַשּׁוּעָלִים." By stating that Noach would have been rated lower in Avraham's outstanding generation, *Rashi* was not degrading Noach's status, but was actually elevating it.

6

PURE OIL

וְאַתָּה תְּצַוֶּה אֶת בְּנֵי יִשְׂרָאֵל וְיִקְחוּ אֵלֶיךָ שֶׁמֶן זַיִת זָךְ כָּתִית לַמָּאוֹר לְהַעֲלֹת נֵר תָּמִיד...מֵעֶרֶב עַד בֹּקֶר.

And you shall command B'nei Yisrael that they shall take to you pure olive oil, crushed for illumination, to produce a continual flame...from evening until morning.

Shemos 27:20–21

THE Torah is discussing the oil used for lighting the *Menorah. Rashi's* comments on this matter, as we shall see, are quite illuminating. In his opening remarks on the *parashah, Rashi* states: "וְאַתָּה תְּצַוֶּה. זָךְ. בְּלִי שְׁמָרִים, כְּמוֹ שֶׁשָּׁנִינוּ בִּמְנָחוֹת מְגַרְגְּרוֹ בְּרֹאשׁ הַזַּיִת וכו'—**'And you shall command** [B'nei Yisrael, and they shall take...olive oil which is] **pure'**—[meaning:] without sediment; as is taught in *Menachos* 86a: 'He leaves it to ripen at the top of the olive tree...'"

A Pure Mechanech

One of the intriguing features of this *Rashi* is the *dibbur ha'maschil*—"וְאַתָּה תְּצַוֶּה. זָךְ." Technically speaking, these words are not connected in the *pasuk*, but appear at some distance from each other: "וְאַתָּה תְּצַוֶּה אֶת בְּנֵי יִשְׂרָאֵל וְיִקְחוּ אֵלֶיךָ שֶׁמֶן זַיִת זָךְ." Why, then, did *Rashi* include them together in the *dibbur ha'maschil*? Furthermore, it doesn't even appear that *Rashi* addresses all these words in his remarks. He goes on to describe the level of the oil's purity, highlighting the requirement that it be free of sediment. This is a proper explanation of the word "זָךְ," but what does it have to do with the words "אַתָּה תְּצַוֶּה"?

It appears that *Rashi* here is actually conveying to us a very important *yesod* relating to *chinuch*. When it comes to "אַתָּה תְּצַוֶּה"—instructing and teaching Klal Yisrael about the mitzvos—the key is that the *mechanech* must be "זָךְ"—pure and unblemished. When teaching or guiding people, one must make sure that his behavior, *middos*, and way of life are pristine, absent any "sediment" or trace of negativity.

In many instances, the outside world abides by the old cliché of, "Do as I say, not as I do," but the Torah demands a higher standard for its teachers and advisors. Imagine someone who warns against a particular form of conduct, when they themselves are guilty of the same. On an intellectual level, of course, they are saying the *emes*—one certainly should avoid improper behavior. In reality, however, it is difficult to accept something from a person who doesn't practice what they preach. This, then, is the lesson *Rashi* here seeks to impart. The *Menorah* requires oil that is free from imperfections, or else it's not worthy to be used for illumination.

As Chazal tell us, the *Menorah* represents Torah, and so the same would apply to the holy endeavor of teaching Torah. "אַתָּה תְּצַוֶּה": When "you"—the *rebbi*, parent, advisor—teach Torah, it is essential that your essence be זָךְ, that is, clear and pure in your actions and mindset. It is only in this manner that your message will be palatable to your listeners.

Rashi proceeds to cite the Gemara in *Menachos* that states "מְגַרְגְּרוֹ בְּרֹאשׁ הַזַּיִת—He leaves it to ripen at the top of the olive tree." This appears to be a further allusion to the idea outlined above. The choicest oil comes from the olives of the top part of the tree because they ripen first; we see that the best and purest oil comes from the top. In a similar fashion, it is from the רֹאשׁ of the family that there emanates the initial drop of guidance for the remainder of the household. For the message he delivers to be properly absorbed, then, it is imperative that the רֹאשׁ be completely זָךְ.

Continuous

Aside from the requirement of pure oil, we find another characteristic regarding the *Menorah*'s lighting: namely, that it be "תָּמִיד—continuous." Now, the *Menorah* was lit only in the evening hours, as the *pasuk* states: "מֵעֶרֶב עַד בֹּקֶר—From evening until morning." But doing so consistently each night satisfies this requirement, as *Rashi* goes on to explain: "כָּל לַיְלָה וְלַיְלָה קָרוּי תָּמִיד—If it is [lit] each and every night—this itself is called continuous." This requirement likewise appears to reflect on the role of the *rebbi*/parent, which must also be characterized by "תָּמִיד." We have already learned of the importance that the *rebbi*/parent be זַךְ, pure in both actions and mindset. The *pasuk* now stresses that this pristine level must be maintained on a consistent and continuous basis.

The timing of the mitzvah—its illumination throughout the night—seems to carry yet another powerful lesson in this regard. Night represents a time when it is more challenging to make good choices. Given its inherent darkness, it is during the night that indecent people tend to assert themselves and engage in improper behavior. "Who will see me?" they tell themselves. The light of the *Menorah* thus comes to remind us not to succumb to this way of thinking, and instead to make proper decisions even when we may think that no one is looking. The Torah expects a *rebbi*/parent to be *zach* on a constant basis—regardless of who may or may not be watching. Only *mechanchim* who are consistently pure can produce the clearest and purest *b'nei Torah*.

7

SHALOM BAYIS
AND THE MENORAH

הֱוֵי מִתַּלְמִידָיו שֶׁל אַהֲרֹן, אוֹהֵב שָׁלוֹם וְרוֹדֵף שָׁלוֹם, אוֹהֵב אֶת
הַבְּרִיּוֹת וּמְקָרְבָן לַתּוֹרָה.

*Be from the disciples of Aharon: loving peace and pursuing
peace, loving others, and drawing them closer to Torah.*

Avos 1:12

A well-known *Rashi* at the beginning of *Parashas Behaalosecha* addresses the connection between that *parashah* and the end of the previous one, *Parashas Naso*. *Naso* concluded with the extensive passage fea-
turing the *Chanukas HaMizbei'ach*; *Behaalosecha* opens with the mitzvah
of lighting the *Menorah*. And as *Rashi* explains, one thing led to another.
Aharon experienced a measure of *chalishas ha'daas* in the aftermath of
the *Chanukas HaMizbei'ach*. Having just watched all of the *nesi'im* bring
their offerings to dedicate the *Mizbei'ach*, he was very despondent that
he and his *shevet* didn't participate. Hashem thus broached the topic of
the *Menorah* in order to comfort Aharon, telling him: ",שֶׁלְּךָ גְדוֹלָה מִשֶּׁלָּהֶם
שֶׁאַתָּה מַדְלִיק וּמֵיטִיב אֶת הַנֵּרוֹת—Yours is greater than theirs, for you light and
prepare the [*Menorah's*] lamps."

141

Aharon's Disappointment

At first glance, *Rashi's* explanation gives rise to a number of questions. First and foremost, the whole notion that Aharon harbored such sentiments in the first place is somewhat curious. We probably would have expected of Aharon to be happy and content with his lot; being dissatisfied and disappointed doesn't seem to fit so well with his elevated character. How, then, could *Rashi* suggest something that appears to reflect negatively upon such a lofty figure?

Aside from this issue, the fact that Aharon in particular would be so bothered seems highly problematic. Consider what occurred in another, earlier instance—by the *sneh*. Hashem was trying to convince Moshe to accept the mission of leading and redeeming Klal Yisrael. Moshe, however, was concerned that his elevation to such a position would hurt the feelings of his brother, Aharon, and he remained adamant in his refusal, until Hashem reassured him that there was no cause for worry. Hashem, Who knows all hidden thoughts and feelings, attested that Aharon would feel no insult; on the contrary: "וְרָאֲךָ וְשָׂמַח בְּלִבּוֹ—He will see you and rejoice in his heart."[1] And so we see that when it came to such a colossally important mission such as saving and leading Klal Yisrael, Aharon had no problem with his brother being selected over him. Why, then, would this very same Aharon have such *chalishas ha'daas* for missing out on the *Chanukas HaMizbei'ach*? What's the difference?

Actually, there is a key distinction between the two cases. Of course, as evidenced by his attitude when Moshe was selected as leader, Aharon was far above petty grievances and jealousies. In that instance, however, the only factor that Aharon had to take into account was his *own* honor; as such, he was perfectly content and happy for Moshe to be the *manhig*. What was different by the *Chanukas HaMizbei'ach* was that the omission affected not only himself, but his whole *shevet* as well. As *Rashi* states: "כְּשֶׁרָאָה אַהֲרֹן חֲנוּכַּת הַנְּשִׂיאִים חָלְשָׁה אָז דַּעְתּוֹ כְּשֶׁלֹּא הָיָה עִמָּהֶם בַּחֲנוּכָּה לֹא הוּא וְלֹא שִׁבְטוֹ—When Aharon saw the dedication ceremony in which the *nesi'im* were engaged, he became despondent; for neither

---

1   *Shemos* 4:14.

he **nor his *shevet*** participated with them in this *Chanukah*." In other
words, Aharon, of course, wasn't bothered by being left out; it was only
when *other people* were involved that he became concerned. Indeed, this
concern for others was the very hallmark of Aharon, as we know from
the familiar Mishnah: "הֱוֵי מִתַּלְמִידָיו שֶׁל אַהֲרֹן, אוֹהֵב שָׁלוֹם וְרוֹדֵף שָׁלוֹם, אוֹהֵב
אֶת הַבְּרִיּוֹת וּמְקָרְבָן לַתּוֹרָה—Be from the disciples of Aharon: loving peace
and pursuing peace, loving others and drawing them closer to Torah."[2]
Aharon's concern was never for himself, only for others. When another
Yid experienced pain or disappointment, Aharon felt it perhaps even
more than the individual himself. And so, we see that Aharon's *chalishas
ha'daas* here does not reflect negatively on him at all; on the contrary, it
highlights the beauty of his love and concern for every Jew.

Aharon's disappointment here can be understood on another level,
also reflecting the qualities outlined above. It wasn't just *any* worthy
endeavor that Aharon had missed out on; rather, it was the *specific
event* of the *Chanukas HaMizbei'ach* that caused him such distress. This
is because Aharon had a strong, personal connection to the *Mizbei'ach*.
At the end of *Maseches Gittin*, the Gemara tells us that the *Mizbei'ach*
sheds tears when a couple gets divorced, *Rachmana litzlan*. And it was
in this very area that Aharon was so deeply invested. As an "אוֹהֵב שָׁלוֹם
וְרוֹדֵף שָׁלוֹם," he simply could not bear to see a lack of peace between husband and wife, and he dedicated his life to helping resolve differences
and preserve harmony. It states in *Maseches Kallah* that Aharon saved
eighty thousand marriages from the brink of divorce; most likely he
improved the quality of countless others. In short, *shalom bayis* was
Aharon's "forte"—he so deeply shared the pain the *Mizbei'ach* felt
that when the *Mizbei'ach* cried, Aharon cried even harder. Thus, while
he already had a strong bond with the *Mizbei'ach*, participating in the
Chanukas HaMizbei'ach would have strengthened that bond even more;
and through this deeper connection, Aharon may have applied himself
to *shalom bayis* with even greater intensity. It is for this reason that
Aharon was so profoundly disappointed by his exclusion from the

2   *Avos* 1:12.

Chanukas HaMizbei'ach. For he saw therein a missed opportunity, one that could have furthered the cause of *shalom bayis* in Klal Yisrael. Once again, we see that Aharon's *chalishas ha'daas* was not a negative, but a strong positive. It was not based on any selfish motives, rather it speaks only to his overwhelming concern for others.

Yours Is Greater Than Theirs

We have seen from the above why it was that Aharon felt such keen disappointment over the lack of participation in the *Chanukas HaMizbei'ach*. To comfort him, as *Rashi* related, Hashem assured him that his *avodah* was superior to theirs: "שֶׁלְּךָ גְדוֹלָה מִשֶּׁלָּהֶם, שֶׁאַתָּה מַדְלִיק וּמֵיטִיב אֶת הַנֵּרוֹת—Yours is greater than theirs, for you light and prepare the [*Menorah*'s] lamps." But this also seems to be a cause for wonder. How, indeed, was this supposed to comfort Aharon? Why would lighting the *Menorah* be more precious to him than dedicating the *Mizbei'ach*?

Actually, this matter can also be clarified along the lines of the above. Aharon's legendary pursuit of *shalom bayis* meant that he had a special connection with the Jewish home. This is evidenced by the fact that, when he was *niftar*, the Torah makes a point of stating: "וַיִּבְכּוּ אֶת אַהֲרֹן...כֹּל בֵּית יִשְׂרָאֵל—And **the entire House of Yisrael** cried for Aharon."[3] The "entire House of Yisrael," *Rashi* explains, includes everyone—both men and women. For Aharon's kindness affected everyone, particularly in the realm of *shalom bayis*, as he restored so much harmony to the Jewish home.

We now understand even further how the *Menorah* would serve as a sense of comfort to Aharon. As we have seen, he was distressed about the *Chanukas HaMizbei'ach* because it represented an opportunity to increase *shalom bayis*. What Hashem was demonstrating to Aharon was that he could do just that through the lighting of the *Menorah*—perhaps on an even greater scale. As we know, the *Menorah* symbolizes Torah. In presiding over its lighting, Aharon would thereby be responsible for channeling the light of Torah into every Jewish home, and the light of Torah has a tremendous effect on the state of *shalom bayis* in the home.

---

3   *Bamidbar* 20:29.

In a Torah home, a husband and wife speak and act differently to each other. They are more careful with what they say and do, thereby creating a warmer, more nurturing atmosphere within their home. A Torah home is marked by peace, calmness, and greater sensitivity toward one another. And most importantly, the light of Torah helps to prevent the outbreak of heated discussions which could potentially destroy the *shalom bayis* of a home, *Rachmana litzlan.*

Aharon's goal was to protect *shalom bayis* and preserve marriages. After all the yelling, screaming, and bitter feelings, he would do everything and anything he could to piece it all back together and avoid a potentially tragic ending. Thus, the *avodah* of lighting the *Menorah* was a tremendous asset for achieving this goal; as we have seen, the light of Torah it imparted to a Jewish home did so much to prevent *machlokes* and preserve *shalom bayis.*

This, then, was the message Hashem conveyed to Aharon, when He declared: "שֶׁלְּךָ גְדוֹלָה מִשֶּׁלָּהֶם—Yours is greater than theirs." Both the *Menorah* and the *Mizbei'ach*, as we have learned, have connections to *shalom bayis*. But in one key respect there is a difference, and it is in this way that the *Menorah* is "greater" than the *Mizbei'ach*. As was previously stated, the *Mizbei'ach* would shed tears upon the occasion of a divorce; thus, its relationship to *shalom bayis* was of a more reactive form. In contrast, the *Menorah*'s stance was a *proactive* one, as the light of Torah it channeled to the Jewish home prevented threats to *shalom bayis* from arising in the first place. In this sense, then, the *avodah* of lighting the *Menorah* was indeed superior to the dedication of the *Mizbei'ach*. By way of its light, Aharon would be in a better position to protect the *shalom bayis* of Klal Yisrael. In this way, neither he nor the *Mizbei'ach* would ever have to shed another tear.

8

LESSONS IN CHINUCH

וַיֶּעְתַּר מָנוֹחַ אֶל ה׳ וַיֹּאמַר בִּי אֲדוֹנָי אִישׁ הָאֱלֹקִים אֲשֶׁר שָׁלַחְתָּ
יָבוֹא נָא עוֹד אֵלֵינוּ וְיוֹרֵנוּ מַה נַּעֲשֶׂה לַנַּעַר הַיּוּלָד.

*And Manoach entreated Hashem, and he said: "Please,
Hashem! The man of G-d whom You sent—may he come again
to us and instruct us what we should do for the boy to be born.*

Shoftim 13:8

RAISING children properly is, simultaneously one of the most rewarding and challenging opportunities a person may face. It takes a lot of time, energy, and cooperation to develop an effective approach. Needless to say, implementing that approach can be an overwhelming experience.

Taking Responsibility

I recently had an experience that gave me an enhanced perspective on the whole notion of *chinuch*. As of this writing, it has been four years since the passing of my mother, and more recently, my father passed away as well. At the *beis ha'kevaros*, as I saw my father buried next to my mother, an interesting thought occurred to me that I shared with my family and friends. The Gemara states: "שְׁלֹשָׁה שֻׁתָּפִין הֵן בָּאָדָם, הַקָּדוֹשׁ

בָּרוּךְ הוּא וְאָבִיו וְאִמּוֹ—There are three partners in [the formation of] a person—Hashem, one's father, and one's mother."[1] With this Gemara in mind, I derived a sense of comfort from looking at my parents. I realized that the three partners in my own creation and development were back together again. The partners were reunited, the partnership stronger than ever.

What, then, does the partnership of *chinuch* entail? I believe, first and foremost, it means taking responsibility for one's children—at all times. A successful partnership is one in which all hands are on deck, 24/7.

Many years ago, I had a student who was giving the yeshiva a challenging time. I called his parents and explained that their son was on the brink of ending up in serious trouble. After hearing me out, the mother offered the following startling comment: "Bottom line, what are you going to do about it?" A bit taken aback, I told the mother that there was something we needed to clarify here. It's not that you're helping me—I'm helping you. This is *your* son. What are *you* going to do for him and how can I help *you*? Taking full responsibility and leading the way is critical in assuring that we are *mechanech* our children in the most optimal way. Whether it's through *tefillah* or hands-on guidance (or both), a parent has to be an active participant. Autopilot is not the Torah way of raising children.

In addition, we may not allow the daily pressures that accumulate to derail us from this most important task. Factors such as age, stressors of paying tuition, and preoccupation with responsibilities can present significant obstacles; nonetheless, they do not absolve us from being *mechanech* our children properly. This we see from the case of Eli, the Kohen Gadol, whose two sons Chofni and Pinchas were guilty of certain misdeeds (on their level). The *pasuk* states: "וְעֵלִי זָקֵן מְאֹד וְשָׁמַע אֵת כָּל אֲשֶׁר יַעֲשׂוּן בָּנָיו לְכָל יִשְׂרָאֵל—And Eli was very old, and he heard all that his sons were doing to all Yisrael."[2] The narrative continues, and Eli goes on to give his sons a gentle reprimand—which they promptly ignore. A *Navi* then approaches Eli and delivers to him a fairly harsh rebuke in which

---

1   *Kiddushin* 30b.
2   *Shmuel I* 2:22.

he insinuates that Eli himself shares in the guilt. Now, it is interesting that the *pasuk* goes out of its way to emphasize Eli's age: "וְעֵלִי זָקֵן מְאֹד וְשָׁמַע אֵת כָּל אֲשֶׁר יַעֲשׂוּן בָּנָיו לְכָל יִשְׂרָאֵל." Perhaps the message being conveyed here is that age is not an excuse, nor are the other factors which may have otherwise exonerated him: He was quite busy in his position of Kohen Gadol, his children were adults with their own high-profile jobs, and he himself didn't observe their improper behavior. Apparently, however, none of these seemingly good excuses absolved Eli of responsibility. He was taken to task because, as a parent, it was still his *obligation* to be *mechanech* his children to the best of his ability.

Lessons from Manoach

There is another key episode in the *Navi* from which we may learn some important principles in the area of *chinuch*. Manoach and his barren wife were told they would be blessed with a son (Shimshon) whom they should raise as a *nazir*. The *malach* actually appeared first to Eishes Manoach bearing the happy tidings. When she relayed the news to her husband, he reacted in the following way: "וַיֶּעְתַּר מָנוֹחַ אֶל ה' וַיֹּאמַר בִּי אֲדוֹנִי אִישׁ הָאֱלֹקִים אֲשֶׁר שָׁלַחְתָּ יָבוֹא נָא עוֹד אֵלֵינוּ וְיוֹרֵנוּ מַה נַּעֲשֶׂה לַנַּעַר הַיּוּלָּד—And Manoach entreated Hashem, and he said: 'Please, My Lord! [Regarding] the man of G-d whom You sent—may he come to us again and instruct us what we should do for the child to be born.'"[3] It is noteworthy that the *pasuk* here uses fairly strong language. Instead of stating that Manoach merely "asked" or "requested"—or even "prayed"—it says "וַיֶּעְתַּר," which literally means: "he begged." This is the same phrase used in connection with the supplications of Yitzchak and Rivkah, who also suffered from childlessness: "וַיֶּעְתַּר יִצְחָק לַה' לְנֹכַח אִשְׁתּוֹ כִּי עֲקָרָה הִוא—And Yitzchak **entreated** Hashem opposite his wife, for she was barren."[4] *Rashi* there points out that the *shoresh* "עתר" denotes an especially strong form of prayer, characterized by increased intensity. In essence, Yitzchak was begging and pleading for a child as if Klal Yisrael depended on it; and this was indeed the case, as without a Yaakov Avinu there would be no

---

3   *Shoftim* 13:8.
4   *Bereishis* 25:21.

continuation of Klal Yisrael. Of course, Hashem was aware of that, and wanted and intended to bring it to fruition; nonetheless, for his part, Yitzchak had to plead for it with every fiber of his being. In a similar way, Klal Yisrael at that time desperately needed Shimshon HaGibor, but it was Manoach's obligation to entreat Hashem for the successful development of his son. This, then, is the first important lesson imparted to us by this episode. We see that if we want to be privileged to have children and raise them as *b'nei* and *b'nos* Torah, we must truly plead with Hashem to answer our *tefillos*.

We see further that Manoach was particular to consult with the "אִישׁ הָאֱלֹקִים" regarding the raising of his child: "אִישׁ הָאֱלֹקִים אֲשֶׁר שָׁלַחְתָּ יָבוֹא נָא עוֹד אֵלֵינוּ וְיוֹרֵנוּ מַה נַּעֲשֶׂה לַנַּעַר הַיּוּלָּד." Of course, it is quicker, more convenient, and more comfortable to make all *chinuch* decisions by ourselves. But it's also riskier. Parents sometimes make the (potentially disastrous) mistake of assuming they're smarter and "know better" about raising children than seasoned *mechanchim*. However, it is essential to recall that the best doctor is not necessarily the one with the highest IQ. When dealing with a serious illness, *Rachmana litzlan*, most people instinctively search out a doctor who has already seen and treated this sickness a thousand times. He is the one who knows what works and what doesn't. Experience is a vital asset in the field of *chinuch*, as well. What is more, an earnest *mechanech* is granted a special measure of *siyata d'Shmaya*. In the case of Manoach, the angel is never referred to as simply a "מַלְאָךְ," but a "מַלְאַךְ ה׳." This indicates that when it comes to *chinuch*, Hashem is always at the ready to provide His *shaliach* with a special *berachah* to ensure the parents are guided correctly. Thus, the second lesson we learn from Manoach is the importance of consulting with upstanding *mechanchim*, such that we may benefit not only from their wisdom and experience, but from the unique *siyata d'Shmaya* that surrounds their holy task.

Yet a third lesson we can learn from this episode relates to the time at which *chinuch* begins. For we see that Manoach sought guidance *even before his son was born*, as he declared: "וְיוֹרֵנוּ מַה נַּעֲשֶׂה לַנַּעַר הַיּוּלָּד"—Let him instruct us what we should do for the child **who is going to be born**." The principle that emerges is that today is a good time to strategize about a child, but yesterday was an even better time. The well-known Gemara in *Tamid* seems to reflect this idea when it states: "אֵיזֶהוּ חָכָם הָרוֹאֶה אֶת הַנּוֹלָד."[5] This of course refers to the importance of foresight in general, but it could apply just as well to a literal "נוֹלָד." The wisdom of foresight is most necessary when it comes to educating children. When a person is driving and is ahead of the curve, he has a number of options—to slow down, stop, or turn around. And such is the case regarding *chinuch* as well. Foresight creates options for guiding one's child in the most optimal way.

A child is a personalized gift to each parent from Hashem. A person can theoretically decide *not* to have children; but no one can guarantee that they will have children. Parents who cry for their children will not cry from their children. If we plead with Hashem, consult with *mechanchim*, and are careful to exercise wisdom and foresight, Hashem will bless us with beautiful *b'nei* and *b'nos Torah* and much *nachas*.

---

5   *Tamid* 32a.

9

MOSHE STRIKES
THE ROCK

וַיְדַבֵּר ה' אֶל מֹשֶׁה לֵּאמֹר...וְדִבַּרְתֶּם אֶל הַסֶּלַע לְעֵינֵיהֶם וְנָתַן
מֵימָיו...וַיָּרֶם מֹשֶׁה אֶת יָדוֹ וַיַּךְ אֶת הַסֶּלַע בְּמַטֵּהוּ פַּעֲמָיִם וַיֵּצְאוּ
מַיִם רַבִּים...

*And Hashem said to Moshe, saying: "...Speak to the rock before
their eyes and it shall give its waters."...And Moshe raised his
hand, and he struck the rock with his staff twice; and much
water emerged...*

Bamidbar 20:7–11

IF there was ever a case that called for leniency, one would think it was
the event of Moshe hitting the rock. This episode is perhaps one of the
most difficult ones in the Torah to comprehend. It certainly seems to be
the case that Moshe deviated from the actual instructions; Hashem had
told him to speak to the rock, whereas Moshe ended up striking it—not
once, but twice. It is of course somewhat mysterious that Moshe took
such action, and what led him to do so is a matter of much discussion
among the *mefarshim*. But in any event, he was censured quite severely
for deviating from the command, losing the right to enter into Eretz

וַיֹּאמֶר ה׳ אֶל מֹשֶׁה וְאֶל אַהֲרֹן יַעַן לֹא הֶאֱמַנְתֶּם בִּי לְהַקְדִּישֵׁנִי לְעֵינֵי בְּנֵי יִשְׂרָאֵל: "Yisrael

לָכֵן לֹא תָבִיאוּ אֶת הַקָּהָל הַזֶּה אֶל הָאָרֶץ אֲשֶׁר נָתַתִּי לָהֶם—And Hashem said to Moshe and Aharon: 'Since you did not show faith in Me, to sanctify Me before the eyes of B'nei Yisrael, therefore you shall not bring this congregation into the land that I have given to them.'"[1]

Magnitude of the Deed

At first glance, it does seem to be a very harsh punishment in relation to the offense. Furthermore, even after receiving these devastating tidings, Moshe continues to serve Hashem with the utmost dedication. A lesser person may have exhibited some resentment and slackened in their measure of devotion. But Moshe was unwavering, living up to his characterization of "בְּכָל בֵּיתִי נֶאֱמָן הוּא"—In all of My household, he is the most faithful,"[2] to the very end. After all he had done for Klal Yisrael, and for his continued loyalty—wouldn't he be deserving of some leniency? Why indeed was his offense accorded such gravity?

As mentioned, this is one of the most enigmatic episodes in the Torah, and the *mefarshim* go to great lengths to provide clarification. I would like to suggest a somewhat novel approach, based on a personal story which I feel sheds some light on the issue. Many years ago, my wife and I were contemplating if we should move. We lived in a beautiful Torah community with many *maalos*, but there was another community we felt offered better opportunities from the standpoint of our children's *chinuch*. Still, I had many good reasons not to move, and I was really unsure of what to do.

I decided to write a letter to Rav Chaim Kanievsky laying out my dilemma. Rav Chaim's response was succinct and powerful: "*Chinuch ha'yeladim kodem*—The education of the children comes first." That settled that. Despite all of the compelling *cheshbonos* for staying, Rav Chaim laid down that *chinuch* outweighs them all, and with that, we made the move. Many parents have been *moser nefesh* for the sake of

---

1   *Bamidbar* 20:12.

2   Ibid., 12:7.

their children's *chinuch*—and rightly so. One is expected to sacrifice the world for their children in order to afford them the best *chinuch* possible.

The above serves to illustrate, in any event, the supreme importance that is accorded to the notion of *chinuch*. And this may have been the factor that determined the severity of Moshe's deed. *Rashi* relates that this whole episode represented the loss of a tremendous opportunity. Had Moshe followed the instructions of *speaking* to the rock, he could have conveyed thereby a most valuable lesson to Klal Yisrael, in the form of a *kal v'chomer*. The people would have deduced the following: If a rock—which doesn't speak, hear, or rely on Hashem for *parnassah*—will nevertheless fulfill *dibburo shel Makom* (the word of Hashem), *kal v'chomer* that we—who do speak, hear, and rely on Hashem for *parnassah*—must respond positively and fulfill *dibburo shel Makom*. This was the great lesson in *chinuch* that seems to have been lost due to the deviation from the plan.

However, one could suggest that even through Moshe's deed, the lesson is not entirely lost; in essence, the *kal v'chomer* remains, only in a somewhat different form. Moshe didn't speak to the rock, but he did hit it (twice)—and in doing so, it responded and provided abundant water. Thus, Klal Yisrael could still deduce that if an inanimate rock responds when hit, *kal v'chomer* should Yisrael respond when Hashem has to deliver a "*potsch*"!

But this "adjustment" to the *kal v'chomer* itself may account for the severity of Moshe's deed, for consequently the whole manner and standard of *chinuch* underwent a certain "downgrade." The original plan—as per Hashem's instructions to speak to the rock—was that Klal Yisrael's *chinuch* would be based on *dibbur*. That is, Hashem desired that they would respond to authority merely by being spoken to, and it is for this reason *Rashi* utilizes the *lashon* of "דִּבּוּרוֹ שֶׁל מָקוֹם" in discussing the *kal v'chomer*. But by hitting the rock (and thus changing the *kal v'chomer*), Moshe in effect *lowered the bar* and set a different standard for the *chinuch* of Klal Yisrael. He conveyed to them that it is the *potsch* that compels one to listen to authority.

Imagine how wonderful it would be if children were trained to always respond to polite requests! But if the standard is more than mere polite requests, then these polite requests lose their impact. For example, if a student knows (and they do) that a *rebbi* doesn't really mean business until he turns red and yells, then polite requests will be ineffective. For when the *rebbi* speaks softly, he thereby sends a signal that he isn't upset yet.

Perhaps, in this way, we may approach the episode of Moshe hitting the rock. Hashem had wanted Moshe to be *mechanech* Klal Yisrael with a standard of polite *dibbur*. By hitting the rock, Moshe lowered that standard, and so his deed constituted not just a regular offense, but one that had a negative effect in the area of *chinuch*. And this, as we have seen, is a weighty matter indeed. As Rav Chaim said, "*Chinuch ha'yeladim kodem*"—educating our children is the priority.

10

NADAV AND AVIHU

הַרְבֵּה תּוֹרָה לָמַדְתִּי מֵרַבּוֹתַי, וּמֵחֲבֵירַי יוֹתֵר מֵהֶם, וּמִתַּלְמִידַי יוֹתֵר מִכּוּלָן.

Much Torah have I learned from my teachers; and even more from my colleagues; and from my students, I have learned more than from all of them.

Makkos 10a

THE sudden death of Nadav and Avihu was obviously quite tragic. It also seems somewhat mysterious. What did they do to deserve such a fate? Numerous explanations of their offense are offered by Chazal and the *mefarshim*. One of these, brought down by the *Kli Yakar*, is that they neglected to have children. This, however, still seems hard to understand. Granted, it's a beautiful thing to have a family, but if one does not, for some reason, have a family, should he really be put to death? The punishment appears to be somewhat on the harsh side!

Perhaps we can clarify this issue based on the famous teaching of Rebbi, who said: "הַרְבֵּה תּוֹרָה לָמַדְתִּי מֵרַבּוֹתַי, וּמֵחֲבֵירַי יוֹתֵר מֵהֶם, וּמִתַּלְמִידַי יוֹתֵר מִכּוּלָן—I have learned much Torah from my teachers, even more from my *chavrusas*, but I learned the most from my students." Rebbi speaks here of progressive stages of learning, with each one greater than the one before. But it is important to note that he is referring to more than just quantity; in actuality, Rebbi is presenting a formula for personal growth. How is it that one learns "the most" from *talmidim*? For a *rebbi*, preparation is critical, so that he can give over the material to his students with absolute clarity. This requires the *rebbi* himself to attain absolute clarity; he must break everything down to its simplest form. What happens, then, is that this process raises the *rebbi's* own understanding of the material. His *talmidim* have contributed to the *rebbi's* own personal growth in Torah—even more than his *rebbeim* and *chaveirim*.

The beautiful thing about this *rebbi-talmid* relationship is that it involves a never-ending cycle of growth on both sides of the equation:

- We have just seen that the *rebbi* himself becomes greater in Torah as a result of his *talmidim*.
- As such, the Torah that he has to offer is of a much higher caliber; when he gives this over to the *talmidim*, they in turn become greater.
- Now the *rebbi* has even greater *talmidim*, which means that, as he prepares and gives over more Torah to them, his own growth will increase.
- And so it continues, with both the *rebbi* and the *talmidim* attaining higher and higher levels.

In light of this idea, we may perhaps better understand the episode of Nadav and Avihu. There is a linkage between children and students. Chazal consider one's *talmidim* as "children,"[1] and, of course, one's own children can be one's students. Nadav and Avihu themselves were on an extremely lofty level; they were the future leaders of Klal Yisrael and had so much to give over. However, without children—who can be one's greatest and most essential *talmidim*—they could not carry on this most valuable *mesorah*. But even more, they lost out on the tremendous opportunity for growth; with their elevated stature, they could have produced the greatest *talmidim*, and these in turn would

---

1   *Sanhedrin* 19b.

have contributed to their own growth—and so on and so forth. We can therefore appreciate the magnitude of the tragedy that resulted from their failure to have children and *talmidim*; and it was for this that they were treated in such a severe way.

In any event, we learn from the above about one of the great benefits of being a *rebbi*/parent: the more we teach our children, the more we can grow in our own learning. It may be beautiful to learn Torah on your own, but it doesn't come close to giving it over to our children.

PART V

מידות,
הכרת הטוב

MIDDOS, HAKARAS HA'TOV

1

HAKARAS HA'TOV
AND THE MAKKOS

> וַיֹּאמֶר ה׳ אֶל מֹשֶׁה אֱמֹר אֶל אַהֲרֹן קַח מַטְּךָ וּנְטֵה יָדְךָ עַל מֵימֵי
> מִצְרַיִם...וְיִהְיוּ דָם...
>
> *And Hashem said to Moshe: "Say to Aharon, 'Take your staff*
> *and stretch your hand over the waters of Egypt...and they shall*
> *become blood...'"*
>
> *Shemos 7:1*

$\mathcal{A}$S we all know, Moshe Rabbeinu was appointed by Hashem to be
the redeemer of Klal Yisrael and many wonders and miracles were performed through his hand in Mitzrayim. Interestingly enough, when it
came to the first three *makkos*, Hashem turned to Aharon instead:

- "וַיֹּאמֶר ה׳ אֶל מֹשֶׁה **אֱמֹר אֶל אַהֲרֹן** קַח מַטְּךָ וּנְטֵה יָדְךָ עַל מֵימֵי מִצְרַיִם...וְיִהְיוּ
  דָם—Hashem said to Moshe: **Say to Aharon,** Take your staff
  and stretch your hand over the waters of Egypt...and they shall
  become blood."[1]

---

1   *Shemos* 7:19.

- "אֱמֹר אֶל אַהֲרֹן נְטֵה אֶת יָדְךָ בְּמַטֶּךָ עַל הַנְּהָרֹת...וְהַעַל אֶת הַצְפַרְדְּעִים"—**Say to Aharon,** Stretch your hand with your staff over the rivers...and bring up the frogs."[2]

- "אֱמֹר אֶל אַהֲרֹן נְטֵה אֶת מַטְּךָ וְהַךְ אֶת עֲפַר הָאָרֶץ וְהָיָה לְכִנִּם"—**Say to Aharon,** Stretch your staff and strike the dirt of the earth, and it shall become lice."[3]

From this point on, the rest of the *makkos* were executed through Moshe.

Why were these original *makkos* performed through Aharon instead of Moshe? *Rashi* explains that it was a matter of *hakaras ha'tov*:

- The first two *makkos* involved the water, which played an important role in preserving Moshe's life; when he was a baby, his mother placed him in a basket upon the river.
- The third *makkah* involved the earth, which protected Moshe when he had killed the Mitzri (by concealing the body).

Since Moshe had benefited from these elements, it was not proper for him to turn around and strike them; therefore, Aharon had to do so instead.

But the question is, did Moshe really have to be instructed to refrain from striking the water and the earth? After all, he was Moshe Rabbeinu—he was the greatest of *tzaddikim*, and, of course, very smart and learned. Surely, he knew all about "appreciation" on his own. Why did he have to be informed about this concept by Hashem?

Now, one may say that there really was a *chiddush* here, even for Moshe Rabbeinu. That is, Moshe of course knew all about *hakaras ha'tov*, but he thought it applied only to animate objects (i.e., people). Hashem had to tell him that it extended even to *inanimate* objects such as water as well. But while this is an important *chiddush*, it only accounts for the first time. Surely Moshe would have learned this lesson during the *makkah* of *dam* alone. Why did Hashem have to repeat it for him when it came to *tzfardei'a*, telling him again to let Aharon perform the *makkah*?

---

2   Ibid., 8:1.
3   Ibid., v. 12.

The truth is, however, that each time contained yet another *chiddush* about the *middah* of gratitude. True, Moshe learned from the first *makkah* that *hakaras ha'tov* applies even to inanimate objects, and so he himself didn't strike the water. But he still thought that once was enough. He had already shown his appreciation to the water during the first *makkah*, and was "*yotzei*" with that; now, he felt he could strike it during the second *makkah*. This is why Hashem had to tell him even during *tzfardei'a* to pass it on to Aharon. Hashem was teaching Moshe that, in fact, once is not enough—*hakaras ha'tov* never ends.

There was yet another lesson in store for Moshe, which is why Hashem still had to instruct him to speak to Aharon for the *makkah* of *kinim*. Yes, Moshe had learned that *hakaras ha'tov* applies even to inanimate objects, such as the earth, and is eternal. But Moshe may have thought that the earth didn't really help him much in the end. While the dirt did cover the body, we know that the deed was eventually discovered—Pharaoh found out that Moshe had killed the Mitzri, forcing him to flee. Moshe concluded that, in the end, he had not actually benefited from the *afar* and so he owed it no *hakaras ha'tov*. And so, even in this final instance Hashem had to impart this idea to Moshe; that even though the attempt was unsuccessful, he still had to show *hakaras ha'tov* simply for the effort. As such, Moshe could not strike the *afar* either, and Aharon had to stand in his stead.

We see, then, that three valuable lessons were conveyed to Moshe over the course of the beginning *makkos*. He learned that *hakaras ha'tov* applied:

- even to inanimate objects,
- for all time,
- even for an unsuccessful effort.

How much the more so, then, must we ourselves appreciate real people—our parents, spouses, family, *rebbeim*, and *chaveirim*. They help us not just once, but constantly. And so, we must show *hakaras ha'tov* to those who expend so much effort on our behalf.

2

SPLITTING THE SEA

וַיֵּט מֹשֶׁה אֶת יָדוֹ עַל הַיָּם וַיּוֹלֶךְ ה' אֶת הַיָּם בְּרוּחַ קָדִים עַזָּה כָּל
הַלַּיְלָה וַיָּשֶׂם אֶת הַיָּם לֶחָרָבָה וַיִּבָּקְעוּ הַמָּיִם.

*And Moshe stretched his hand over the sea, and Hashem
guided the sea with a strong east wind the entire night; and He
set the sea to dry land, and the waters split.*

Shemos 14:21

THE midrash tells us that when Moshe set out to perform *k'rias Yam
Suf*, he initially met with some opposition—from the Yam Suf itself.[1]
The water was being asked to change its regular nature, and nothing—including, apparently, the water—wants to go against its nature.
It therefore denied Moshe's request, with the claim that it had no obligation to listen. "Why should I submit to you?" it said to Moshe. "After
all, I am greater; I was created on the third day of Creation, while you
were only created on the sixth day." The midrash concludes that Moshe
then sought Hashem's intervention, and the sea acquiesced.

---

1   *Shemos Rabbah* 21:6.

The Sea's Complaint

A very intriguing midrash, of course; but let us focus on one particular aspect.

Why did the Yam Suf choose this specific line of argument? It is a good point, to be sure—the sea was created before man, and therefore could claim seniority. But it would seem that there was an even better *tainah* the sea could have made, based on the principle of *hakaras ha'tov*. This issue played a prominent role in the first three *makkos*, which were administered by Aharon instead of Moshe. The reason, as *Rashi* explains in *Parashas Va'eira*, is that the water and the earth were stricken during these *makkos*. It would have been improper for Moshe himself to strike these entities, as at various points they had afforded him much needed protection. Out of *hakaras ha'tov*, then, the task of initiating these *makkos* was given to Aharon instead. In a similar vein, it would seem that the Yam Suf could make an identical claim. "The water was instrumental in saving your life as a baby," the sea could assert. "If not for me, you would have been killed by Pharaoh's henchmen. And now you're asking me to go against my nature, and split on *your* behalf?" This would seem to be a more compelling argument than the seniority issue. Moreover, as we have seen, Hashem Himself had made this very point in connection with the first three *makkos*. Why, then, did the water neglect to make this claim?

It appears that this episode is teaching us a most important lesson about the parameters of this essential quality. Yes, one who receives benefit from another is certainly obligated to display *hakaras ha'tov*. But that is a responsibility that rests upon the recipient; the benefactor himself cannot *demand* gratitude. *Hakaras ha'tov* is defined by deeply felt gratitude and appreciation emanating from the recipient's heart.

The concept of "I owe you" is central to Torah thought, however the feeling that "you owe me" is not a Torah one. The *middah* of *hakaras ha'tov* is not just an ongoing scorecard that enables the recipient to declare: "Now we are even." It may often happen that favors are performed in a sort of reciprocal fashion; one person benefits from another, and he later does a kind act on behalf of his original benefactor. In truth, though, these two acts of goodness should not be seen as connected to each other. Rather than plain "payback," they ideally should function as independent actions, resulting from goodwill and heartfelt appreciation. The bottom line is that *hakaras ha'tov* should arise naturally; it is not something that you can lay claim to. It was for this reason that the Yam Suf had to resort to a different line of argument.

This leaves us with another question. We may understand the conduct of the sea, but Moshe's behavior itself seems perplexing. True, the Yam Suf could not demand of Moshe to show *hakaras ha'tov*, but why didn't Moshe display it on his own? As stated, he was the beneficiary, and we would thus expect him to fulfill his responsibility and defer to the Yam Suf on these grounds. Why, then, did Moshe insist on proceeding even in the face of the sea's refusal?

It appears that Moshe took his cue from Hashem: When it came to the issue of the first three *makkos*, He explicitly instructed Moshe to pass the matter off to Aharon, stating repeatedly: "אֱמֹר אֶל אַהֲרֹן...." This was not the case at the Yam Suf, as Hashem there charged Moshe himself with the task. But this itself requires clarification. Why did Hashem view the event of *k'rias Yam Suf* in a different light? Why didn't it require the same level of *hakaras ha'tov* that applied to the *makkos*?

A Positive Experience

If we look more closely, however, we do find a number of significant distinctions between these two episodes. Let us focus on two:

- The initiation of the *makkah* of *dam*, for example, called for an actual striking of the water: "וַיָּרֶם בַּמַּטֶּה וַיַּךְ אֶת הַמַּיִם אֲשֶׁר בַּיְאֹר"—And he raised the staff and **struck** the waters of the river."[2] No such factor applied to *k'rias Yam Suf*, which entailed a mere stretching of the hand: "וְאַתָּה הָרֵם אֶת מַטְּךָ וּנְטֵה אֶת יָדְךָ עַל הַיָּם וּבְקָעֵהוּ"—And you shall raise your staff, and stretch your hand over the sea and split it."[3]

- Much negativity was associated with the water in the case of the *makkos*; it was enlisted for the purpose of such repulsive

---

2   *Shemos* 7:20.

3   Ibid., 14:16.

entities as blood and frogs, and it served only as a conduit for pain and punishment. But the splitting of the sea did not involve any negative qualities (the drowning of the Mitzrim was a function of the *closing* of the sea). On the contrary, the water was being granted a tremendous *zechus*—to participate in saving the Jewish People and furthering their ultimate goal of receiving the Torah at Sinai and reaching Eretz Yisrael.

Based on the above, we see indeed that it was only in the case of the *makkos* that Moshe's involvement would have reflected a lack of *hakaras ha'tov*. But as there was nothing inherently negative associated with *k'rias Yam Suf*, there was no real reason for Moshe to retreat. In fact, it could even be that this was the nature of Hashem's intervention. By presenting the positive factors outlined above, Hashem convinced the Yam Suf to split after all.

3

RIVALRY OF YOSEF
AND HIS BROTHERS

וַיַּחֲלֹם עוֹד חֲלוֹם אַחֵר...וַיְסַפֵּר אֶל אָבִיו וְאֶל אֶחָיו וַיִּגְעַר בּוֹ אָבִיו
וַיֹּאמֶר לוֹ מָה הַחֲלוֹם הַזֶּה אֲשֶׁר חָלָמְתָּ...וַיְקַנְאוּ בוֹ אֶחָיו וְאָבִיו
שָׁמַר אֶת הַדָּבָר.

*And he further dreamed another dream...And he related it to
his father and to his brothers, and his father rebuked him, and
said to him: "What is this dream that you have dreamt...?" And
his brothers were jealous of him, and his father kept watch over
the matter.*

Bereishis 37:9–11

THE episode involving Yosef and his brothers is one of the most
perplexing and dramatic narratives in the Torah. We find the righteous
Shivtei Kah seemingly embroiled in the most fierce and personal rivalry
with Yosef at the center. Of course, the *mefarshim* go to great lengths to
clarify this whole matter, revealing the true profundity underlying these
events. But here we focus on the part of Yaakov Avinu: Where exactly
was he throughout this affair? What role did he play while the events
were unfolding? Did he try to intervene and rectify the situation?

The Torah does record Yaakov's reaction to Yosef's second dream. Yosef had just related how the sun, moon, and stars—representative of his family members—had all bowed to him. This elicited a pointed response from his father, who noted that the dream was flawed (on account of its reference to his deceased mother): "וַיִּגְעַר בּוֹ אָבִיו וַיֹּאמֶר לוֹ—And his father rebuked him, and he said to him: 'What is this dream that you have dreamt? Shall I, your mother, and your brothers come to bow to you upon the ground?'"[1]

Inwardly, Yaakov really did give credence to the dream, as the *pasuk* proceeds to state: "וַיְקַנְאוּ בּוֹ אֶחָיו וְאָבִיו שָׁמַר אֶת הַדָּבָר"—And his brothers were jealous of him, and his father kept watch over the matter."[2] *Rashi* comments that Yaakov was "waiting in anticipation of its fulfillment." It seems, then, that he knew there was something to the dream. Why, then, did he reprimand Yosef with the claim that it wasn't viable? What was Yaakov's strategy here?

This seems to indicate that Yaakov was indeed aware of what was transpiring, and he aimed to put a stop to it. He saw that an intense hatred had developed toward Yosef among the members of his household. Yaakov knew this trait could only prove detrimental to Klal Yisrael, and thus had to be eradicated. He also identified that it was his own display of unconditional love toward Yosef—through his gifts, his exclusive teaching of Yosef—that had greatly contributed to this *sinah*. He therefore seized the opportunity to publicly demonstrate his disapproval of Yosef. This, he hoped, would counteract the impression of favoritism toward Yosef, which in turn would tamp down the hatred.

At first glance, it may appear that as well-intentioned as these efforts were, they were unsuccessful. We, of course, know the rest of the story—the ill feelings perpetuated, leading to most tragic results.

However, if we look more closely at the *pesukim*, we discover that Yaakov's intervention *did* indeed foster a change. Up to this point, the brothers were infused with hatred for Yosef. Time and again the Torah

---

1   *Bereishis* 37:10.
2   Ibid., v. 11.

makes reference to their mounting *sinah* for their brother: "וַיִּרְאוּ אֶחָיו כִּי
אֹתוֹ אָהַב אֲבִיהֶם מִכָּל אֶחָיו וַיִּשְׂנְאוּ אֹתוֹ—And his brothers saw that their father
loved him from all of his brothers, and they **hated** him;"[3] "וַיּוֹסִפוּ עוֹד שְׂנֹא
אֹתוֹ עַל חֲלֹמֹתָיו וְעַל דְּבָרָיו—And their **hatred** for him increased, on account
of his dreams and his words;"[4] and so forth. But interestingly enough,
from the time that Yaakov issued his rebuke, no more mention is made
of the brothers' hatred. It was replaced instead with *kinah* (envy): "וַיִּגְעַר
בּוֹ אָבִיו וַיֹּאמֶר לוֹ מָה הַחֲלוֹם הַזֶּה אֲשֶׁר חָלָמְתָּ...וַיְקַנְאוּ בוֹ אֶחָיו וְאָבִיו שָׁמַר אֶת הַדָּבָר." Thus,
we see that Yaakov's intervention succeeded in transforming their
sinah to *kinah*.

Is that really an improvement? The answer, it would appear, is—absolutely yes. Of course, both traits are highly undesirable. But *sinah* is
so insidious it is in a league of its own. It is a consuming fire that fuels
itself, as *sinah* only breeds more *sinah*. Twice the *pasuk* states that their
initial *sinah* for Yosef increased even more: "וַיּוֹסִפוּ עוֹד שְׂנֹא אֹתוֹ."[5]

Even when it comes to the mitzvah of wiping out Amalek, there is
only a mitzvah to actually eliminate them; we do not find any explicit
command to bear them hatred. In short, we see that *sinah* is simply a
destructive force with almost no redeeming elements.

Kinah, on the other hand, can also be detrimental, of course. There are
people who can't seem to get past their friend having what appears as
a better life than they. But unlike *sinah*, *kinah* can also breed greatness.
As Chazal famously declare: "קִנְאַת סוֹפְרִים תַּרְבֶּה חָכְמָה—Jealousy among
scholars increases wisdom."[6] When properly channeled, such *kinah* can
serve to motivate and inspire one to exert himself more and climb in
ruchniyus. This, then, is what lay at the core of Yaakov Avinu's strategy.
He hoped that the *Shevatim* would appreciate and accept their brother's
destiny, and then utilize the opportunity for their own self-growth.

---

3   Ibid., v. 4.
4   Ibid., v. 8.
5   Ibid., v. 5, 8.
6   *Bava Basra* 21b.

4

CHEIT HA'EIGEL II:
SHOCKING BETRAYAL

וַיַּעֲשֵׂהוּ עֵגֶל מַסֵּכָה וַיֹּאמְרוּ אֵלֶּה אֱלֹהֶיךָ יִשְׂרָאֵל אֲשֶׁר הֶעֱלוּךָ מֵאֶרֶץ מִצְרָיִם.

And they made it into a molten calf, and they said, "This is your god, O Yisrael, who has taken you out of the land of Egypt."

Shemos 32:3

IMAGINE the following scenario:

A certain couple remained childless for many years. During this whole time, they poured their hearts out to Hashem, crying and beseeching Him to send them a child. After many years, the long-awaited day finally came—Hashem blessed them with a baby boy! Needless to say, the boy was their pride and joy. They showered him with love and provided him with the best of everything. Whether it was school, camp, vacations, or anything else—the child had it all.

The boy thrived and did very well in school. He eventually ended up in a top medical school where he continued to excel; he was at the top of his class and was even chosen to be valedictorian. On that fateful day, as thousands packed the auditorium for graduation, his parents sat in the front row beaming. Their son was called to the podium to deliver his valedictory address. Throughout the speech, his parents glowed with pride and, of course, listened with rapt attention. Their son then reached the conclusion of his speech, the part customarily reserved for expressing appreciation. And this is what he said:

"This is the proudest moment of my life. There are two people in the audience to whom I owe everything. If not for them, I don't think I would be standing here today addressing you as valedictorian. These two very special people were my pillars and constant support whenever times were tough, and I attribute all of my success to them. In fact, I would like to ask these two people to come up. Everyone, please join me in welcoming to the podium...my two roommates, Steve and Bob!"

As the crowd burst into applause, the two parents looked at each other in utter shock and disbelief. After all they had done for their son, everything they sacrificed to give him a beautiful life, he cast them aside and instead credited two people they'd never heard of. As happy as they had been when he was born, that's how brokenhearted they felt at this moment. They quickly left the auditorium in tears.

The *Cheit Ha'eigel* is, of course, one of the most tragic and unfortunate episodes, the repercussions of which reverberate down to this very day. The questions abound as to the nature of this sin, especially asking how Yisrael could have stumbled into something so egregious so quickly. The *mefarshim* devote much space to elucidating these weighty matters. Before we even begin to address these particulars, it is worthwhile to first contemplate for a moment the enormity of the disappointment this event must have been for Hashem. And that is the purpose of the sad scenario outlined above, which to a significant degree mirrors the conduct of Klal Yisrael. Hashem had done so much for them, His children. He had performed countless *nissim* on their behalf and had granted them so many *yeshuos*—through the *makkos, yetzias Mitzrayim, milchemes Amalek,* and, of course, *Matan Torah.* And after all that, they turned around and made the *eigel!* In fact, it would have been more than enough had they simply made the *eigel* after having experienced all of Hashem's goodness. They went a step further. As with the graduate in the above scenario, they placed the credit elsewhere. Referring to the *eigel*, they declared: "אֵלֶּה אֱלֹהֶיךָ יִשְׂרָאֵל אֲשֶׁר הֶעֱלוּךָ מֵאֶרֶץ מִצְרָיִם—This is your god, O Yisrael, **who has taken you out of the land of Egypt.**"

This must have been almost too much for Hashem to bear, *Ka'veyachol*. It was the lowest point in our history, and practically brought Hashem to the point of wanting to destroy the nation and start all over. True, it was the *eirev rav* that instigated the action, but Yisrael was still held responsible for participating, on some level.

Thankfully, Hashem loves Yisrael so much and therefore allowed them to return to Him; so much so that every generation has the opportunity to gradually wipe away the *Cheit Ha'eigel* until we are restored to our previous exalted level.

The question of course, as mentioned, is how it was possible for Klal Yisrael to come to the point where they could perpetrate such a deed in the first place? This is a matter that we shall yet explore, *b'ezras Hashem*.

5

CHEIT HA'EIGEL III:
EXTENT OF INGRATITUDE

וַיַּרְא הָעָם כִּי בֹשֵׁשׁ מֹשֶׁה לָרֶדֶת מִן הָהָר וַיִּקָּהֵל הָעָם עַל אַהֲרֹן
וַיֹּאמְרוּ אֵלָיו קוּם עֲשֵׂה לָנוּ אֱלֹהִים אֲשֶׁר יֵלְכוּ לְפָנֵינוּ, כִּי זֶה מֹשֶׁה
הָאִישׁ אֲשֶׁר הֶעֱלָנוּ מֵאֶרֶץ מִצְרַיִם לֹא יָדַעְנוּ מֶה הָיָה לוֹ.

*And the people saw that Moshe tarried in descending from the
mountain. And the people congregated against Aharon, and
they said to him: "Arise, and fashion for us a deity who shall
walk before us; for this man, Moshe, who has taken us out
of the Land of Egypt—we do not know what has happened
to him."*

Shemos 32:1

THE *Cheit Ha'eigel*, of course, is a most perplexing episode, and we have already attempted to address some of its complexities. But it may be worthwhile to approach it now from a certain basic standpoint. One of the most fundamental *middah tovah* is the attribute of *hakaras ha'tov*. This trait was particularly near and dear to Moshe Rabbeinu. We have previously discussed the fact that Hashem personally taught Moshe the lengths to which one must go in practicing this *middah*. It was for this reason that Moshe could not strike the water or the land during the first three *makkos* in Mitzrayim; these elements had offered him protection, and he thus had to treat them with the proper level of gratitude and respect. Given Moshe's strong connection to this *middah*, one would have expected him to have imparted its importance to Yisrael in the strongest possible way.

If so, the perpetration of the *Cheit Ha'eigel* becomes all the more in-triguing from this angle—whatever happened to simple *hakaras ha'tov*? After all, Hashem had just performed for Yisrael a series of the most remarkable miracles and wondrous salvations: in the form of *Yetzias Mitzrayim, k'rias Yam Suf, Milchemes Amalek, Matan Torah*, etc. Even a single *neis* would have obligated Yisrael to display outstanding grati-tude; all the more so a whole string of *nissim*! But instead—after all that Hashem had done for them—they turned around and committed this grave act. It appears that there wasn't even a trace of *hakaras ha'tov*. How could Klal Yisrael seem to ignore the obvious?

Who Shall Walk before Us

We have already seen that the *Cheit Ha'eigel* originated not with Yisrael themselves, but with the *eirev rav*; and this lack of *hakaras ha'tov* may well have trickled down from these instigators too. For the truth is that the *eirev rav* themselves displayed a total disregard for *hakaras ha'tov* in the most overt manner. Recall that it was solely on account of Moshe Rabbeinu that the *eirev rav* was able to join with Yisrael in the first place. As has been previously mentioned, *Rashi* relates that Moshe did not even consult with Hashem; he included the *eirev rav* on his own initiative, feeling it would be a great *kiddush Hashem*.[1] If not for Moshe's intervention, then the *eirev rav* would have been left in Mitzrayim to suffer the same fate as the rest of their nation. And so, even if they had not completely abandoned their idolatrous ways, surely they must have realized, at the very least, that Moshe himself would not approve of this deed. Shouldn't they have felt some obligation toward him? How could they repay what he did for them with this egregious betrayal?

---

1   *Shemos* 32:7.

We may get some idea of their mindset from their demand to Aharon. The *pasuk* records their response to Moshe's absence: "וַיַּרְא הָעָם כִּי בֹשֵׁשׁ מֹשֶׁה לָרֶדֶת מִן הָהָר וַיִּקָּהֵל הָעָם עַל אַהֲרֹן וַיֹּאמְרוּ אֵלָיו קוּם עֲשֵׂה לָנוּ אֱלֹהִים אֲשֶׁר יֵלְכוּ לְפָנֵינוּ כִּי זֶה מֹשֶׁה הָאִישׁ אֲשֶׁר הֶעֱלָנוּ מֵאֶרֶץ מִצְרַיִם לֹא יָדַעְנוּ מֶה הָיָה לוֹ—And the people saw that Moshe tarried in descending from the mountain. And the people congregated against Aharon, and they said to him: 'Arise, and fashion for us a deity **who shall walk before us**; for this man, Moshe, who has taken us out of the land of Egypt—we do not know what has happened to him.'"

Their utterance of the phrase "לְפָנֵינוּ—**in front of us**" is quite telling, and it seems to hold the key to understanding their conduct. Basically, the implication is that they wouldn't behave this way if Moshe were **in front of us**. "Sure," they were saying, "we appreciate what he did by accepting us among the Jewish People. And we wouldn't think of doing this if he were here now. But he's not, so let's get on with it."

To the *eirev rav*, *hakaras ha'tov* was basically limited to the here and now. They needed something "לְפָנֵינוּ" in order to feel any real appreciation. Past kindnesses were not on their radar. As far as they were concerned, whatever Moshe had done for them was yesterday's news.

Keeping the Memory Fresh

This attitude, of course, is not the Torah's idea of proper *hakaras ha'tov*. There is a poignant story from my family's past that I feel beautifully illustrates the true Torah ideal in displaying gratitude.

My great-grandfather, Aharon Asher Wolinetz, *zt"l*, escaped from the dangers of Europe around 1935. He eventually ended up in the Bronx where he would give a Mishnayos *shiur* each evening between *Minchah* and *Maariv*. One day, a stranger walked in during that time, looking a bit lost. My *zaidy* approached him and asked what he could do to help. The stranger said that he had come to say Kaddish for his father but was not sure how to do it. And so, my *zaidy* stood next to the man during the service and said Kaddish together with him. The process repeated itself the next morning; the man came back and, standing by his side, my *zaidy* once again guided him through Kaddish.

The man was very grateful and thanked my *zaidy* profusely. He revealed that he was the head of a political organization known as the Star Democratic Club. "Please contact me if I can be of any assistance," he said. My *zaidy* immediately mentioned the fact that he had children and grandchildren still stuck in Europe, and to date had been unsuccessful in obtaining visas for them. Perhaps, suggested my *zaidy*, the man could ask a local congressman to write a letter to the United States embassy in Warsaw requesting the visas. To make a long story short, his children were able to come to Warsaw three months later to pick up their visas, and my maternal grandparents and their children arrived safely in America in 1939. We see then the tremendous effect of an act of kindness. My *zaidy* performed a single good deed for a fellow Jew. This triggered a reaction of *hakaras ha'tov*, whereby the beneficiary was moved to return the favor. As a result of his intervention, my *zaidy*'s family was rescued from Europe, and thus dozens of his descendants were *oseik baTorah u'mitzvos* for many years to come.

The story doesn't end there. Thirty years later, an uncle of mine—by then a highly successful lawyer—arranged to meet this politician to personally thank him for what he had done years back. When the politician, who was now a judge, saw the results of his efforts, he hugged my uncle and together they cried tears of joy.

This, in any event, is the Torah's notion of *hakaras ha'tov*. Indeed, it was precisely this aspect about which Hashem taught Moshe when it came to hitting the water. As *Rashi* points out, Moshe was prevented from striking the water because it had afforded him protection when he was set afloat on the Nile.[2] That episode took place when Moshe was just a baby. It was now *eighty years later*—and still, Moshe was expected to display his gratitude. We see that it doesn't matter if the event occurred recently or many years ago; a good deed deserves to be remembered and acknowledged, even after the passage of generations.

Unfortunately, however, not everyone shares this perspective when it comes to showing appreciation. It used to be that *hakaras ha'tov*

---

2   *Shemos* 7:19.

truly endured for generations. If Reuven benefited from Shimon, then Reuven's grandchildren would show appreciation to the grandchildren of Shimon. But today, many people consider our grandfathers' favors to each other to be ancient history. Actually, the downward trend has gotten even worse, whereby some people don't show proper appreciation even when they themselves were the beneficiaries. Instead, they adopt the attitude of "What have you done for me lately?"—"lately" meaning "yesterday." And some have really hit rock bottom in this regard. They don't care what happened ten years ago, or even yesterday. Their focus is entirely on the present: "What are you doing for me right now?"

This was the mentality of the *eirev rav*. Their whole emphasis was on "לְפָנֵינוּ—in front of us." They surmised: Right now, we have no Moshe. He may have once helped us; but he is no longer לְפָנֵינוּ, and so we owe him nothing. It was with this attitude that they were able to construct the *eigel* without any pangs of conscience.

It seems that this mentality of "now" trickled down to Klal Yisrael as well, and this was why they did not respond with proper *hakaras ha'tov* to the great miracles that Hashem had performed for them. The *eirev rav's* negative influence exerted itself upon them to the extent that these wonders became to them as a mere distant memory. As such, they felt no urgency to prevent the sin and protest the lack of gratitude in the *Cheit Ha'eigel*.

The above may actually give us some insight into some of the elements of *tefillah*. Chazal understood just how detrimental this kind of thinking was to Klal Yisrael, so, rather than allowing these great events to be relegated to "ancient history," they incorporated their remembrance into the daily prayers.

- We mention *yetzias Mitzrayim* twice a day in *K'rias Shema*.
- *K'rias Yam Suf* is recalled through *Az Yashir* and the *berachah* recited after *K'rias Shema*.
- *Milchemes Amalek* and *Maamad Har Sinai* are part of the *Sheish Zechiros*.

These are four miracles that should have engendered much *hakaras ha'tov* within the hearts of Klal Yisrael. In truth, we have to constantly remind ourselves of all the miracles Hashem did, does, and will continue to do for us. Each person should keep track of all the good Hashem does for him on a constant basis. The point of all this, of course, is to increase our sense of *hakaras ha'tov* to Hashem. In this way, the attitude displayed by the *eigel* will never surface again.

6

IMPACT OF LEITZANUS

בְּעֶשְׂרִים וַחֲמִשָּׁה בְּכִסְלֵיו נִגְמְרָה מְלֶאכֶת הַמִּשְׁכָּן...הֵקִימוֹ מֹשֶׁה אֶחָד בְּנִיסָן...שֶׁבְּנִיסָן נוֹלַד יִצְחָק.

On the twenty-fifth of Kislev, the production of the Mishkan was completed...Moshe erected it on the first of Nissan...for in Nissan, Yitzchak was born.

Pesiksa Rabasi

"**AND** it was, on the day that Moshe finished erecting the *Mishkan*—מִשְׁכָּן אֶת לְהָקִים מֹשֶׁה כַּלּוֹת בְּיוֹם וַיְהִי."[1] This day, *Rashi* informs us, was Rosh Chodesh Nissan. And it was somewhat of a novelty that the *Mishkan* was erected then, because it had really been completed long before—on the date of Chanukah (25 Kislev). The midrash points out, however, that its actual establishment was deliberately delayed until Nissan, so that it would take place in the same month as Yitzchak Avinu's birth.

---

1   *Bamidbar* 7:1.

Moshe and Yitzchak

This arrangement may seem somewhat surprising. Let us recall, after all, that we are dealing with the *Mishkan*, a place to house the Shechinah. And this was not even its only function, for it also served as a *kapparah* for the *Cheit Ha'eigel*.[2] Surely, every moment of delay was most significant. It would be nice, of course, to have the establishment of the *Mishkan* coincide with the month of Yitzchak's birth, but was it really so imperative? Why indeed was it considered so important that it was worthwhile to postpone the *Mishkan*'s initiation for so long?

We may perhaps gain some insight on this matter from *Parashas Pekudei*, which begins: "אֵלֶּה פְקוּדֵי הַמִּשְׁכָּן...אֲשֶׁר פֻּקַּד עַל פִּי מֹשֶׁה"—These are the accountings of the *Mishkan*...which were counted by the word of Moshe."[3] Moshe felt the need to make a strict and thorough accounting of every gift donated for the *Mishkan*'s construction. The reason he felt compelled to do so, explains the midrash, is because he overheard the *leitzanim* accusing him of pocketing the money.[4] Moshe could have rightfully turned to them and given them a sharp reprimand for their utter chutzpah. Instead, he responded by sharing the records, accounting to the public for every last penny.

Let us analyze this for a moment. Among Moshe's many *maalos*, he was renowned for his loyalty and honesty, as Hashem Himself attested about him: "בְּכָל בֵּיתִי נֶאֱמָן הוּא"—He is the most trustworthy of My entire household."[5] Furthermore, he was extremely wealthy, having become enriched from the shavings of the *Luchos*.[6] He was not lacking in funds, and was the last person to be suspected of dishonesty. Nonetheless, he felt it important to clear himself of any suspicion, even that spread by such lowly characters as the *leitzanim*.

It was in this vein, perhaps, that Hashem encouraged Moshe to establish the *Mishkan* in the month of Yitzchak's birth. For there is indeed a significant parallel, as Yitzchak was likewise the subject of spurious

---

2   *Rashi, Shemos* 38:21.
3   *Shemos* 38:21.
4   *Shemos Rabbah* 51:6.
5   *Bamidbar* 12:7.
6   *Rashi, Shemos* 34:1.

speculation. At the beginning of *Parashas Toldos*, it states: "וְאֵלֶּה תּוֹלְדֹת יִצְחָק בֶּן אַבְרָהָם אַבְרָהָם הוֹלִיד אֶת יִצְחָק—These are the chronicles of Yitzchak son of Avraham; Avraham gave birth to Yitzchak."[7] The obvious question, of course, relates to the repetition: having just mentioned that Yitzchak was the son of Avraham, why was it necessary to then repeat that "Avraham gave birth to Yitzchak"?

Addressing the issue, *Rashi* explains that the *leitzanei ha'dor* advanced some defamatory claims in connection with Yitzchak's birth. For so many years Sarah had not borne Avraham any children. Then she was taken by Avimelech, and shortly thereafter, a child was born? In this way they sought to cast doubt on the issue of Yitzchak's *yichus*, claiming that Avimelech was the real father. Hashem quelled this bout of *leitzanus* by making Yitzchak look exactly like his real father, Avraham. Thus, the Torah emphasizes that it was indeed Avraham who gave birth to Yitzchak, as testified by their exact likeness.

This is why the effort was made to link the establishment of the *Mishkan* with the birth of Yitzchak. In doing so, Hashem was being *mechazek* Moshe, who was also hounded by *leitzanim*. The message Hashem was sending to Moshe was that he should not be overly concerned about their chatter. After all, Hashem was reminding him, it did not last in the case of Yitzchak Avinu, so here too, its effects will be minimized. Thus, Moshe was able to respond to the "allegations" of theft with confidence instead of desperation and resentment.

By dealing with it in the manner that he did, Moshe Rabbeinu was able to contain the impact of *leitzanus*. But this is not to imply that *leitzanus* is inherently a minor offense. In fact, it can be a formidable power, and is thus referred to by the *Mesilas Yesharim* with the term "כֹּחַ שֶׁל לֵיצָנוּת." From the standpoint of those who engage in such behavior, *leitzanus* is a potent weapon capable of wreaking devastation—on the scale of a spiritual nuclear bomb. The real purpose of *leitzanus* is to destroy the very foundation of the Torah, as we see from the incidents sighted above. On the surface, it may seem that Yitzchak was the intended target of

7   *Bereishis* 25:19.

the scornful reports. But on a deeper level, this *leitzanus* was really aimed at the basis of all Klal Yisrael. Hashem had promised Avraham that a great nation would emanate from him; the potential impact of the *leitzanus* was to undermine this promise. By attributing Yitzchak's parentage to Avimelech, the *leitzanei ha'dor* sought to annul the link between Avraham and Yitzchak. And if that link is broken, there is no Klal Yisrael, *Rachmana litzlan*.

The *leitzanus* in the case of Moshe Rabbeinu can be viewed in a similar manner. The *leitzim* weren't only disparaging Moshe. Yes, they were accusing him of stealing *mamon hekdesh*, but by doing so, they were asserting that the *Mishkan* itself was founded on thievery. Had this been so, it would certainly not be a place worthy of housing the Shechinah. Such is the potential devastation that can be wrought by *leitzanus*.

Korach and Noach

The episode of Korach's rebellion serves as another prime example of this idea. Part of their campaign, as *Rashi* relates, entailed a series of mock "*sh'eilos*."[8] One of these involved the mitzvah of tzitzis; they asked Moshe if a tallis that is entirely *techeiles* requires tzitzis. When Moshe answered in the affirmative, they responded condescendingly: "A regular tallis is exempted by a single strand of *techeiles*. Surely, then, a tallis comprised entirely of *techeiles* should be exempt!" Thus the phenomenon played itself out once again. On the surface, they were seeking just to mock Moshe, but in reality, their intentions were even more sinister: Tzitzis, as we know, is the key to observing all the mitzvos, as we say in *K'rias Shema*: "וּרְאִיתֶם אֹתוֹ וּזְכַרְתֶּם אֶת כָּל מִצְוֹת ה' וַעֲשִׂיתֶם אֹתָם—And you shall see it, and remember all of the mitzvos of Hashem and do them."[9] Furthermore, as *Rashi* points out, the *gematria* of tzitzis (when we add the five knots and eight strings to the numerical value of the word) is 613. What emerges, then, is that these *leitzim* were not only mocking Moshe, but they were trying to uproot one of our main pillars that connects us to the entire Torah.

---

8   *Bamidbar* 16:1.
9   Ibid., 15:39.

A final example appears in the episode of the *mabul*, in connection with Noach's *teivah*. It took an inordinately long time—120 years—for Noach to build the *teivah*. But this was a purposeful arrangement, intended to draw attention to Noach. At the very least, then, people would become curious, and thus stop to ask him what he was doing. This would give Noach the opportunity to engage them in conversation and gear the topic toward *teshuvah*. But as the *Midrash Tanchuma* relates, instead of sincere questions, the people responded with constant harassment and *leitzanus*. They hurled insults at Noach and mocked him for wasting 120 years of his life. "This region doesn't produce enough yearly rainfall to fill a schnapps cup," they would tell him, "and you're preparing for a major flood!?" For 120 years they made Noach into a laughingstock. He was an easy target—but not the main target. The purpose of Noach building the *teivah* was to encourage them to do *teshuvah*, and thereby spare the world. Through their *leitzanus*, the people effectively undermined the whole effort. Because of their mockery, nobody took Noach seriously and thus no one did *teshuvah*. And so, the end result of their *leitzanus* was the destruction of the world.

The examples above serve to illustrate the real *ko'ach* of *leitzanus*. It may often appear as just a witty comment. But in reality, it's a nuclear bomb with devastating consequences—capable of uprooting *teshuvah*, *emunah*, Torah, and all that is holy.

7

YERAVAM'S OPPORTUNITY

תָּפְשׂוֹ הַקָּדוֹשׁ בָּרוּךְ הוּא לְיָרָבְעָם בְּבִגְדוֹ וְאָמַר לוֹ, חֲזוֹר בָּךְ, וַאֲנִי וְאַתָּה וּבֶן יִשַׁי נְטַיֵּיל בְּגַן עֵדֶן, אָמַר לוֹ מִי בָּרֹאשׁ, בֶּן יִשַׁי בָּרֹאשׁ, אִי הָכִי לֹא בָּעֵינָא.

Hashem grabbed hold of Yeravam's garment and said to him: "Repent, and I, you, and ben Yishai will stroll together in Gan Eden." He said to Him: "Who will be in front?" [Hashem answered:] "Ben Yishai will be in front." [Yeravam said:] "If so, I'm not interested."

Sanhedrin 102a

$\mathcal{Y}$ERAVAM ben Nevat is known, of course, for his total wickedness. Not only did he immerse himself in *avodah zarah*, but he led Klal Yisrael astray as well. Nonetheless, Hashem's abundant mercies extended even to such a sinful figure. The Gemara relates that Hashem grabbed hold of his garment, and urged him to repent: חֲזוֹר בָּךְ, וַאֲנִי וְאַתָּה וּבֶן יִשַׁי נְטַיֵּיל בְּגַן עֵדֶן—Repent, and I, you, and ben Yishai will stroll together in Gan Eden." It would seem to be an offer that couldn't be refused. But Yeravam immediately asked: "מִי בָּרֹאשׁ—Who will be in front?" Hashem

185

answered, "בֶּן יִשַׁי בְּרֹאשׁ." Upon hearing that David HaMelech would go first, Yeravam declined. "אִי הָכִי לֹא בָּעֵינָא—If so, I'm not interested." Having rejected the offer of a lifetime, he continued in his sinful ways.

Now, if you look carefully at this dialogue, you'll notice that something changed along the way. When initially presenting the offer, Hashem placed Yeravam before David: "חֲזוֹר בָּךְ, וַאֲנִי וְאַתָּה וּבֶן יִשַׁי נְטַיֵּיל בְּגַן עֵדֶן." But in response to Yeravam's question of "מִי בְּרֹאשׁ," the order was reversed, and Hashem responded that ben Yishai would go first. We see that Yeravam was originally slated to be at the head, but by asking his question, he forfeited the lead position. The question is, why was he knocked down a notch just for asking "מִי בְּרֹאשׁ?" Was it really such a terrible thing to want to know?

For that matter, Yeravam's question itself seems somewhat odd. What, indeed, was bothering him? It can't be that he was jealous of David, for he had heard Hashem tell him that he himself would go first: "אֲנִי וְאַתָּה וּבֶן יִשַׁי נְטַיֵּיל בְּגַן עֵדֶן." It must be, then, that what was really bothering Yeravam was the fact that *Hashem* would be at the very front. And so we can understand why his response was so deplorable; apparently, Yeravam felt that he "deserved" to go even before Hashem.

At first glance, this *p'shat* may seem somewhat drastic. Could anyone—even someone as far gone as Yeravam—be so arrogant to really think this way? Was he so twisted as to actually believe that he should go before Hashem Himself?

The sad truth, however, is that we ourselves may not be too different.

This idea can be illustrated by a famous story. A boy on his way to yeshiva was given two quarters by his mother—one for *tzedakah*, and one to buy a snack. On the way, one quarter falls out of his pocket and rolls into the sewer. The boy thinks for a moment, and then says, "Sorry, Hashem, that was Your quarter."

In our day-to-day lives, we encounter many *nisyonos*. We are constantly faced with having to make decisions, and it's not always so easy to do the right thing. But in the end, it really comes down to the question of whose needs come first—ours or Hashem's?

- When we make bad choices, we are actually announcing "מִי בָּרֹאשׁ" loudly and clearly, putting ourselves before Hashem.
- When we think straight and actually do the right thing, our choices give *nachas ru'ach* to Hashem. In these instances, we are announcing, "*Hashem ba'rosh*—Hashem is first."

And when we make Hashem first, we may be *zocheh* one day to stroll with Him in Gan Eden.

8

THE SONS OF AHARON: LESSONS IN SILENCE

וַיִּקְחוּ בְנֵי אַהֲרֹן נָדָב וַאֲבִיהוּא...וַיַּקְרִיבוּ לִפְנֵי ה' אֵשׁ זָרָה...וַתֵּצֵא
אֵשׁ מִלִּפְנֵי ה' וַתֹּאכַל אוֹתָם וַיָּמֻתוּ לִפְנֵי ה'...וַיִּדֹּם אַהֲרֹן.

*And the sons of Aharon, Nadav, and Avihu took...and they
brought before Hashem a foreign fire...And a fire went forth
from before Hashem and it consumed them, and they died
before Hashem...And Aharon remained silent.*

Vayikra 10:1–3

$\mathcal{A}$ number of questions, addressed by the *mefarshim*, surround the tragic episode of the death of Nadav and Avihu, Aharon's sons. One of the most obvious, of course, involves the guilt of Nadav and Avihu. What exactly did they do to warrant such a harsh punishment?

Chazal offer a number of approaches. One of these, cited by the *Kli Yakar*, relates to a conversation that took place between the brothers. Walking behind Moshe and Aharon, Nadav remarked to Avihu: "When will these two *zekeinim* die so that we may take over?" And so, asserts the *Kli Yakar*, it was due to such charged words about the *gedolei Yisrael* that they incurred the death penalty.

The issue, however, is that this explanation seems to account for only one side. We may understand the offense committed by Nadav—after all, he was the one who actually expressed this sentiment. Avihu, however, said nothing; at most, he was a passive listener. Why, then, was he dealt with so severely? The answer, as the *Toras Kohanim* explains, is that Avihu shared the same guilt because of his failure to protest! Avihu really should have spoken out upon hearing Nadav's comments; remaining silent signaled his agreement—"*shetikah k'hodaah*." By neglecting to protest he was effectively complicit in Nadav's deed, and thus shared in his *onesh*.

In stark contrast stands Aharon's response to the tragic events. His simple yet celebrated reaction, as recorded in the Torah, is: "וַיִּדֹּם אַהֲרֹן—And Aharon remained silent." Aharon had just suffered a colossal loss, and another, lesser individual may have cried out and reacted with bitterness. But although he had been bereaved, Aharon retained his peace: "וַיִּדֹּם אַהֲרֹן." And for this he was greatly rewarded. The following section deals with the *inyan* of *shesuyei yayin*, the prohibition against performing the *avodah* while intoxicated.[1] Hashem transmitted this section exclusively through Aharon: "וַיְדַבֵּר ה' אֶל אַהֲרֹן לֵאמֹר יַיִן וְשֵׁכָר אַל תֵּשְׁתְּ אַתָּה וּבָנֶיךָ אִתָּךְ בְּבֹאֲכֶם אֶל אֹהֶל מוֹעֵד...." He was accorded this supreme honor, *Rashi* states, as a reward for his measured silence.

This story imparts to us a most valuable lesson on the topic of silence. A Yid must always be vigilant and know when and where to be silent—and when to speak up. In the case of Avihu, he actually should have spoken up and issued a protest; thus, he was punished severely for remaining silent. But for Aharon, on the other hand, silence was the most appropriate response. One may have assumed he had true reason to protest, yet he remained firm in his faith, retained his composure, and practiced silence. And for this, he received eternal reward.

---

1   *Vayikra* 10:8–11.

9

CULTIVATING AND
SPREADING SIMCHAH

THERE is a fairly common phenomenon that many of us may have experienced. A neighbor of yours is making a *chasunah*. You're not necessarily so close to him, but you want to do the proper thing, so you attend. At the *chasunah*, you go over to wish him *mazal tov*, and he responds with a huge smile and effusive words of *berachah* for you and your family. Of course, you answer with an equally warm amen. Such a nice moment. A few days later, you see this same neighbor in a store and give him a pleasant greeting. Only this time, he barely acknowledges you. You are now left to wonder if this is indeed the same person who just a few days ago seemed so friendly and enthusiastic. Then, he showered you with blessing, while now, he can hardly afford to give you a nod.

A Flow of Simchah

Actually, this scenario illustrates a common pitfall. *Baruch Hashem*, many people are aware of the importance of doing *chessed* and helping others. But what people tend to overlook is the "simple" act of making another Jew feel good about himself. This is unfortunate, for it really is one of the greatest forms of *chessed* one can perform. Telling someone how talented, special, etc., they are can make a meaningful difference in their life. However, many people hesitate to do so, finding it difficult to compliment another person. Actually, there is a simple reason for this. An inability to build up another person usually stems from a feeling of insecurity within one's own self. They feel as if boosting another person somehow minimizes their own standing. In reality, nothing could be further from the truth. Boosting someone else doesn't cause insecurity, but it may very well be insecurity that stops one from boosting another person.

As simple and obvious as it may be, the bottom line is that in order to make someone else feel good, you need to feel good about yourself. And thus, we may understand the *baal simchah* of our scenario. When he was making a *simchah*, he was on cloud nine and felt great, so it was fairly easy for him to make you feel great as well—the positivity flowed naturally. But when you meet him a few days later in the store, he's no longer on that high that produced such beautiful *berachos*. Instead, he's back to the old mindset, complete with the usual concerns and insecurities.

The question, then, is how to acquire and maintain a proper and positive mindset. Do we really need a band, buffet, and hundreds of people wishing us *mazal tov* to put us in the frame of mind for making others feel good? Is there, perhaps, a simpler (and less expensive) way to increase our own feelings of happiness, such that we can spread it to others?

The Right Tools

It appears that the familiar Mishnah in *Avos* (4:1) contains the key. The Mishnah states: "אֵיזֶהוּ עָשִׁיר הַשָּׂמֵחַ בְּחֶלְקוֹ"—Who is wealthy? One who is happy with his portion." Significantly, the Mishnah does not attach any specific size or amount to this "portion." This underscores the fact that the amount is really irrelevant. There are billionaires who are miserable, while others could be short on rent money but still feel like they're the most fortunate people in the world. Essentially, what the Mishnah is conveying to us is that happiness is a state of mind, not a product of worldly possessions and material success.

How do we achieve that state of mind? We can gain much insight from the latter part of the Mishnah's statement, which promises one who follows this formula to find fortune in both this world and the next: "אַשְׁרֶיךָ בָּעוֹלָם הַזֶּה, וְטוֹב לָךְ לָעוֹלָם הַבָּא." The same Mishnah also deals with other qualities: "אֵיזֶהוּ חָכָם...גִּבּוֹר...מְכֻבָּד..." But it is only in connection with *ashirus* that the Mishnah invoked the idea of *Olam Haba* and *Olam Hazeh*. For Chazal understood that in order to cultivate true happiness, one must have a clear picture of what the world is all about and what his purpose is in it.

Every Jew has a specific mission to fulfill in this world, and by doing so faithfully and completely he earns an ever-greater share in the World to Come. Hashem, of course, is perfect and fair, and thus provides every person with whatever tools he needs to fulfil his purpose to perfection. Someone who is fully aware of these simple truths is indeed extremely fortunate. He remains focused on utilizing this world as an opportunity to earn the highest level in the next world, and he knows that he has been granted all the right tools to do exactly that. As such, he will be filled with contentment in this world and reap the benefits in the World to Come.

It may be easier said than done, however, because the *yetzer hara* tries constantly to distract us. We might see someone who has more money, a bigger house, or something else that seems desirable, and we may react by thinking, "Now, that's a portion I think I could be happy with." But it's pure *sheker*; because if our own situation were any different, we would be lacking the tools we need to fulfill our role and purpose in the world.

This idea may perhaps be illustrated by the following fanciful scenario. The word went out that a great contest was about to take place, and an eager crowd gathered to watch. They saw before them two contestants, each of whom had brought along a certain implement. One of them was brandishing a brand-new, high-quality, industrial-sized jackhammer, while the other had with him only a flimsy fly swatter. Not surprisingly, all bets were on the huge jackhammer, while the owner of the fly swatter was roundly mocked. But then the competition began. The audience was quite shocked when they realized what the contest was—a race to kill a fly. Their initial smiles quickly turned to frowns as they realized that the fellow with the fly swatter was perfectly positioned to win the contest; the one with the jackhammer didn't have a chance.

In real life, this scenario takes place on a daily basis. We think that someone else's portion is better than ours and would bring us much happiness if we had it. But what we fail to realize is that having a different *chelek* means having a different purpose. In fact, we each have the exact portion we need to fulfill that purpose for which we were sent to this world in the first place. If a person is wise enough to realize this, he can truly be "שָׂמֵחַ בְּחֶלְקוֹ," and will indeed be most fortunate—in both this world and the next. Infused with constant *simchah*, he will always be ready and able to bring *simchah* to others.

10

DONATION
OF THE NESI'IM

וְהַנְּשִׂאָם הֵבִיאוּ אֵת אַבְנֵי הַשֹּׁהַם וְאֵת אַבְנֵי הַמִּלֻּאִים לָאֵפוֹד
וְלַחֹשֶׁן.

And the tribal chiefs brought the shoham-stones and the filling-stones for the ephod and the choshen.

Shemos 35:27

IN describing their contribution to the *Mishkan*'s construction, the Torah spells "נְשִׂאָם" in an irregular fashion, removing the letter *yud* from their title. Citing the midrash, *Rashi* provides the background for this omission. The *nesi'im* approached the whole donation campaign with a certain *cheshbon*. "Let the *tzibbur* donate," they said, "and in the end, we will fill in whatever is missing." What ended up happening, however, is that Klal Yisrael basically provided all of the necessary materials. All the *nesi'im* could come up with to donate at that point were the *avnei shoham* and *avnei miluim*. In any event, they were somewhat faulted for their conduct, which, as *Rashi* explains, constituted a display of *atzlus*. To reflect their deficiency, the term "נְשִׂאָם" was spelled in a deficient manner.

Now, there are a few points here that could use some clarification. The *nesi'im*, of course, were not just regular people, but righteous and respected figures of a very high caliber. What indeed were they thinking? Weren't they concerned that their delay could cause them to miss out entirely on the opportunity to participate in this great communal mitzvah? What is also intriguing is the fact that *Rashi* attributes their behavior to laziness. But was this really the case? At first glance, it would appear that the trait of stinginess played more of a role. This is akin to a story of a shul member who makes a similar offer at the shul dinner. The congregation had set a certain fundraising goal, and this individual pledged to write a check in the end for whatever may be missing from the total. As the dinner progressed, this "donor" was found to be immersed in prayer. He was davening his heart out for the goal to be reached before the end of the night; this way, his generous donation would become unnecessary. Perhaps the *nesi'im* had been thinking along similar lines. How was *Rashi* so sure that the real issue was laziness?

In fact, there was a good reason the *nesi'im* weren't afraid of totally missing out on the donations—for they were the only ones in possession of the *avnei shoham*. From the start, then, they knew they had a definitive part in contributing to the *Mishkan*. And it is for this very reason that there was no issue of stinginess here; they were secure in the knowledge that they would eventually bring their exclusive *avanim*. This is how *Rashi* was able to identify the underlying issue as one of *atzlus*. Now, they may even have had some good intentions in holding off with their donation, allowing the rest of Klal Yisrael some time to procure their own contributions. But *Rashi* perceived that this *cheshbon* was not free from the taint of laziness. At the end of the day, pushing off something you will inevitably have to do is an act of procrastination, indicative of some measure of laziness. Especially for people on the level of the *nesi'im*—and in connection with such a worthy event as the building of the *Mishkan*—it was unseemly to display even a trace of *atzlus*. And so, the Torah removed the *yud* from their name, to drive home this important lesson.

PART VI

עֵשָׂו, עֲמָלֵק, הָמָן

EISAV, AMALEK, HAMAN

1

AMALEK AND THE MIDDAH OF PERFECTION

כָּכָה יֵעָשֶׂה לַשּׁוֹר הָאֶחָד אוֹ לָאַיִל הָאֶחָד אוֹ לַשֶּׂה בַכְּבָשִׂים אוֹ בָעִזִּים, כַּמִּסְפָּר אֲשֶׁר תַּעֲשׂוּ כָּכָה תַּעֲשׂוּ לָאֶחָד כְּמִסְפָּרָם.

So shall be done for one ox or one sheep or goat; in accordance with the number that you shall offer, so shall you do for one according to their number.

Bamidbar 15:11–12

THE *pasuk* "כָּכָה יֵעָשֶׂה—So shall be done" comes near the conclusion of the *parashah* of the *nesachim*, instructing Klal Yisrael to ensure that they include the proper measure of *menachos* and *nesachim* when they bring their offerings. And the Torah is very exact in this regard. The Gemara *darshens* from this *pasuk* that if any of these ingredients is missing even the slightest amount, the *korban* is *passul*.[1] Every detail, we see, is deemed essential.

---

1   *Menachos* 27b.

This same concept can be extended to the quality of *emes*. For something to be true, it has to be completely true. Even if it is 99 percent *emes*, it is essentially *sheker*.

Indeed, this idea can and should be applied to the entirety of our *avodas Hashem*. And we find that it has far-reaching ramifications. Such emerges from the story of *Megillas Esther*, in which the beginning of Haman's downfall is marked by the very same phrase ("כָּכָה יֵעָשֶׂה"). Haman HaRasha, "riding high" and at the climax of his power, had come to speak to Achashveirosh to secure Mordechai's execution. When he came before the king, however, he was presented with a question: "מַה לַעֲשׂוֹת בָּאִישׁ אֲשֶׁר הַמֶּלֶךְ חָפֵץ בִּיקָרוֹ—What should be done for the person whom the king wishes to honor?"[2] The question intrigued Haman, as he was certain that the glory was intended for himself. He answered by devising an elaborate ceremony: the recipient of the honor would be clothed in the king's royal garments and be led in public by a royal servant upon the king's own horse. And then he added: "וְקָרְאוּ לְפָנָיו **כָּכָה** יֵעָשֶׂה לָאִישׁ אֲשֶׁר הַמֶּלֶךְ חָפֵץ בִּיקָרוֹ—And they should call before him: 'So shall be done** to the person whom the king wishes to be honored.'"[3] And so, in a dramatic turn of events, this "כָּכָה יֵעָשֶׂה," brought about Haman's complete denigration. Achashveirosh immediately seized upon the idea and instructed Haman to do this very thing to Mordechai—down to the very last detail. As the king emphasized: "אַל תַּפֵּל דָּבָר מִכֹּל אֲשֶׁר דִּבַּרְתָּ—Do not leave out a thing from all that you have spoken!"[4] The ordeal, of course, must have been torturous for Haman. This event was one that set into motion a chain of fast-moving events that ultimately led to Haman's own demise.

The means of defeating Amalek through perfection in *avodas Hashem* has its roots in a much earlier episode. The progenitor of Amalek was Eisav. When Yaakov was preparing to confront Eisav and his four hundred men, he sent the following message: "עִם לָבָן גַּרְתִּי—I have dwelled

---

2   *Esther* 6:6.
3   Ibid., v. 9.
4   Ibid., v. 10.

with Lavan."⁵ *Rashi* comments that גַּרְתִּי is a reference to תרי"ג, the 613 mitzvos of the Torah, which he was able to keep even while living with Lavan HaRasha.

It would seem that Yaakov really could have sufficed with a much simpler communication. He could have mentioned that he had maintained a high standard of honesty even while around Lavan HaRamai (the "trickster"), or that he managed to learn Torah despite his grueling work schedule. Why didn't he say this? It seems that Yaakov realized that Eisav would not have been particularly impressed with these accomplishments. He understood that it was only through the power of perfection that he could overcome Eisav. Even having kept 612 mitzvos would not have been enough; what was needed was the observance of the total, complete array of all 613 mitzvos under the challenging conditions of Lavan's house.

It is somewhat ironic that, to some extent, this penchant for perfection was adopted by Haman himself. It became deeply embedded in his personality but manifested itself in a negative way. Haman had engineered that all the land would bow to him, including all the Jews. They all did, except for one: Mordechai HaYehudi. Haman had achieved *almost* 100 percent success in his self-aggrandizing goals. But Mordechai's refusal to bow so enraged him that he felt he had nothing at all. Haman was the most exalted official in the entire kingdom, but he had this to say about his unparalleled status: "וְכָל זֶה אֵינֶנּוּ שֹׁוֶה לִי בְּכָל עֵת אֲשֶׁר אֲנִי רֹאֶה אֶת מָרְדֳּכַי הַיְּהוּדִי יוֹשֵׁב בְּשַׁעַר הַמֶּלֶךְ—All of this is worth nothing to me, as long as I see Mordechai HaYehudi sitting by the king's gate."⁶ On the one hand, he had "כָּל זֶה," everything. But without perfection, he felt like he had nothing. Mordechai's refusal to bow could be compared to a tiny ink spot on a perfectly white shirt. Just as the ink spot ruins the shirt, so did Mordechai's solitary refusal ruin all of his glory.

At the same time that Haman desired perfection for himself, he also realized that the only way to defeat Klal Yisrael was to detract from their own perfection. This he may have learned from the episode involving

5   *Bereishis* 32:5.
6   *Esther* 5:13.

his ancestor Agag, king of Amalek, who had also been involved in a battle with Yisrael. As related in *Sefer Shmuel I*, Shmuel instructed Shaul to wage war against Amalek and wipe them out *completely*—men, women, children, and animals.[7] In an unfortunate turn of events, however, Shaul ended up taking pity on Agag, allowing him to be the lone survivor. With this, Yisrael's "armor" of perfection was pierced. When Shmuel found out, his reaction was quite harsh. Despite Shaul's otherwise sweeping success against Amalek, Shmuel tells him: "לֹא שָׁמַעְתָּ בְּקוֹל ה׳—You did not listen to Hashem's voice."[8] Shmuel was telling him that he shouldn't think he succeeded if he did a 99 percent job. Even if there is only one remaining, it was as if he hadn't listened at all.

The result of this imperfection led eventually to the birth of Haman HaRasha, a direct descendant of Agag.

Our archenemies—Eisav, Amalek, Haman—realize that imperfection is our greatest weakness. Therefore, we must do all we can to strive for perfection in Torah and mitzvos, each of us on our own level, as this is our ultimate protection.

---

7   *Shmuel I*, ch. 15.
8   Ibid., v. 19.

2

LEARNING FROM AMALEK

זָכוֹר אֵת אֲשֶׁר עָשָׂה לְךָ עֲמָלֵק...אֲשֶׁר קָרְךָ בַּדֶּרֶךְ.

Remember that which Amalek did to you...that he happened upon you in the way.

Devarim 25:17–18

DAVID HaMelech declares: "מֵאֹיְבַי תְּחַכְּמֵנִי—Make me wiser than my enemies."[1] While this is the conventional understanding, others learn that David was saying: "Make me wiser—*from* my enemies." The implication is that it is sometimes possible to glean important lessons even from the *resha'im* who rise against us. They employ their strategies to commit more evil deeds, but we can sometimes adopt these same strategies and apply them positively to *avodas Hashem*. As we shall see, there is a most important lesson we can learn from even our most sinister enemy—the nation of Amalek.

We have previously learned that Klal Yisrael possesses a certain *ko'ach* of perfection, which of course serves them as a tremendous asset. We also learned that Eisav and his descendants recognized this trait and aimed to defeat Yisrael by weakening their quality of perfection.

---

1   *Tehillim* 119:98.

Perhaps no one personified this strategy more than Amalek. When B'nei Yisrael went out of Mitzrayim, Amalek realized that given their lofty spiritual level it would be impossible to defeat them right away. Indeed, the whole world was shaking in fear from B'nei Yisrael after seeing the great miracles Hashem performed on their behalf in taking them out of Mitzrayim. As such, no one dared to approach them.

However, Amalek persevered and devised a strategy they felt could succeed in defeating Yisrael. True, they could not be overcome instantaneously, but the key, Amalek felt, was to *gradually* wear down their armor of perfection. The matter can be compared to a situation in which a man wishes to cool down a pot of boiling water so he takes an ice cube and throws it into the pot.

His watching friends start to mock him. "You're wasting your time," they tell him. "The ice cube dissolved right away and the water is still boiling hot." But the man stands ready with his reply. "You're correct," he tells them, "the water is still very hot; but it is a drop cooler than before. The next ice cube will also dissolve immediately, but it will do its job in a minimal fashion. Every ice cube will cool the water down about a half of a degree. It may take twenty, thirty, or fifty ice cubes. But in the end, you will see—not only will the water have lost its heat, it'll be freezing cold." This was Amalek's aim as well. In fact, *Rashi* interprets the wording of *Parashas Zachor* as reflecting this very idea (and he provides a *mashal* along the lines of the above). The *pasuk* remarks about Amalek: "אֲשֶׁר קָרְךָ בַּדֶּרֶךְ," and *Rashi* explains that the root of the term "קָרְךָ" is קֹר—coldness. For this was precisely Amalek's approach in fighting Yisrael. They understood it may be too difficult to defeat them immediately, but they geared up for a protracted battle. If the Amalek of each generation attacks the Jewish People, they reasoned, we will eventually be able to "cool them down." It may take years, or even generations; but if we persist, we will ultimately succeed.

As we know, Amalek's plan is destined to fail, and we are promised that Amalek themselves will ultimately be defeated. In and of itself, however, the strategy is a solid one; and it is one we ourselves should learn from and adapt to *avodas Hashem*. This is the great lesson we may derive from Amalek.

Many people—with plenty of help from the *yetzer hara*—tend to get overwhelmed from the considerable task that lies before them. They view the great volume of Torah and mitzvos and allow themselves to become discouraged. "*Shas* is so huge," they may say, or, "How can I go to yeshiva/get up for minyan, day after day after day?" In short, the *yetzer hara* turns everything into a mountain; and with this type of thinking, it is no wonder that many give up before even starting. But if we were to apply the principle of Amalek, the task at hand can actually become more doable. If one takes small steps toward the goal, he will find a much smoother path than he may have anticipated.

One individual who employed this strategy with outstanding success was the great Rabbi Meir Shapiro of Lublin, initiator of the *daf yomi* learning cycle. The concept of *daf yomi* serves as a perfect example of this idea; by learning a single *daf* a day, completing the entire *Shas* becomes a most attainable goal. In fact, many *thousands* of people have indeed finished *Shas*, through this (or other similar) programs. It all begins with the first *daf*.

We learn, in any event, that the way to avoid being overwhelmed is to gradually progress in the right direction. It may take time, but eventually we will succeed. Every person, family, and generation that strives for perfection in this manner gives Hashem *nachas*, and helps to solidify the iron wall of Torah that protects us from our archenemy, Amalek, *yimach shemam v'zichram*.

3

EISAV'S CRY

וַיֶּחֱרַד יִצְחָק חֲרָדָה גְדֹלָה עַד מְאֹד וַיֹּאמֶר מִי אֵפוֹא הוּא הַצָּד צַיִד
וַיָּבֵא לִי וָאֹכַל מִכֹּל בְּטֶרֶם תָּבוֹא וָאֲבָרֲכֵהוּ גַּם בָּרוּךְ יִהְיֶה, כִּשְׁמֹעַ
עֵשָׂו אֶת דִּבְרֵי אָבִיו וַיִּצְעַק צְעָקָה גְּדֹלָה וּמָרָה עַד מְאֹד.

*And Yitzchak trembled an exceedingly great trembling, and he
said: "Who was the one who [already] hunted game, brought it
to me, and I ate from it all—before you arrived—and I blessed
him; even he shall be blessed." When Eisav heard the words of
his father, he emitted an exceedingly great and bitter cry.*

Bereishis 27:33–34

THE Torah describes how Eisav undergoes a dramatic transformation. This seems to be the case, at the very least, when it comes to his
attitude toward the *bechorah*. At first, Eisav thinks nothing of his *bechorah*, as the *pasuk* attests: "וַיִּבֶז עֵשָׂו אֶת הַבְּכֹרָה—And Eisav disdained the
bechorah."[1] Thus, he traded away his *bechorah* for a mere bowl of lentils
with hardly an afterthought. Later on, things change. Eisav enters his
father's presence just as Yaakov was leaving and discovers that he lost
out on the *berachos* designated for the *bechor*. When Eisav presents his

---

1   *Bereishis* 25:34.

prepared food to his father, Yitzchak remarks in wonderment that he had already been served by "someone else"—to whom he had delivered the *berachos*. Upon hearing the news that his brother had secured the *berachos* in his place, Eisav responds in a most striking way: "כִּשְׁמֹעַ עֵשָׂו אֶת דִּבְרֵי אָבִיו וַיִּצְעַק צְעָקָה גְּדֹלָה וּמָרָה עַד מְאֹד—When Eisav heard the words of his father, he emitted an exceedingly great and bitter cry."[2] This was quite a reaction for someone who had previously thought nothing of the *bechorah*. The obvious question, of course, is—what changed?

The key may lay in the conclusion of Yitzchak's statement to Eisav: "וַיֹּאמֶר מִי אֵפוֹא הוּא הַצָּד צַיִד וַיָּבֵא לִי וָאֹכַל מִכֹּל בְּטֶרֶם תָּבוֹא וָאֲבָרֲכֵהוּ גַּם־בָּרוּךְ יִהְיֶה—And he said: 'Who was the one who [already] hunted game, brought it to me, and I ate from it all—before you arrived—and I blessed him; **even he shall be blessed.**'"[3] Here, Eisav is informed that his brother had engaged in a subterfuge to receive the blessings. But that fact itself was not what elicited such an intense reaction. We see, rather, that Eisav did not respond until he heard these words—"גַּם־בָּרוּךְ יִהְיֶה." This phrase laid bare to Eisav the fallacy of his whole thinking. He initially disdained the *bechorah* because he thought only of the here and now. He had entered famished and demanded food, declaring: "הִנֵּה אָנֹכִי הוֹלֵךְ לָמוּת וְלָמָּה זֶּה לִי בְּכֹרָה—Behold, I am going to die; what do I need the *bechorah* for?"[4] He gave no thought to and attached no importance to the future; for Eisav, today was everything, tomorrow was nothing. But when he heard his father's proclamation—"גַּם בָּרוּךְ יִהְיֶה"—the reality hit him between the eyes. The word "יִהְיֶה," of course, is in future tense, and connotes the fact that the effects of the *berachos* last forever. Eisav was being told that Yaakov's descendants would *eternally* prevail over his own. The phrase, furthermore, alludes to a specific example: Mordechai, who is referred to as "בָּרוּךְ" (as in: "עַד דְּלֹא יָדַע בֵּין אָרוּר הָמָן לְבָרוּךְ מָרְדֳּכַי"), and who defeated Eisav's *einikel*, the wicked Haman. Thus, Eisav understood that Yaakov's victory over him did not represent just a temporary setback; it would

---

2   Ibid., 27:34.

3   Ibid., v. 33.

4   Ibid., 25:32.

endure for the long term. The dawning of this reality was too much for Eisav to bear and caused him to let out a strong and bitter cry.

It happens to be that the pain Eisav experienced from this episode was so great that, to some extent, Yaakov was held responsible, and his progeny were punished in kind. As the midrash points out, Hashem is always concerned for the *nirdaf*—even if it is a *rasha* who is "pursued" and distressed by a *tzaddik*.[5] Nonetheless, this indeed was only a temporary situation, something that Eisav himself understood. He knew of the inverse relationship between his descendants and those of Yaakov—when one is up, the other is down. For the moment, then, "וְהַמֶּלֶךְ וְהָמָן יָשְׁבוּ לִשְׁתּוֹת"—The king and Haman sat down to drink;" while at the same time: "וְהָעִיר שׁוּשָׁן נָבוֹכָה"—The [Jews of the] city of Shushan were confounded."[6] But of course, as had been foretold to Eisav, this was soon to change. For ultimately—"גַּם בָּרוּךְ יִהְיֶה."

Klal Yisrael emerged victorious then, and will prevail in the future, for all eternity.

---

5   *Vayikra Rabbah* 25:7.
6   *Esther* 3:15.

4

AMALEK, CHAZARAS HA'SHATZ, AND THE INTERNET

וְהָסֵר שָׂטָן מִלְּפָנֵינוּ וּמֵאַחֲרֵינוּ.

Please remove the Satan from before us and from behind us.

Maariv

WE have learned previously of Amalek's nefarious strategy in battling against Klal Yisrael. Amalek seeks Yisrael's destruction—not only physically, but in the spiritual sense as well. Realizing, however, that a full-scale assault is doomed to failure, Amalek adopts a gradual approach. This sinister idea entails piercing Yisrael's armor in even some minor way; but once gaining just a toehold, Amalek wears down Yisrael's defenses little by little. And this is the grave danger posed by this most determined foe. Before one realizes it, he turns around to find that Amalek has indeed wrought extensive damage.

Infiltration through a Mitzvah

In a sense, the matter can be characterized as a spider web. Picture a person driving along the highway. He suddenly hears a slight "clink"

209

upon his windshield, the result of a pebble kicked up by the truck in front of him. The driver is able to identify the exact point of impact, because—lo and behold—a tiny crack has appeared in that area. Now, it is tempting to simply ignore the miniscule crack; after all, it hardly obscures his view. But we all know what will happen if he indeed leaves it unattended: it will slowly but surely expand ever more, branching this way and that into a substantial "spider web" type of crack.

The term is quite an apt one, as such is the nature of an actual spider web. The spider constructs it with patience and deliberation, stretching out its web little by little—until, eventually, it constitutes a formidable trap in which to ensnare its prey. The point is that it is very advisable to repair the crack in the windshield right away. For although it is hardly noticeable at first, if left alone it will gradually mushroom into a big and expensive problem.

Such is the stratagem of the *kochos ha'ra* in the endeavor to ensnare and bring down a Yid. One striking example of this idea is manifest in *chazaras ha'shatz* of all places. The *Mechaber* is quite clear about the need for every person to focus on and really listen to the *berachos* recited by the chazzan: "בְּשֶׁשַׁ"צ חוֹזֵר הַתְּפִלָּה הַקָּהָל יֵשׁ לָהֶם לִשְׁתּוֹק וּלְכַוֵּין לִבְרָכוֹת שֶׁמְּבָרֵךְ הַחַזָּן וְלַעֲנוֹת אָמֵן—When the chazzan recites *chazaras ha'shatz*, the congregation should remain silent and follow the *berachos* recited by the chazzan with *kavanah* and answer amen [to them]."[1] Given the need to concentrate upon the chazzan's *berachos*, writes the Chafetz Chaim, a person should not even engage in learning during *chazaras ha'shatz*.[2]

Now, this (apparently) comes as a surprise to some people, who would be tempted to do precisely that. "Why just stand here?" they may think to themselves. "May as well make the most of the time and get in some extra learning." However, continues the Chafetz Chaim, one should not think this way. In fact, he should not learn at this time *even if he is particular to hear the end of each berachah and answer amen*. For this itself may lead to some significant consequences. Unlearned people will see and conclude that listening to *chazaras ha'shatz* is not so important

---

1   *Orach Chayim* 124:4.
2   *Mishnah Berurah* ibid., § 17.

after all, and they will start to schmooze with their neighbors—a truly serious *aveirah*! What emerges, concludes the Chafetz Chaim, is that the "learner" has actually committed a grave offense. He may have thought he was doing something fairly innocent and enjoyable—even a mitzvah! In truth, however, he ended up being *machti es ha'rabim*, which Chazal count as one of the most severe transgressions.[3] In short, we see that learning during *chazaras ha'shatz* constitutes a "crack in the system." One may think it is no "big deal"; what's he doing after all—just looking into a *sefer* during the chazzan's rendition. But we see the types of major *aveiros* that may end up happening as a result.

Ensnared in the Web

There is another manifestation of this "spider web" which is perhaps all too familiar and common in our times. The Internet serves as a prime example of a crack which develops into a large crevice, with disastrous outcomes. It is tragically appropriate that the Internet refers to one of its primary services as a "**web**site." Many people have become ensnared in them and have thereby ruined their lives. True, the Internet offers Torah lectures, *chizuk*, and *chessed* opportunities. There appear to be endless possibilities for good emanating from the Internet. However, this aspect itself can actually be a "crack in the system," a way for the *ko'ach ha'ra* to insert itself into the lives of otherwise upstanding people. People may approach these opportunities with good intentions; the truth is, however, that many have thereby been exposed to certain sights and images that are most spiritually destructive. While most are aware of the dangers of the Internet, those who are honest with themselves know that even the best filter is not foolproof. It may start with good intentions and appropriate sites, but it is not so hard to lose control quite quickly of what appears on the screen. And so, it truly functions as a "**web**site," as little by little a person succumbs, being drawn in deeper and deeper. The crack slowly develops into a crater of *aveiros*, *Rachmana litzlan*.

---

3   See *Avos*, ch. 5.

We make reference in *Maariv* to two forms of *yetzer hara*, as we recite in *Hashkiveinu*: "וְהָסֵר שָׂטָן מִלְּפָנֵינוּ וּמֵאַחֲרֵינוּ—Remove the Satan **that is before us and that is behind us**." The "שָׂטָן מִלְּפָנֵינוּ" is the standard form; it is overt and stands right in front of us, either to prevent us from learning Torah and doing mitzvos, or to entice us into an *aveirah*. But then there is a *yetzer hara* that is more subtle—he is "behind us" and less detectable. This Satan tries to lead us into sin in a much more deceitful way, "hooking" us with some mitzvah aspect. And this strategy, it appears, is very much in play when it comes to the Internet. It may very well be that the Satan is baiting us with some Torah, so that we get caught in the web of spiritual destruction.

Furthermore, it would seem that the Chafetz Chaim's admonition with regard to *chazaras ha'shatz* would apply to Internet usage as well. The Chafetz Chaim had stated a concern of being *machti es ha'rabbim*; when people see that a *talmid chacham* treats *chazaras ha'shatz* with leniency, they may follow suit in an even more serious manner. This likewise poses a danger when it comes to the Internet. People who are indeed great Torah scholars may wish to utilize the Internet for Torah-true purposes. But then arises the issue of perception, and the potential pitfalls that may result. The masses look up to such individuals, and when they see such elevated figures using the Internet, they may take it as a general seal of approval. Needless to say, the consequences may be disastrous, as they may come to use it in ways that propel them to the depths.

In short, it behooves us to be aware of the strategy of Amalek/the *ko'ach ha'ra* so that we may be on guard for such pitfalls. The key is to recall that the smallest crack can become the biggest canyon. We therefore daven to Hashem to remove the Satan "מִלְּפָנֵינוּ וּמֵאַחֲרֵינוּ"—to help us avoid all cracks and instead maintain real *sheleimus*.

5

LEARNING PATIENCE
AND PROVIDENCE

בִּימֵי מָרְדְּכַי וְאֶסְתֵּר בְּשׁוּשַׁן הַבִּירָה, כְּשֶׁעָמַד עֲלֵיהֶם הָמָן הָרָשָׁע, בִּקֵּשׁ לְהַשְׁמִיד לַהֲרֹג וּלְאַבֵּד אֶת כָּל הַיְּהוּדִים...בִּשְׁלוֹשָׁה עָשָׂר לְחֹדֶשׁ שְׁנֵים עָשָׂר...וְאַתָּה בְּרַחֲמֶיךָ הָרַבִּים הֵפַרְתָּ אֶת עֲצָתוֹ...וְתָלוּ אוֹתוֹ וְאֶת בָּנָיו עַל הָעֵץ.

In the days of Mordechai and Esther in the capital city of Shushan, when Haman the Wicked stood against them, he sought to destroy, kill, and wipe out all of the Jews...on the thirteenth day of the twelfth month...But You, in Your abundant mercy, foiled his design...and they hung him and his sons on the gallows.

Al Hanissim

THE *Al Hanissim* we recite on Purim provides a concise but complete summary of the Purim story. It relates how, in the days of Mordechai and Esther, the wicked Haman tried to wipe out all of the Jews. Through Hashem's mercy, however, his designs were foiled, and Haman himself ended up hanging from the gallows he had prepared for Mordechai. This rendition seems to contain all the vital information and is very much to

213

the point. It could almost make one wonder—why wasn't the *Megillah* itself written in the same fashion? Perhaps a few more sentences could be added to account for additional details such as the party, Esther's petition before the king, etc., but it still seems that the entire story could really be condensed into one paragraph. Yet, when we compare *Al Hanissim* to the actual *Megillah*, the difference in length is fairly astounding. Why, indeed, was "the whole *Megillah*" necessary?

The answer is that as the *Megillah* was written with *ruach ha'kodesh*; every single word is certainly essential. On a superficial level, it may seem long to us, but in truth, every aspect of the *Megillah* demonstrates the operation of Divine Providence, every step of the way.

Lesson in Hashgachah

One of the principle elements around which the *Megillah* revolves is the phenomenon of "וְנַהֲפוֹךְ הוּא," the remarkable reversal Hashem orchestrated at that time. This element served a most vital function—namely, to awaken Klal Yisrael and bring them closer to each other and to Hashem. In order for the "וְנַהֲפוֹךְ הוּא" to have a maximum impact, it was necessary for the reversal to be of a most dramatic nature. This itself accounts for much of the apparent "lengthiness" of the *Megillah*; Hashem was laying the groundwork to ensure that the reversal would in fact be of the grandest nature.

Take the stature of Haman, for example. Chazal tell us that he started out as a lowly barber. Hashem, of course, could have removed Haman at any point in the story. But the defeat of a mere barber is not as impactful as the defeat of one of the most powerful men in the world. As the common expression goes: "The bigger they are, the harder they fall." And so, in order for the "וְנַהֲפוֹךְ הוּא" to provide the maximum benefit, it was necessary to give Haman the time and space to gradually climb the royal ladder.

There were other necessary developments that had to take place, such as Haman's intense fury toward Mordechai. We have already seen that Haman had ascended the ranks, becoming one of the most prestigious members of the kingdom to whom all subjects had to bow. He felt himself on top of the world, invited to the exclusive party with the king and queen. It was just as he was at the pinnacle of his success that he encountered Mordechai who—in his eyes—robbed him of his deserved happiness: "וַיֵּצֵא הָמָן בַּיּוֹם הַהוּא שָׂמֵחַ וְטוֹב לֵב וְכִרְאוֹת הָמָן אֶת מָרְדְּכַי בְּשַׁעַר הַמֶּלֶךְ

וְלֹא קָם וְלֹא זָע מִמֶּנּוּ וַיִּמָּלֵא הָמָן עַל מָרְדְּכַי חֵמָה—And Haman went out on that day joyous, and of good heart; and when Haman saw Mordechai by the king's gate—not arising or trembling before him—Haman was filled with rage against Mordechai."[1] That is how he arrived at home, burning with anger and ready to express it. Of course, he didn't hold back from bragging about all of his successes. But after expounding at length about his wealth, family, power, and glory, he declared: "וְכָל זֶה אֵינֶנּוּ שֹׁוֶה לִי

בְּכָל עֵת אֲשֶׁר אֲנִי רֹאֶה אֶת מָרְדְּכַי הַיְּהוּדִי יוֹשֵׁב בְּשַׁעַר הַמֶּלֶךְ—And all of this is worth nothing to me—as long as I see Mordechai the Jew sitting by the king's gate."[2] Thus, the plan is crafted to erect a tall gallows for the purpose of ridding himself of the obstacle to his complete happiness—Mordechai. Haman is thrilled with the plan and begins to implement it. In this way, the stage is set for the great reversal and the self-destruction of Haman.

Now, there was yet another element that had to be established in preparation of the great reversal—and that was the situation of Yisrael themselves. Haman had to reach the very top before he could fall, but Yisrael had to reach the bottom before they could be lifted up; there-fore, the *Megillah* depicts at some length how Yisrael reached a point of utter desperation. Certain tragedies affect only a segment of people; others may affect more people but in a minimal way. During the Purim episode, however, the decree was issued that encompassed the entirety of the nation, and posed a threat of the greatest magnitude: "לְהַשְׁמִיד

לַהֲרֹג וּלְאַבֵּד אֶת כָּל הַיְּהוּדִים מִנַּעַר וְעַד זָקֵן טַף וְנָשִׁים בְּיוֹם אֶחָד...—To destroy, kill, and exterminate all of the Jews—from youth until the elderly, children, and women—on a single day..."[3] With the critical moment looming, the nation was indeed brought to the point of desperation, and they responded with fasting, tears, and beseeching Hashem. The stage was

---

1   *Esther* 5:9.
2   Ibid., v. 13.
3   Ibid., 3:13.

now set for the great reversal on Yisrael's end, as they were lifted from the depths of despair to the heights of exultation, "מֵאֵבֶל לְיוֹם טוֹב."[4]

We can see, then, that a mere paragraph would not have done justice to this episode. In order to fully appreciate the grand nature of the miracle, the *Megillah* had to outline the groundwork laid by *Shamayim*, the various necessary steps that were taken in order that the deliverance would have maximum effect.

The truth is that this is an important lesson for everyday living. Life works much the same way: there are no extraneous details, and each step is necessary and has something to teach us. As with the *Megillah*, the challenge is to appreciate the message in the details and to realize that each step brings us closer to "אוֹרָה וְשִׂמְחָה."[5]

Lesson in Patience

In a more general sense, it could be that the extensive account in the *Megillah* comes to impart yet another lesson. My son once came home from playgroup and made a remark. He had been doing a project on the *Megillah* and he commented to my wife: "The *Megillah* is sooo long." Now, this may not be surprising coming from a three-year-old. The issue, however, is that there are some adults who voice the same sentiment. This attitude is one of the symptoms of a society that only wants and expects instant gratification. It is possible nowadays to accomplish a number of complex tasks with the push of a single button or a touch on a screen.

This, then, is yet another important lesson that we surely need to learn today. A summary version hardly would have done real justice to the magnitude of the Purim miracle. It may be sufficient to mention the day's event in the course of davening, but in order to fully absorb the message of the day, more contemplation is needed throughout the Yom Tov. And so, it may be that the *Megillah* is imparting to us this vital lesson, emphasizing the need for patience and deliberation.

---

4   Ibid., 9:22.
5   Ibid., 8:16.

6

KIDDUSH HASHEM OF ACHDUS

וַיֹּאמְרוּ לוֹ חֲכָמָיו וְזֶרֶשׁ אִשְׁתּוֹ אִם מִזֶּרַע הַיְּהוּדִים מָרְדֳּכַי אֲשֶׁר הַחִלּוֹתָ לִנְפֹּל לְפָנָיו לֹא תוּכַל לוֹ כִּי נָפוֹל תִּפּוֹל לְפָנָיו.

And [Haman's] wise men and his wife Zeresh said to him: "If Mordechai, before whom you have begun to falter, is from the offspring of the Jews, you will not be able to overcome him, but will continue to falter before him."

Esther 6:13

"A person should never absent himself from the *beis midrash*—not even for a moment—לְעוֹלָם אַל יִמְנַע אָדָם עַצְמוֹ מִבֵּית הַמֶּדְרָשׁ אֲפִילוּ שָׁעָה אֶחָת."[1] At first glance, this statement of Chazal seems to be another teaching emphasizing the importance of *hasmadah* in learning, as they exhort a Yid to utilize every possible minute for *talmud Torah*. Rabbi Chaim Shmuelevitz, however, has a bit of a different take.[2] Of course, it is essential to avoid wasting time, but that is not the focus of this particular

---

1   *Beitzah* 24b.
2   *Sichos Mussar* §12.

declaration. In fact, Rav Chaim understands that the Gemara is referring even to a situation where a person will be learning at home; Chazal
still urge him to opt instead for learning specifically in the *beis midrash*.
The *maalah* of learning in this location—even if he will be learning
there on his own—is that he still learns together with a *tzibbur* in the
same *beis midrash*. In other words, the Gemara here means to highlight
the value of *achdus*. When Hashem observes His children functioning as
a cohesive unit, it brings Him tremendous *nachas*.

Power of Achdus

My *rebbi*, Rabbi Wein, would actually point to the episode of Sodom as
containing a great lesson in *achdus*. As we know, Sodom was the epitome
of evil, with its people attaining a level of wickedness that warranted
its destruction. When Avraham Avinu heard about its looming fate, he
tried to intervene by "negotiating" for its salvation. He asked Hashem
to spare the city if it contained fifty *tzaddikim* and Hashem agrees, but
there are not enough. Avraham persists, going down to forty-five, then
forty, and so on and so forth. Finally, Hashem agrees to spare the city
if there are even just ten *tzaddikim*. Now, even this number couldn't be
found—but we do learn something quite extraordinary. As thoroughly
evil as Sodom was, ten *tzaddikim*—had they existed—would have saved
it. Ten, of course, constitutes a minyan—a cohesive unit of goodness.
Such, then, is the power of *achdus*, which can overpower the thousands
upon thousands of evildoers.

The tremendous *ko'ach* of *achdus* also appears in the Purim story in a
most interesting way. The *Megillah* relates two conversations Haman
held with Zeresh and his friends about dealing with Mordechai—but
with very different outcomes.

In the first instance, Haman had just left Esther's party feeling quite
elated, having been the only one (aside from the king) to be invited.
But seeing Mordechai persist in his refusal to bow ignited his fury. He
comes home and first speaks of his great successes. Then he turns to
the subject which is uppermost in his mind: "וְכָל זֶה אֵינֶנּוּ שֹׁוֶה לִי בְּכָל עֵת
אֲשֶׁר אֲנִי רֹאֶה אֶת מָרְדְּכַי הַיְּהוּדִי יוֹשֵׁב בְּשַׁעַר הַמֶּלֶךְ—And all of this is not worth
anything to me, as long as I see Mordechai the Jew sitting by the king's

gate."[3] Right away, Zeresh comes up with a simple solution that Haman eagerly accepts: build a gallows on which to hang Mordechai.

Shortly thereafter, Haman goes through the whole humiliating ordeal of leading Mordechai on the king's horse and proclaiming before him: "כָּכָה יֵעָשֶׂה לָאִישׁ אֲשֶׁר הַמֶּלֶךְ חָפֵץ בִּיקָרוֹ"—So shall be done to the man whom the king desires to honor."[4] Haman then returns home in disgrace, more depressed than ever. Once again, he turns to his wife and friends to relate the occurrence, but this time, the response is markedly different. The first time around, Zeresh had reacted with confidence, telling her husband to eliminate his adversary. But now she is profoundly pessimistic: אִם מִזֶּרַע הַיְּהוּדִים מָרְדֳּכַי אֲשֶׁר הַחִלּוֹתָ לִנְפֹּל לְפָנָיו לֹא תוּכַל לוֹ כִּי נָפוֹל תִּפּוֹל לְפָנָיו—If Mordechai, before whom you have begun to falter, is from the offspring of the Jews, you will not be able to overcome him, but will continue to falter before him."[5]

This is quite a turnaround! Zeresh essentially went from saying "Hang him" to "You're finished." What accounts for this dramatic change?

We begin to get some indication from the slight shift in the way Mordechai is referred to. In the first instance, Haman called him "מָרְדֳּכַי הַיְּהוּדִי," using the singular form. That is, he was viewed as just an individual Jew, and from this perspective, they felt it would be no problem to simply destroy him. In the second encounter, Haman provided a lot of detail, telling his company "כָּל אֲשֶׁר קָרָהוּ—all that happened to him." Hearing all of these details, Zeresh and Haman's friends got very nervous, for they started to realize that there was something very powerful at play here. Putting the pieces together, Zeresh verbalized what it was: "אִם מִזֶּרַע הַיְּהוּדִים מָרְדֳּכַי...לֹא תוּכַל לוֹ." Here she refers to Mordechai together with all of the Yidden, for she understood that he was not just an "individual" Jew, but part of a unified Klal Yisrael. This being the case, she knew there was no way to overcome this power. Because of the *achdus* of the Yehudim, it was clear that "לֹא תוּכַל לוֹ—you will be unable to overcome him."

3 *Esther* 5:13.
4 Ibid., 6:11.
5 Ibid., v. 13.

Recognized by All

The above serves to illustrate the tremendous *ko'ach* of *achdus*. Actually, there is another element that emerges from the Purim episode that relates to the whole notion of *achdus*. In addition to the power of *achdus* itself, Klal Yisrael enjoys another *zechus*—and that is the *kiddush Hashem* that results from the nations' recognition of our special unity. In this *zechus*, Klal Yisrael is afforded even greater protection from Hashem. Such seems to have been the case when it came to Zeresh and company, who were sworn enemies of the Jews and sought only their harm. We have already seen how quick and eager they were, at the beginning, to condemn Mordechai and have him hung. But when the *ko'ach* of Klal Yisrael's *achdus* later dawned on them, they just as quickly backed off. Once they recognized that Mordechai was part of the greater body of "זֶרַע הַיְּהוּדִים," they readily acknowledged their own powerlessness: "לֹא תוּכַל לוֹ."

I once personally witnessed a similar phenomenon play itself out. Not so long ago, a terrible tragedy was visited upon the Jewish community of Pittsburgh: a *rasha* went on a murderous rampage, killing several Jews who were attending services. At some point on that day, I happened to go to the local gas station (in my hometown of Lakewood) to fill up my car. When the gas-station attendant saw me, he came over to my window and told me how sorry he was for my loss. I understood that he was referring to the tragedy in Pittsburgh, and his gesture made an impression on me. We had an assembly about the event the next day in yeshiva. I shared this story with my students, conveying the following message. The gas attendant didn't know me; all he knew about me was what he saw—namely, that I was a Yid. But that was enough for him to know that the tragedy affected me on a personal level. Obviously, his perspective was that all Jews are connected. I didn't personally know these Jews in Pittsburgh; in fact, I have never even been to Pittsburgh. Nonetheless, the attendant instinctively knew that because we are all Jews, we must experience such an event as if it were a family tragedy, *Rachmana litzlan*. I'm sure that many non-Jews also got gas that day, and the attendant probably said nothing about it. Or if he did, the conversation probably went something along the following lines: "Sad story in

Pittsburgh. Glad I'm not there. What can I do for you today?" No need
to offer consolation or sympathy, just business as usual. But when it
came to me—because I am a Jew—the attendant knew right away how
pained I would be. This simple gentile immediately and clearly grasped
the situation. He knew that I didn't know these other Jews, yet he also
knew we are a united family, and feel for each other's pain.

Here, then, was yet another instance where our *achdus*—so apparent
even to the goyim—was the source of a *kiddush Hashem*. The inherent
power of *achdus* grows even stronger due to the *kiddush Hashem* in its
wake. In this *zechus*, our enemies, like Zeresh before them, will back
off and retreat, as they come to realize the truth of "אִם מִזֶּרַע הַיְּהוּדִים...לֹא
תוּכַל לוֹ."

7

EISAV'S KIBBUD AV

וְעֵשָׂו אָחִיו בָּא מִצֵּידוֹ, וַיַּעַשׂ גַּם הוּא מַטְעַמִּים וַיָּבֵא לְאָבִיו וַיֹּאמֶר
לְאָבִיו יָקֻם אָבִי וְיֹאכַל מִצֵּיד בְּנוֹ בַּעֲבֻר תְּבָרֲכַנִּי נַפְשֶׁךָ.

And Eisav, his brother, arrived from having hunted. And he
also prepared tasty foods, and he brought [them] to his father;
and he said to his father: "May my father arise and eat from his
son's game, so that your soul shall bless me."

Bereishis 27:30–31

AS much of a *rasha* that Eisav was, it appears that there was one mitzvah with which he was very particular. Chazal tell us that he excelled in the area of *kibbud av*—honoring his father.

Still, the question arises about just how genuine his *kibbud av* really was. Rav Chaim Kanievsky makes a most poignant observation in this regard, shedding much light on the mitzvah itself. In describing the act of serving his father, the *pasuk* states: "וַיַּעַשׂ גַּם הוּא מַטְעַמִּים וַיָּבֵא לְאָבִיו—And he also prepared tasty foods, and he brought [them] to his father."[1] Rav Chaim notes that the phrase "וַיָּבֵא לְאָבִיו" is what we call a palindrome—a word or phrase that reads the same forward and

---

1   *Bereishis* 27:31.

222

backward (such as "mom" or "pop"). The significance of this is that *kibbud av va'eim* is indeed a "two-way street"; the way a person treats his parents determines the way his own children will end up treating him. As we shall see, this notion played itself out in a most interesting way in Eisav's case.

Soon after, the Torah relates that Yaakov cried upon meeting Rachel for the first time.[2] In one explanation, *Rashi* attributes this reaction to his dire situation. When Avraham's servant Eliezer approached Rivkah, he presented her with elegant gifts; by contrast, Yaakov was empty-handed. What happened? As *Rashi* proceeds to recount, such was the outcome of Yaakov's encounter with Eliphaz. Eisav had sent his son Eliphaz to track down and kill Yaakov as the latter was fleeing. Eliphaz indeed caught up with Yaakov, but he found himself in a quandary. Growing up in the lap of his righteous grandfather Yitzchak had an effect on him; as such, he could not bring himself to kill Yaakov. On the other hand, there was also the issue of fulfilling his father's command. "What should I do?" he asked Yaakov. "Take all of my possessions," Yaakov counseled. "In this way, I shall be left an *ani* (pauper). Since an *ani* is considered as if he were a *meis*, you will be listening to your father without committing actual murder." Thus, Yaakov was left penniless, unable to provide Rachel with any gift.

We see, then, that the matter really came full circle. Yes, Eisav's *kibbud av* was legendary. But at the same time that he was honoring and serving his father, he was also deceiving him. As *Rashi* explains, Eisav tricked Yitzchak into thinking he was righteous by asking questions about taking *maaser* from salt or straw.[3] And so, while Eisav may have provided his father with exemplary service, he also dealt with him in an underhanded way.

"וַיָּבֵא לְאָבִיו"—A similar thing ended up happening to Eisav himself with his own son. Eliphaz, as we have seen, was mindful of *kibbud av*, and sought to fulfill his father's command. By taking Yaakov's advice, he did just that—but only in a technical sense. Rather than actually

---

2   Ibid., 29:11.
3   Ibid., 25:27–28.

killing Yaakov, he left him destitute and hence equivalent to being dead. Like father, like son—Eliphaz indeed honored his father, if only with a touch of cunning.

8

ESTHER'S MEGILLAH

אִם הַחֲרֵשׁ תַּחֲרִישִׁי בָּעֵת הַזֹּאת רֶוַח וְהַצָּלָה יַעֲמוֹד לַיְּהוּדִים מִמָּקוֹם
אַחֵר וְאַתְּ וּבֵית אָבִיךְ תֹּאבֵדוּ וּמִי יוֹדֵעַ אִם לְעֵת כָּזֹאת הִגַּעַתְּ
לַמַּלְכוּת.

*For if you remain silent at this time, relief and salvation shall
arise for the Jews from another quarter—and you and your
father's house shall go lost. And who knows if it was not for a
time such as this that you have attained royalty?*

Esther 4:13

THERE is a certain intriguing quality about *Megillas Esther*, one
that it seems to share with the episode of *Akeidas Yitzchak*. The latter, of course, features the most challenging *nisayon* Avraham Avinu
had to face. After so many years of waiting, Avraham and Sarah had
been blessed with a son, one who was destined to be the father of the
Jewish nation. All of a sudden, it appeared that the promise was re-
voked, as Avraham was charged with sacrificing Yitzchak. But despite
the difficulty involved—including the various attempts of the Satan
to intervene and prevent the accumulation of eternal *zechus* for Klal
Yisrael—Avraham forged ahead. He displayed an unparalleled sense

of *emunah* and determination to fulfill Hashem's will, and in this way passed the test with flying colors.

And yet, despite the colossal strength and effort put forth by Avraham, the event is not called by his name. Rather, as we know, it is referred to as "*Akeidas Yitzchak.*"

Life on the Line

A similar situation occurs in the Purim episode. Mordechai was the essential leader of the Jewish People at the time. He served as the rock of *emunah*, guiding the Jews through a period of great transformation—from the *Churban Bayis Rishon* to the building of *Bayis Sheini*. He stood at the forefront even as the people had to face tears, pain, low morale, and the threat of annihilation during the seventy years of *galus*. Through it all, he was the source of inspiration for his nation. He single-handedly stood up to a kingdom that despised Klal Yisrael, demonstrating remarkable fortitude in refusing to bow to the wicked Haman—one of the most powerful people of the realm and archenemy of the Jewish People. In short, Mordechai was a central figure in the whole episode, which culminated with the great reversal—signified by Haman's downfall, Mordechai's ascendancy, and the salvation of Klal Yisrael. The accomplishments of Mordechai HaTzaddik in the realm of *avodas Hashem* and leading his nation almost defy comprehension. And yet, the very *Megillah* which recounts this narrative is not called "*Megillas Mordechai*" but "*Megillas Esther.*"

What, then, are we to make of the apparent irony surrounding "*Akeidas Yitzchak*" and "*Megillas Esther*"? There is a traditional explanation offered, which holds true in both instances. It is undoubtedly the case, as outlined above, that both Avraham and Mordechai displayed their deep love for Klal Yisrael and played a most significant role in furthering their cause. But there was a certain element that applied specifically to Yitzchak and Esther in their respective instances: that is, they each placed themselves in danger of losing their lives. It was on account of their willingness to be *moser nefesh mamash* that the events mentioned above were attributed to Yitzchak and Esther.

Filling in the Blank

It may be possible, however, to suggest another approach to this issue. This emerges from a closer examination of the conversation that takes place between Mordechai and Esther, in which Mordechai aims to convince the queen on Yisrael's behalf.

Understandably, Esther initially voices some hesitation. It had been some time since she was summoned by the king, and she was well aware of the potential consequences of an unauthorized entry: "כָּל אִישׁ וְאִשָּׁה אֲשֶׁר יָבוֹא אֶל הַמֶּלֶךְ...אֲשֶׁר לֹא יִקָּרֵא אַחַת דָּתוֹ לְהָמִית לְבַד מֵאֲשֶׁר יוֹשִׁיט לוֹ הַמֶּלֶךְ אֶת שַׁרְבִיט הַזָּהָב...וַאֲנִי לֹא נִקְרֵאתִי לָבוֹא אֶל הַמֶּלֶךְ זֶה שְׁלוֹשִׁים יוֹם—[Regarding] any man or woman who shall come before the king...who has not been called, only one law applies: death; except for one for whom the king stretches forth his golden scepter...And I have not been called to come before the king for thirty days now."[1] Now, Mordechai's response to Esther's apparently reasonable claim is quite telling. One may have expected him to intensify his pleas on behalf of Klal Yisrael, spelling out just what dire straits they are in and how important it is to take a risk for their deliverance. But that was not Mordechai's tactic! Rather than emphasizing Yisrael's desperate situation, Mordechai turns the focus on Esther herself: "אִם הַחֲרֵשׁ תַּחֲרִישִׁי בָּעֵת הַזֹּאת רֶוַח וְהַצָּלָה יַעֲמוֹד לַיְּהוּדִים מִמָּקוֹם אַחֵר וְאַתְּ וּבֵית אָבִיךְ תֹּאבֵדוּ וּמִי יוֹדֵעַ אִם לְעֵת כָּזֹאת הִגַּעַתְּ לַמַּלְכוּת—If you remain silent at this time, relief and salvation shall arise for the Jews from another quarter—**and you and your father's house shall go lost**. And who knows if it was not for a time such as this that you have succeeded to royalty?" From his response, it almost appears that Mordechai was, in fact, not too worried about Klal Yisrael's welfare. He was telling Esther that the Jewish People are fine, and so they always will be; Hashem will take care of them. The only question concerns Esther herself—will she be fine? If you don't step up, Mordechai was telling Esther, salvation will come from somewhere else. The Jewish people will continue to exist, but you and your lineage will be imperiled.

---

1   *Esther* 4:11.

It seems that there is precedent for such a concept, for there is another instance where someone's failure to seize the moment indeed bore eternal consequences. Such occurred in *Parashas Shemos*, when Hashem was seeking to persuade Moshe Rabbeinu to accept the mission of redeeming Yisrael. For various reasons, Moshe resisted the request—to the point where, in accordance with his level, Hashem felt that his refusal was improper. And as a result, Moshe suffered an eternal loss. Previously, he had been slated to receive the *kehunah*. However, for failing to step up and seize the opportunity before him, this privilege was taken away and granted to Aharon instead.[2]

This was the message Mordechai was seeking to convey to Esther. He was trying to get her to realize that her eternity was at stake. The salvation of the Jewish People was assured; the only question was who would merit to be the savior. In a sense, there was a "blank space" next to this "position"; Mordechai was urging Esther to seize the opportunity and insert her name in that space. She took his advice and indeed heeded the call, agreeing to risk her life by appearing before the king. And it is for this reason the *sefer* is called "*Megillas Esther*"; the title reflects the fact that it was her moment, and she did not shirk her responsibility.

This lesson of *Megillas Esther* bears relevance to each and every one of us. The Mishnah informs us that each person has his designated "*sefer*," in which are recorded the deeds and moments of one's life: "וְכָל מַעֲשֶׂיךָ בַּסֵּפֶר נִכְתָּבִין."[3] Perhaps we may understand this idea in the following manner. There is a *sefer* designated for every person born into this world—a "*megillah*" of sorts in which is portrayed all that they are capable of accomplishing in their lifetime. Every opportunity is listed: moments of learning, davening, *chessed*, *tzedakah*, speaking kind words, etc. But there is a blank line next to each of these opportunities, and the goal in life is to ensure that our name is placed on as many of these lines as possible. We know that "הַרְבֵּה שְׁלוּחִים לַמָּקוֹם—Hashem has many agents"; if a person passes up an opportunity, there is always someone else who can step in and seize it in his place. Imagine what would happen

---

2   *Rashi, Shemos* 4:14.
3   *Avos* 2:1.

if a person ascends to *Shamayim* after 120 years, only to find that "his" *megillah* is filled with the names of other people! And so *Megillas Esther* exhorts us to grasp these opportunities and to fill in these spaces with our own names.

ABOUT THE AUTHOR

Born and raised in the Bronx, Rabbi Buddy Berkowitz learned in Yeshiva Sha'arei Torah in Monsey for many years and received *semichah* from Rabbi Berel Wein, *shlita*. He has been involved in *chinuch* for over thirty years and has taught in many adult education programs around the world. He lives in Lakewood, NJ, with his wife and children.

לעילוי נשמת

תמרה בת אברהם אבינו

. . . .

לעילוי נשמת

צביה לאה בת אברהם מרדכי

LYNN KORNFELD
DR. SHAMSHY AND TOBI EISENBERGER

. . . .

לעילוי נשמת
Beloved grandparents

שבתי בן ישעיה יצחק

אסנה בת יוסף

MINDY AND JEFFREY KAZAN

Rothenberg Law Firm LLP

. . . .

לרפואה שלימה
זלדא בת הינדא GROSS
RABBI AND MRS. SHIMONE BENDER

· · · · · · · · ·

לעילוי נשמת
משה דוד בן שרגא פייבל · אסתר ליבא בת אפרים מיכל הלוי
RABBI AND MRS. ELIYAHU ARONSON

· · · · · · · · ·

לעילוי נשמת
דוד נחמי' בן ברוך
DR. AND MRS. SHALOM MEHLER AND FAMILY

· · · · · · · · ·

לעילוי נשמת
משה דוד בן שרגא פייבל · אסתר ליבא בת אפרים מיכל הלוי
MR. AND MRS. BOB BROMBERG

· · · · · · · · ·

לעילוי נשמת
הרב נחמן בן אריה לייב הלוי
YOSEF ZALMAN MORGAN AND FAMILY

· · · · · · · · ·

לעילוי נשמת
חיים יוסף בן יעקב · אשר יעקב בן חיים יוסף
RABBI AND MRS. AVRUMY BERLINER

· · · · · · · · ·

לעילוי נשמת
מרדכי בן יחזקאל הכהן
RABBI AND MRS. CHESKY SCHONFELD

· · · · · · · · ·

לעילוי נשמת
זהבה גולדא לאה בת יעקב
MR. AND MRS. J.J. HUTMAN

· · · · · · · · ·

לעילוי נשמת
שמעון בער בן יהושוע מיכל
MR. AND MRS. YECHIEL AND ATARA LENCH

לעילוי נשמת

חיים יוסף ליב בן שאול יצחק

RABBI AND MRS. USHI SMITH

· · · · · · · · ·

לעילוי נשמת

משה דוד בן שרגא פייבל • אסתר ליבא בת אפרים מיכל הלוי

RABBI AND MRS. OZER YONA KUSHNER

· · · · · · · · ·

לעילוי נשמת

האשה החשובה אלטע צפורה בת הרב קלונימוס קלמן

RABBI AND MRS. ARON MILSTEIN

· · · · · · · · ·

לעילוי נשמת

ישראל בן דוד

RABBI AND MRS. AVROHOM FLAM

· · · · · · · · ·

לעילוי נשמת

אבי מורי ר׳מרדכי בן ר׳חיים • אמי מורתי לאה בת ר׳ אפרים שלמה ROTHBARD

RABBI AND MRS PINCHOS HELBERG

· · · · · · · · ·

לזכות

חיה פריידא בת רבקה

MR. AND MRS. ARI HUTMAN

· · · · · · · · ·

לעילוי נשמת

אהרון בן שמחה הלוי CHASE

RABBI AND MRS. AVROHOM CHASE AND FAMILY

· · · · · · · · ·

לעילוי נשמת

רוחמה נחמה זלטא בת הרב משה שמואל זנוויל

RABBI NAFTALI HASS AND FAMILY

· · · · · · · · ·

לעילוי נשמת

דוד דוב בן יהודה • דוד בן אברהם אליעזר

MR. AND MRS. MENDEL SUSSMAN

ר׳ אהרן אשר בן ר׳ אברהם

תמר בת ר׳ אליעזר

ר׳ אפרים מיכל בן ר׳ זאב נחמיה הלוי

פעשע ביילה בת ר׳ אהרן אשר

ר׳ שרגא פייבל בן ר׳ יעקב

משא בת ר׳ זכריה

ר׳ יוסף בן ר׳ שמואל

דינה עלקא בת ר׳ מרדכי הלוי

ר׳ שמואל בן ר׳ יעקב

וויטע בת ר׳ משה נפתלי

MOSAICA PRESS

BOOK PUBLISHERS

Elegant, Meaningful & Bold

info@MosaicaPress.com
www.MosaicaPress.com

The Mosaica Press team of
acclaimed editors and designers
is attracting some of the most
compelling thinkers and teachers
in the Jewish community today.
Our books are available around
the world.

HARAV YAACOV HABER
RABBI DORON KORNBLUTH